Betty Brooks

Betty Brooks

STAGE
DIALECTS

Three reels of sound tapes to accompany STAGE DIALECTS are available:

Reel 1: The Phonetic Alphabet; Japanese; Brooklyn-
    ese; American Southern
Reel 2: Standard English; Cockney; Irish; Scots
Reel 3: French; Italian; German; Russian

STAGE DIALECTS

*

Jerry Blunt

*

Chandler
HARPER & ROW, PUBLISHERS
New York   Hagerstown   San Francisco   London

*

To Betty

CONTENTS

*

FOREWORD

*

The need among American actors for a source of study of the most-used stage dialects has been obvious for some time. In today's theatre—community, educational, professional—and on today's film the variety of material being performed is extremely diversified, dealing with many voices from many lands. In most cases these voices would sound better if they spoke in the accents and idiom of the source material. A proper dialect properly delivered adds attractive and informative qualities to every kind of interpretive work.

It used to be that an American actor, if he traveled to any extent, could hear at first hand numerous native and foreign dialects. Unfortunately, such sources are drying up throughout the American scene. Variations of speech patterns, once heard in abundance in the cross-currents of daily life, have disappeared under the impact of modern education and the influence of our communications media, a condition as noticeable in rural as urban areas. For example, the author recently completed a 2,000-mile trek along the ridge of the Rockies from northern New Mexico to Jasper Township in Canada in search of a full-bodied western-rural-mountain dialect, such as he had known as a boy growing up on a ranch in western Colorado. As far as the desired dialect was concerned, the journey produced meager results. By actual count, more tourist than native voices were taped.[1] Even former grammar- and high-school classmates had changed speech both in manner and in forms. As a result of these nation-wide alterations, today's performer is left with only an uncertain reliance on vague traditions of pronunciation and phraseology. This book seeks to aid him in remedying this situation.

To their credit be it said that most actors not only welcome the opportunity to obtain a dialect role but even show an eagerness for dialect study well in advance of any future chances. In a great many cases, role or no

role, individuals respond to the appeal of the various dialects themselves. Sometimes the response is to the vocal challenge a dialect presents; sometimes the reaction shows as an awareness of the dramatic enrichment a dialect provides to a part or a play. Whatever the motivation, most players know that increased expressiveness, through added depth, strength, and beauty, is the result when an actor speaks a dialect as master of his material.

During the collection and organization of source material for this study it was felt that more than one kind of performer would find a need for the book. Certain individuals and groups, such as those at work in the educational theatre, have by the very nature of their effort a need to accomplish studies in depth. For them, extensive discussions identified with the sound symbols of the International Phonetic Alphabet have been prepared; these discussions and symbols are later linked with the accompanying sound tracks in similar formats for each separate dialect. For such individuals and groups subtleties of pronunciation and idiom are available along with the broader aspect of each subject.

Other persons have a less intensive but equally legitimate need for study material in this field. These can range from the professional performer who has a quick-study problem to the after-dinner speaker and social raconteur. For such individuals the linking of taped sound to the practice words and phrases of the text should provide an adequate source of study for their objectives—the material was planned and arranged with this in mind.

The information in this book and on the tapes has

---

[1] Among the many tourist items recorded the principal ones were: 1 Korean, 2 Scots, 2 English (Essex and London), 1 East Indian, 1 Cree Indian, and 2 Lithuanian.

been collected from many places, east and west, and collated over a long period of time with help from many sources. Variable as the results can be from the study of an imperfect science, the author accepts responsibility where one pronunciation or idiomatic expression has been chosen or emphasized over another; in many cases the selection was treated as a matter of reasoned choice and advanced as such, not presented as an unalterable decision. Variance of pronunciation, in dialects as in ordinary conversational speech, is widespread enough to cause the author to want to make it quite clear that while he believes that his suggestions, if achieved vocally, will produce a good dialect, he knows at the same time that his suggestions are not the only way to achieve desirable results.

If it is a proper act for an author to accept responsi-bility, it is a pleasurable act to express thanks. The materials presented here represent the contribution of many helpful individuals. To all those performers whose voices are recorded on the accompanying tapes and whose names are listed in the text the author's sincere appreciation is extended. Very special thanks are expressed to Mr. Timothy Eckersley, Central Programme Operations, the B.B.C., for cooperation over a period of years, and to Stella Hillier of the B.B.C. Radio Enterprises. Barry McGee's contribution at the sound controls is much appreciated. Additional thanks go to the many individuals in such diverse places as Alabama and New Zealand, Vancouver, Venice, and Kyoto, who over the years were helpful in contributing primary source material to add to the bulk of items available for study.

STAGE
DIALECTS

I

*

INTRODUCTION

*

Since the days of Aristophanes, playwrights have written lines in dialect and actors have spoken them on all the stages of the world. That playwrights and actors will continue to use such expressive and attractive kinds of speech is beyond question. Accordingly, it becomes a purposeful act for a player to prepare himself to meet future needs by becoming expert in those major dialects for which his profession has the greatest use.

DEFINITION

A *dialect* is a distinctive form of pronunciation, language structure, and vocabulary which is identified with a geographical area or a social class. In varying degrees it possesses notable melodic and rhythmic patterns. It develops its own idiom. Further, a dialect is created whenever anyone speaks in a language not his own. Although such speech is often referred to as a foreign accent, it is one more form of dialectal expression.

A *stage dialect* is a normal dialect altered as needed to fit the requirements of theatrical clarity and dramatic interpretation. The alteration may create differences between the work of a regional-speech expert and that of a stage dialectician.

The alteration may be slight or marked, may be merely suggested or strongly distorted, may make sounds more melodious or more harsh, dramatic or comedic. Consequently, a stage dialect has the double duty of achieving factual truthfulness through fidelity to its primary sources and artistic truthfulness through fidelity to a dramatic interpretation. Neither form of truthfulness is incompatible with the other. Instead, each complements the other to a remarkable degree, so much so that no dialect need ever be either untruthful or ineffective. It must be stated, however, that to meet the double demands of a good dialect, it is often necessary to break free from many of the traditional concepts and cliché expressions that have plagued dialectal delivery through the years.

THE USES OF DIALECT

If a dialect is nothing else, it is distinctive. Pronunciation and a peculiar use of idiom set one type of speech apart from another. The resultant contrast acts to sharpen an auditor's awareness of the special qualities each possesses. The difference is attractive—one of the reasons why a dialect compels attention as ordinary speech does not. It is no wonder that playwrights and actors, aware of this attractiveness, continually make use of it.

Even as a dialect attracts, it instructs. The sounds of a dialect inform the ear in much the same way that a costume instructs the eye. *Where*, and, in part, *who*, are revealed by dialect. The place where a person is, or comes from, and his socioeconomic standing can simply and concisely be told by his form of speech. A dialect, then, is an expressive tool.

In the interpretive process, a dialect also serves to

* 1

complement the actions of a person or a character. The sharp stop and go of Cockney speech reinforces the visual image of a body that, forever alert, reaches for or darts after desired objects in motions mixed in equal portions of boldness and fear. And what is the Cockney's glottal stop other than the arrested movement of a person instinctually cautious?

As a dialect takes character from its locality, so does it give character back, intensifying the interpretive significance of its use. This aspect of a dialect can be heard in the accents of the Welsh, a people still tentatively melodious in speech, as if not quite able to shake the inherited mysticism of hills and valleys out of their terminal phrases. A like aspect is asserted by the presence of the hard "r" of the American Midwest and Far West, a sound often strong enough to scratch an eardrum the way a diamond scratches glass, one which was inherited from seventeenth-century England and which probably kept its edge by the grindstone quality of frontier life.

MAJOR STAGE DIALECTS

The dialects chosen for study and practice in this book are those of greatest use to an actor. A simple criterion determined the choice: Which dialects in the last three decades were most employed on the American stage and screen? From the American side of the English-speaking world they were: Standard American, American Southern, and the speech of New York City. The dialects of such areas as New England and the hill country of Kentucky, or the patois of New Orleans, for all the distinctiveness each possesses, received but minimal attention.

There was marked difference in the degree of employment of the various British dialects. Those most used come from the British Isles. Standard English, Irish, and Cockney comprise the major share, with Scotch somewhat behind in extent of stage use; Welsh and such regional dialects as Lancashire and Yorkshire were but rarely called for.

Among the continental dialects, French and German were used in about equal degree, and have a corresponding importance beyond the other European groupings, with Russian and Italian next in order.

As a result of World War II and our present relations with Japan, the Japanese dialect has recently moved onto the list of working dialects.

STANDARD AMERICAN AND STANDARD ENGLISH

There are two principal "Standard" dialects, Standard American and Standard English.

"Standard American" is a term which has no authoritative standing, but is needed to specify the most widely employed form of American speech. It is the dialectal utterance of Midwestern and, more recently, Western groupings. It is the speech of the majority of educated persons in this country, and its pronunciation of most words is listed by our semiauthoritarian dictionaries as first or preferred. Naturally this dialect is not listed here for study, since it already is the speech of the majority of professional actors.

Standard English is analogous to its American counterpart. It, too, is the speech of the educated person and, is further identified with an upper-level social class. Like its American kin, it has the authoritarian status of dictionary backing. But it must be treated and learned by the American actor as a separate dialect, just as Irish or Scotch. And it is not the easiest of the lot.

Other "standards" may be considered, but in a sense somewhat different from that applied to the two above. They are "standard" because there are dialects within dialects. Pronunciation and idiom may change from town to town within a rural area and from block to block within a city's limits, even when each is within a major dialectal grouping. This circumstance could create serious problems for the dialect student. Were the stage dialectician under the same obligation as the phonetician or regional-speech expert, he would of necessity be concerned with the minutiae of each variant. But an actor's work, like the drama of which it is a part, is in this respect interpretive rather than scientific. The result is that, within the entities of the various dialects, the player seeks a standard which represents the variations.

Fortunately, such a standard can be established for each dialect. Against the divisive forces of terrain and historical continuity and local custom which exist in every major dialect area, certain and sufficient norms of pronunciation, grammatical usage, and idiomatic expression can be found and put to use. In this circumstance it is proper to learn a "standard" Irish, French, Cockney, or even American Southern, as extensive as that widespread area is.

Perhaps one day the results of the educative process

will be forceful enough to bring the bulk of a national population within one standard speech form. But those of us who are conscious of the distinctiveness presently contained in most dialects question how desirable such a linguistic revolution would be. To those who must manage a language—writers, speakers, actors—hard second thoughts would be in order before the melodic pitch pattern of the Welsh were dropped, before the expressiveness of rural Midwestern speech were allowed to dwindle into disuse, before the burr of the Scotch or the music of the Irish were lost.

STRENGTH

In a life situation, the strength or fullness of a dialect varies from native speaker to native speaker, according to persons and circumstances. Not all sections of a community are equally strong in pronunciation and idiom, no more than all members of the same family are. In like manner, dramatic requirements for strength and fullness vary from character to character, play to play, and director to director. Even in a piece as dialect-conscious as Shaw's *Pygmalion*, the dialect strength to be used by Eliza and Professor Higgins can be increased or decreased within limits from one company or director or actor to another.

Knowing in advance the extent to which such circumstances will have a future application, the dialect student is wise who would base his study and practice upon the premise that it is easier to cut down on the strength of a dialect than it is to build it up. For this reason, all dialects in this book are presented full-strength, with the suggestion that they be mastered in like manner. Later, if a production or a director so requires, the strength of the delivery can immediately be scaled down on suggestion. But if more strength is required than the player possesses, it may take days of renewed study to build up to the desired level, if indeed the role has not already been forfeited.

CONSISTENCY

One of the first marks of quality in the work of a stage dialectician is consistency. Regardless of the degree of strength employed or the fullness of idiom, the consistency of a dialect should be evenly maintained. This means that when a key sound is established as an integral part of a dialect, it should be delivered with the same phonetic value each time it is sounded. If a "broad a" is to be employed in the first syllable of *rather*, as it would be in Standard English, then it must be so repeated each time the word appears.

Consistency is accomplished in preparation. As a major element contributing to excellence, it should be established as a constant conditioner in each work session ahead.

PRIMARY SOURCES

The characteristic sounds of most dialects are available for study in written form, the work of the many regional-speech experts who labor in this field. Still, every dialect to be mastered wants hearing. That is the reason, in *Stage Dialects*, for coordinating a written script with the sounds of a recorded voice. By this means, our two most active senses are brought to bear on each dialect problem.

For exactly the same reason a sufficient quantity of primary source material—the sounds of a dialect as spoken by one who is native to it—had to be heard at first-hand before the materials in this book could be assembled. The process extended over three decades. Numerous voices, speaking in the major dialects of America, Europe, the Far East, and the South Pacific were recorded at home and abroad. Correspondence and exchange programs with interested persons in established institutions were carried on.

The gathering of good dialect material is a fascinating search, one in which the dialect student quickly becomes absorbed. At the same time it is often a frustrating activity. Not every voice with a noticeable accent is a fit subject for collection; indeed, only a few out of hundreds prove suitable for recording. The rewarding ones are remembered: A Greek actor, self-taught in English; an Italian elevator boy in Venice; an Austrian cook, taped in his hotel kitchen at St. Anton in the Tyrol; a Cockney shoemaker, knowledgeable in world affairs; the English gentleman-farmer, whose Standard English was almost classic in strength and consistency; a Kyoto guide in Japan—the list could continue indefinitely.

Most often, frustration came from failure to discover a good foreign accent in non-English speaking countries. The reason was first demonstrated by an Italian-American lady in a small town in the Dolomites. Recently returned from the United States, she asked, with near-kinship feeling, "What's-uh your state? Mine's-uh Boston." Her voluble speech was a prototype for an Italian-American accent, learned in America. It was the first such one heard in weeks. Yet each day there had been conversation with many persons who extended the courtesy of speaking to us in English. The core of the problem lay in the fact that the Italian living in Italy learns his English in school under the eye and ear of a teacher who places emphasis upon correct grammar and pronunciation. In contrast, the foreign accent we Americans have come to know is a slightly taught patois developed by the foreign-born living in America.

For those foreign-born, the exigencies of everyday American life, the need for immediate communication, must of necessity bypass rules of grammar and the niceties of pronunciation. The result is that more usable foreign accents can be found at home than abroad. What we might call our Swedish accent—little used dramatically—is a disappearing product of Swedish settlers in the North Central states; such a speech is seldom heard in Sweden. As a consequence of this circumstance, an American-grown, untutored utterance provides the best primary source for a foreign dialect.

For all the challenge and stimulation of dialect hunting, it is neither the exotic circumstance nor the romantic locale which determines the worth of a primary source. Because of the variance found among those who speak the same dialect, it is often necessary for the dialect seeker to gather bits and pieces in order to make a composite whole. Seldom does one voice stand out, exact, strong, and consistent in every detail. On the other hand, many voices piece imperfections out, emphasizing the essential key sounds through repetition.

Nor is it always easy to get the primary-source performer to remain true to his dialect, a point of which the student searcher needs to be aware. Native patterns can be disrupted by self-consciousness. It is one thing to tape ordinary talk; it is quite another to ask the primary source to read from a prepared script. Hesitancies and error creep in, augmenting a stilted delivery. For example: A leathergoods shopkeeper of Crown Passage in London's West End spoke with a richly full Cockney dialect, not as explosive or as extreme as a shopkeeper in Bethnal Green might have done, but one that was strong and consistent and a delight to hear. But when reading from script, this primary-source performer doggedly placed an "h" every place where he had

dropped one in the ordinary conversation of just moments before. Upon appeal, he tried to correct the error, but to no avail: ". . . got bashed by teacher every time I dropped a ruddy 'aich' readin' in school," he explained.

For exactly the same reason, the manageress of a *pensione* in Florence, when taping a script, failed to insert the characteristic "uh" [ə] sound between words and phrases, although she had consistently done it immediately before. "It's-uh not right to read-uh that way," she said.

RECORDED VOICES ON THE ACCOMPANYING TAPES

The selection and arrangement of voices on the accompanying tapes is designed to mirror the fact just stated, that the makeup of any "standard" dialect is a composite of multiple individual norms. Many voices of all kinds must be heard to achieve such a composite. Consequently each reel that you will use features, on the one hand, the steadiness, strength, and consistency of a dialect expert, and on the other the fluctuations of a primary-source character, replete with individual idiosyncrasies. Some voices you will study are trained, others are not; some are male, others female. Some sections of material were recorded in studios under optimum conditions for fidelity in reproduction, others were taped in difficult circumstances: out of doors; in offices, hotel lobbies, or rooms; on buses. Whenever a good source is found, the essential thing is to get it fixed in a permanent record before it gets away or is lost, which means that poor reproduction and intruding noises must be put up with in the effort to capture needed primary-source material. A tolerance for difficulties is an essential part of the makeup of a dialectician. This tolerance you will be required to practice several times in the work ahead.

In the matter of delivery by the voice on tape, a strong inclination to enliven passages by increased expressiveness, so that the material itself becomes more interesting to the listener, is always present in the work of any performer. In dialect after dialect unique sounds invite dramatic or comedic interpretations, motivated by the speech itself or by the characteristics we impose upon that speech. However, if yielded to, the inclination to heightened expression tends to produce a body of work that seeks to entertain rather than to instruct.

Since instruction is our paramount purpose, most passages (but not all) that invite a more dramatic delivery—even those that are flamboyant in nature, like the speeches from Boucicault's *Arrah-Na-Pogue* in the Irish chapter—have been deliberately restricted in both expressiveness and tempo, to give the listener a better opportunity to locate and analyze the key sounds of the dialect. Further, in place of the usual nervous rapidity, a deliberate tempo has even been accomplished by some of the primary-source voices you will hear; the readings of the French and Russian ladies, France Rouard, and Irene Zmurkevych are cases in point.

To anticipate a possible criticism, it is granted in advance that some sense of fluency is lost when the more deliberate tempo is used in reading the passages, but at this stage of study the loss in fluency is less important than the gain that accrues in clarity, consistency, and strength.

GUIDELINES FOR STUDY

The format for each practice chapter in this book is similar. In each case preparatory comments on a particular dialect are followed by an explanation of its key vowel and consonant sounds. Then come illustrative words, sentences, and paragraphs which are set down in correlation with a recorded voice. In this way, the audio reinforces the visual in a twin attack on each problem. In all key-sound drills, pauses follow each word, so that you may repeat what was heard. A pause is also made after the sentences which contain key sounds. Unfortunately, the pause is not always long enough to permit a slow repetition of the sentence by the listener. The restricted time allowed by the length of tape requires that the recorded voice move forward with more speed than is sometimes desired. Accordingly, it is suggested that the *pause button* on the tape recorder be employed. Its use permits adequate time for repetition, and with no sacrifice to the amount of study material.

The act of hearing and then exactly repeating the sounds just made by the voice on tape requires the development of certain sensory and muscular skills.

The first skill is *auditory.* The ability to hear each enunciated sound correctly and fully is essential to progress. Made lazy by familiarity with the commonplace communications which fill our lives, a potential for acute listening remains dormant in most of us. Clear and analytical hearing, *both of the model and of yourself,* is essential.

Your mastery of a dialect is not an intellectual process, although much thought must go into the activity. Nor is it a creative action, even though you will later use your dialectal accomplishments in creative ways. Essentially, it is an imitative process. A *muscular* skill must accompany the auditory one mentioned above. Awareness, flexibility, and control are the key elements in your progress.

Unless tongue, jaw, and lips are in a proper position, the desired sounds of any dialect cannot be made. Presently, your positional habits are firmly set for the syllabic formations of your own speech, but new habits have to be added as new formations are accomplished. Muscular skill is required to break old habits and institute new ones. Such an accomplishment must occur before as simple a change as the substitution of the "broad a" [ɑ] for a "short a" [æ] is effected for the purpose of pronouncing the word *master* ['mɑstə] in Standard English. In a typical case of another sort, a new muscular skill must be acquired to activate the uvular [r] of a French or German accent. Until you develop the ability to achieve the exact position and action required, syllabification will be deficient.

A premium is placed upon *mimicry* in such a study as this. It is not a new process; each of us learned to speak that way. Under the tutelage of the recorded voice you will initiate your own vocal patterns. Sounds will match phonetic symbols to bring the faculties of eyes and ears into conjunction. Multiple repetitions will drill the voice into new and proper habits of enunciation.

The final section of each chapter is yours to work on without benefit of symbol or recorded voice. Space is left between lines for the transcription of sounds into phonetic symbols. Sight reading for strength, consistency, and fluency is the purpose.

Memorizing and repeating with exactness and fluency any paragraph which contains a mixture of essential key sounds is an excellent way to achieve a like competence when reading other material.

The Key-Sound Word Drill, at the beginning of each chapter's last section, is organized so that the various key sounds of the dialect may come snug against each other. Vocalizing, you must move tongue, jaw, and lips from one critical position to another. Practice on this drill leads to consistency and fluency.

As will be seen, the sense of sentences and paragraphs is not of crucial importance. Indeed, the best material for dialect study is that which has many key sounds within it, mixed in a text that does not, of itself, demand attention.

KEY SOUNDS

The number of key vowel and consonant sounds which differentiate one dialect from another is surprisingly small. In contrast, the number of identical sounds in all dialects is gratifyingly large. Consequently, it is not the number of vocal changes which must be made that is critical, it is the degree of distinctive alteration. Even then, in the majority of instances, it is not so much the fact that new vowel and consonant formations must be made as it is that old ones are to be inserted in unaccustomed places. For example, the "broad a" [ɑ] with which you are familiar must be substituted in Standard English for the "short a" [æ] that you usually use when you say *demand*, making [dɪˈmɑnd] instead of [dɪˈmænd]. Or where you have always used a "broad a" to say *father* [ˈfɑðɚ] in your Standard American, you must now enunciate a "middle a" [a], as in *ask*, to say *father* [ˈfaðɚ] in an Irish dialect.

In contrast, most American actors must learn from scratch how to achieve a uvular [r] by trilling the back of the tongue, or how to effect the glottal stop [ʔ] employed by a Cockney or Scotsman, or how to effect the half [l], half [r] of a Japanese dialect.

In the chapters ahead the term *key sounds* will be uniformly used to indicate the specific vowel, diphthong and consonant usages which differentiate one dialect from another.

Because the number of key-sound differentiations in the various dialects is relatively small as compared to the bulk of similarities, the distinctions take on added importance. Achieve these distinctions and a dialect can be mastered; fail in their achievement and the new speech will never come into being.

MASTERY

Mastery can be defined as a practical action in which every necessary movement is properly accomplished as a matter of habit. Mastery indicates exactness without conscious thought. You will have acquired mastery in a dialect when you can sight read in that dialect with full strength and consistency and without error.

In the simplest terms, the steps to mastery are: that you be able to hear distinctly the key sounds of each dialect; that you know how those sounds are produced by the muscular action of tongue, jaw, and lips and are able to produce them without error; that you combine the separate sounds with accuracy and fluency in sentence and paragraph form.

It will become obvious as you proceed that some dialects require more practice than others. The full body of Scottish speech is much more difficult to "seat" in the mouth than is the neighboring Irish. Some of the non-English vowels in a French accent may delay the full accomplishment of that dialect, just as the [r-l]-[l-r] combination in Japanese generally requires more than normal drill. Even the dropped [r] of Standard English, as in *there* [ðɛə] and *year* [jɪə], may take considerable time before the sound is properly spoken with full strength.

The last statements in this chapter are ones of caution. It is singularly easy, in sport or for relief, to make mock of a dialect or to caricature it. But the very extremity of the process, and sometimes its attractiveness, can well block proper practice to the detriment of all future work. To so play with a dialect before it has been mastered is hazardous in the extreme.

In the matter of use of foreign dialects, it is the commonsense view that a play whose scene is Italian or French and whose characters presumably are speaking the language of that country, even though we hear them in English, needs no accent imposed on line delivery; to speak so would truly gild the lily of dialect speech. The falseness of such a practice would be apparent if *Hamlet* were to be acted in English with a Danish accent.

If you would try out the quality of your dialect on someone who is native to the region from which it comes, or even if you attempt to check your new speech with an acquaintance, you should know that there are as many authorities on dialects as there are experts on the common cold. Innocent of knowledge, many persons yet hold an unconscious conviction that they "know dialects." As a matter of established fact, not one individual in a hundred is really aware of how he forms his syllables and how they actually sound. But many in that large number are quick to express with authority an unauthoritative opinion. Foremost in this group is the individual who is native to a certain dialect. If you are not possessed of his specific variations, he is sure that you are not correct in this sound or that. The advice here is that you listen to the native speaker with the respect due a primary source, and accept his comments with minimal disturbance.

THE PHONETIC
ALPHABET

The first of several purposes of this book is to provide a means whereby an individual actor can achieve proficiency during performance in the use of the most needed stage dialects. The second is to make sure that the representation of each dialect is faithful to its primary sources, free from the multiple malpractices and the time-ridden clichés which have always plagued this aspect of stage work. A third purpose is to make study procedures as simply utilitarian as possible, unencumbered by the plethora of detail which necessarily must be part of the work of the regional-speech expert. To this end it may seem a contradiction of purpose to present the phonetic listings given below. The addition, however, has the capability of decreasing labor even as it increases the validity of the work done.

The international phonetic alphabet, designed by the International Phonetic Association, establishes as standard one special mark or symbol for each separate human sound, thus freeing that sound from the uncertainties of our confused methods of spelling and the dissimilarities of various regional pronunciations. If the human voice can make a certain number of vocal sounds and each sound is represented by one symbol, certainty of analysis and understanding is assured. In this respect the phonetic alphabet has done more than any other means to achieve that assurance. It is unfortunate to relate, however, that the achievement is not entire.

Phonetics is not an exact science, mainly because of the element of human variability. A single symbol may represent a single human sound, but various humans produce different shapes for that sound; further, different ears hear the sounds differently. The result is that the best system yet devised to aid in the study and production of human sound is still an imperfect one, and phoneticians fuss at each other because of that fact.

Fortunately for the dialectician, imperfections arise mainly from subtleties, from shadings of inexactness which, although they must concern the speech expert, need not be part of our concern to nearly the same extent. Consequently, by avoiding the complexities and using only the basic elements of the phonetic system, the student can gain maximum benefit from his effort, even as he uses the system to make his study more accurate. In addition, a large number of actors already have some knowledge of phonetics; many of them undoubtedly possess degrees of expertness in the subject. At any rate the inclusion of the phonetic approach is intended as an aid in the studies ahead, not as an end in itself.

The student should know that differences of opinion among authorities (who in this inexact science can be authorities and still differ) result in different statements about many items of sound production and its scoring. Such differences apply to the formation and stress of certain vowels and to efforts to select a standard set of diphthongs. For us, the source of reference in matters of question will be Kenyon and Knott, *A Pronouncing Dictionary of American English*, or Daniel Jones' *Eng-*

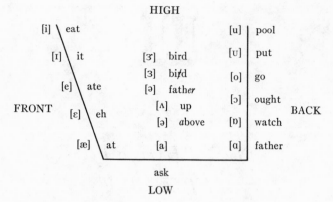

HIGH

[i] eat			[u] pool
[ɪ] it	[ɝ] bird		[ʊ] put
	[ɜ] biʳd		[o] go
[e] ate	[ə] fath*er*		
FRONT		[ʌ] up	[ɔ] ought	BACK
[ɛ] eh		[ə] *above*	[ɒ] watch
[æ] at		[a]	[ɑ] father

ask

LOW

lish Pronouncing Dictionary.[1] The ultimate sources of reference, of course, are the many on-the-street and in-the-shop studies conducted at home and abroad over a long period of years and now recorded on thousands of feet of tape. From the multiple individual differences heard and listed in every country comes the composite dialect which is an essentially just representation of the speech of all users.

The standard set of symbols of the international phonetic alphabet includes markings which distinguish subtle variations of sounds. To the trained ear these graded symbols are essential, indicating, for example, the difference between a regular or tapped [r] (see page 10), or the primary and secondary stress in a multisyllable word, or whether [m, n, l] are regular or syllabic consonants.

To the dialectician with his limited objectives such additions are cumbersome, beyond the needs of actor and audience alike. Consequently the symbols below have been kept as few in number as will serve our purpose. Further, explanations of the symbols are simple rather than complex. Although there are written descriptions of vowel, diphthong, and consonant formations, the main reliance is on the interrelation of written text and accompanying tape—eye reinforcing ear and ear supporting eye. Only such special symbols have been added to the phonetic alphabet as are necessary for representing sounds beyond the range of usual American usage.

In the vowel section of the alphabet, key words have been chosen to represent the vowel sound in an initial, medial, and terminal position. In some instances, however, the vowel may not figure in an initial or terminal

position. As the chart on the left shows, a vowel is categorized by the placement of sound in the mouth at the time of phonation, hence the employment of such terms as high front [i] and middle back [o].

In the list of diphthongs below, if a comparison is made, more will be found than are included in many standard texts (nearly every text has a slightly different list). They are needed because of variability of use in the many different dialects we will study. If your pronunciation of some of the key words differs from that of the speaker, the difference undoubtedly will be an aspect of regional variation. You will note, in the second part of each diphthong, a reliance upon just three vowels: [ə, ɪ, ʊ].

Consonants are conveniently grouped in categories in which the name indicates how the consonant itself is formed. Thus:

Plosives. Temporarily blocked air is suddenly released: [p, b, t, d, k, g].

Nasals. The sound wave is directed through the nasal resonating chambers rather than through the mouth: [m, n, ŋ].

Fricatives. Air is restricted by a partial closure in the throat or mouth so that an audible friction results: [f, v, ð, θ, ʃ, s, ʒ, z, h].

Semivowels: The sound of the consonant is full enough to achieve a vowel-like quality: [l, r].

Glides: Movement of articulators while forming a consonant causes a change of sound during pronunciation: [hw, w, j].

Combinations: A plosive and a fricative consonant are put together as one sound: [tʃ, dʒ].

	Voiced	*Voiceless*
Plosives	[b, d, g]	[p, t, k]
Nasals	[m, n, ŋ]	none
Fricatives	[v, ð, z, ʒ]	[f, θ, s, ʃ, h]
Semivowels	[l, r]	none
Glides	[w, j]	[hw]
Combinations	[dʒ]	[tʃ]

All consonants are either *voiced* or *voiceless*. The difference is determined by whether the vocal folds are or are not vibrating when the consonant is enunciated. In the table above you will notice that most but not all of

---

[1] John S. Kenyon and Thomas A. Knott, *A Pronouncing Dictionary of American English* (Springfield, Mass.: G. and C. Merriam Company, 1953). Daniel Jones, *English Pronouncing Dictionary*, twelfth edition (New York: E. P. Dutton and Company, 1964).

the voiced consonants are matched by voiceless ones. The only point of difficulty for the nonexpert user in this respect is that the consonant written *th* is both voiced and voiceless. Voiced, the symbol is [ð], voiceless, it is [θ]. In this same regard it will be noted later in several dialects that the voiced *th*, [ð], is replaced by the voiced [d] or [z], while the voiceless *th*, [θ], receives a substitution of the voiceless [t] or [s].

THE SYMBOLS AND SOUNDS OF THE PHONETIC ALPHABET

The phonetic alphabet and the additional symbols (page 10) are recorded on tape so that you may associate symbol with sound. To emphasize the sound being enunciated, the stress in the pronounced word is in some instances altered from the normal.

(*Voice:* Jerry Blunt.)

Vowels

Symbol	Key Word	Phonetic Representation
[i]	eat, believe, agree	[it, bə'liv, ə'gri]
[ɪ]	it, think, complicity	[ɪt, θɪŋk, kəm'plɪsətɪ]
[e]	ate, chaotic, hurricane	[et, ke'ɑtɪk, 'hɜɪken]
[ɛ]	ebb, bet, tent	[ɛb, bɛt, tɛnt]
[æ]	at, bat, habitat	[æt, bæt, 'hæbətæt]
[a]	car (*Brooklynese*), ask, dance	[ask, dans, ka:]
[ɑ]	on, father, schwa	[ɑn, 'fɑðɚ, ʃwɑ]
[ɒ]	watch, wander, Gotham	[wɒtʃ, 'wɒndɚ, 'gɒθəm]
[ɔ]	ought, gnawed, Shaw	[ɔt, nɔd, ʃɔ]
[o]	oboe, shrove, poncho	['obo, ʃrov, 'pɑntʃo]
[ʊ]	umlaut, put, took	['ʊmlaʊt, pʊt, tʊk]
[u]	pool, true	[pul, tru]
[ʌ] accented	up, above, Dutch	[ʌp, ə'bʌv, dʌtʃ]
[ə] unaccented, the schwa vowel	*a*bove, gen*e*sis, dat*a*	[ə'bʌv, 'dʒɛnəsɪs, 'detə]

Symbol	Key Word	Phonetic Representation
[ɝ] accented syllable, *r* sounded	further, bird	['fɝðɚ, bɝd]
[ɜ] accented syllable, *r* not sounded	further, bird	['fɜðə, bɜd]
[ɚ] unaccented syllable, *r* sounded	further, mother	['fɝðɚ, 'mʌðɚ]

Diphthongs

Symbol	Key Word	Phonetic Representation
[ɪə]	beer, here, steer (*Southern*)	[bɪə, hɪə, stɪə]
[ɛə]	there, head, west (*Southern*)	[ðɛə, hɛəd, wɛəst]
[eɪ]	eight, great, weigh	[eɪt, greɪt, weɪ]
[aɪ]	aisle, time, cry	[aɪl, taɪm, kraɪ]
[aʊ]	ouch, how, allow	[aʊtʃ, haʊ, ə'laʊ]
[ɔɪ]	oil, choice, employ	[ɔɪl, tʃɔɪs, ɪm'plɔɪ]
[oʊ]	oat, toad, throw	[oʊt, toʊd, θroʊ]
[ju]	union, you, review	['junjən, ju, rɪ'vju]

Consonants

Note that audibility is supplied to the voiceless consonants by the accompanying vowel.

Symbol	Key Word	Phonetic Representation
[p]	peep	[pip]
[b]	bob	[bɑb]
[t]	tat	[tæt]
[d]	dad	[dæd]
[k]	kick	[kɪk]
[g]	gag	[gæg]
[m]	mam	[mæm]
[n]	Nan	[næn]
[ŋ]	singing	[sɪŋɪŋ]
[f]	fife	[faɪf]

Symbol	Key Word	*Phonetic Representation*
[v]	vivid	['vɪvɪd]
[s]	seal	[sil]
[z]	zeal	[zil]
[θ]	think	[θiŋk]
[ð]	the *or* that	[ðə, ðæt]
[ʃ]	sheep	[ʃip]
[ʒ]	vision	['vɪʒən]
[h]	hot	[hɑt]
[r]	rear	[rɪr]
[l]	lily	['lɪlɪ]
[hw]	what	[hwɑt]
[w]	watt	[wɑt]
[j]	yet	[jɛt]
[tʃ]	church	[tʃɝtʃ]
[dʒ]	judge	['dʒʌdʒ]

Additional Symbols

1. [']. This single mark indicates the accented syllable in a multisyllable word. The symbol always precedes the syllable accented, as in '*running*, a'*bout*, *abso*'*lutely*. It will also be used to indicate the misplaced stress in a foreign dialect, as in the French pronunciation of '*about* and *run*'*ning*, or the Japanese double stress of '*abuso*'*rutery*.

2. [:]. Two dots indicate a prolonged vowel sound which should be held as such, not made into a diphthong. It is heard in the Brooklynese pronunciation of *there* [ðɛr], which becomes [ðɛ:], or *car*, which is [kɑ:].

3. [ɔ:]. This is the Daniel Jones symbol for the Standard English pronunciation of a fuller, rounder [ɔ] as in *ought* than Americans are used to making. It will be heard in such words as *ought, all, law, awful*.

4. [ʔ]. The question mark without a bottom dot is the glottal-stop symbol and is used primarily in the Cockney and Scotch dialects. To effect the sound the vocal folds close momentarily, causing a build-up of air pressure which is suddenly released and allowed to come out freely, but without being made into the particular consonant, usually *t*, the glottal stop replaces. With the use of the glottal stop the word *bottle* ['batl] becomes ['bɔ:ʔl], and *bet you* changes to [bɛʔjə].

5. [ɛʳ]. This symbol is a variant of the actual [ɛr] as heard in *air*. Its principal use is in the Scotch, Russian, and Italian dialects, where it mainly replaces the [ɝ] symbol as pronounced in *bird* [bɝd], in which case [ɝ] becomes [ɛʳ] and *bird* is [bɛʳd], just as *first* [fɝst] is [fɛʳst].

The raised [ʳ] signifies a tongue tap [ɛʳ—ɛʳ] (see p. 93).

6. [~]. Placed over a regular phonetic symbol, a wavy mark indicates nasality. Distinctly French, the sound is commonly heard, for example, as either [ɔ̃] as in *bon* [bɔ̃] (*good*), or *vin* [væ̃] (*wine*), although it also is heard in such combinations as the *ment* [mɔ̃], *ant* [ɔ̃], and *tion* [siɔ̃] endings in many French words, such as *département, distant*, and *attention*.

7. [y]. This French sound is made by pursing the lips in a tight circle with the tip and the sides of the tongue against the lower teeth and with the jaw dropped a little as the vowel [u], as in *pool*, is pronounced, thus [y]. In a French dialect this sound would be heard in the pronunciation of English words such as *sue* [su] or *just* [dʒʌst], making [sy] and [ʒyst].

8. [œ:]. This thoroughly French vowel is made by forming [ɛr] as in *air*, but with lips pursed, jaw dropped, and pharyngeal cavity hollowed so that [œ:] results. [œ:] is heard in the French word *acteur* or in a French pronunciation of the English word *course*, making [kœ:rs] (*of course, but of course*).

9. [x]. This symbol represents a sound in both a German and Scotch dialect. It is produced by a relatively heavy expulsion of breath on the vowel [ɑ] as in *on*, or the vowel [ɔ] as in *ought*. The German exclamation *ach!* or the Scotch word for *lake*, which is *loch* [lɔx], both use the sound.

10. [ç]. This is another German and Scotch sound, heavily aspirated. The extra expulsion of breath which forms the [ç] sound is stopped in Scots by a partial closure of the consonant *k*, making [çk]. Good illustrations are found in the two words *right* and *bright*, pronounced in Scots as *ri-k-t* [rɪçt] and *bri-k-t* [brɪçt].

11. [β]. Although this marking is principally employed in scoring a unique *b-v* combination in the Spanish language, we make use of it in the Japanese dialect. The sound the symbol represents is a cross between *b* and *v* and is made by bringing the upper and lower lips together as for *b* until they almost close, and in this position saying *v*. Since the Japanese have no *v* they intrude a portion of the sound of its closest consonantal neighbor, the *b*, and the result is the one heard and listed as [β—β].

ADDITIONAL COMMENT

Some comment is required on certain of the above symbols to clarify their use.

1. [e]. It is held by many speech experts that [e] is not

a pure vowel but part of the diphthong [eɪ]. Since Kenyon and Knott list it singly as [e] (*rate*), and the simplification helps rather than hinders, it suits our purpose to use it as such.

2. [a]. This vowel has a restricted use in America, mainly limited to the areas of New England and New York. Consequently its formation is difficult for many. The sound lies halfway between the [æ] of *at* and the [ɑ] of *father*. Since it is used in several dialects it is included here.

3. [ɒ]. This is another vowel of limited use—Eastern and American Southern—and consequently is difficult to hear and form by nonusers. Halfway between [ɑ] (*father*) and [ɔ] (*ought*), it is best made by saying [ɑ] then holding that sound while rounding the lips for the word *wall*.

4. [ɝ], [ɜ], [ɚ]. Regional differences and the need to indicate whether or not the vowel is stressed require the above series of symbols. [ɝ] is the mark for *er* when the syllable is stressed and the [r] sounded, as when *bird* [bɝd] is pronounced by most Americans. However, for those Southerners and Easterners who do not sound the [r], the symbol is [ɜ]. In a third use of *er*, the mark [ɚ] denotes that the vowel is sounded with [r], but that the syllable itself is unstressed, as in the last syllable of *father* ['fɑðɚ]. (If the pronunciation is Southern, the final syllable will not be any form of *er*, instead it will be the schwa vowel [ə], which is discussed next.)

5. [ʌ, ə]. Here are two symbols for the same sound. The use of the first, [ʌ] as in *up*, denotes that the vowel is accented. The use of the second, [ə], as in the first syllable of *above* [ə'bʌv], indicates that it is not. Unlike other vowels, [ə] has been given a name, the schwa vowel, and the status of a neutral sound, probably the most commonly used vowel sound in any language. If sufficient air is expelled to make a sound, but no particular one is intended, the chances are the resultant sound will be the schwa, [ə]. More often than not, dropped final syllables in any language are heard as this sound, almost as an unformed residual.

6. The flexibility of use to which some of the sounds listed above are going to be put in the studies ahead is best illustrated by the variability of that most versatile of all vocal sounds, the phoneme [r]: it is slurred or dropped in American Southern, Japanese, and Standard English; hardened in Midwestern American and Irish; single tapped in Standard English, Japanese, and others; trilled with tip of tongue in Scotch, Russian, and Italian; trilled with back of tongue and uvula in French and German; and changed to a half or a full [l] in Japanese.

III

JAPANESE

A Japanese dialect takes special character from the fact that no other native speech has so great a contrast with spoken English. Inasmuch as it provides the basis for an unusual and distinctive delivery, the contrast is fortunate—a clear and understandable Japanese dialect is a most attractive speech.

But it also presents challenges. First, it requires a mastery of new and unusual combinations in the articulatory process. Second, it demands a knowledge of what to select and what to reject in authentic reproductions of primary-source material. The first of these problems is solved by practice and will be fully treated in the exercises which follow. The second is solved by developing a good ear, one that will accurately indicate what key sounds should or should not be used.

Crossovers in vocal action, as the sounds of one language try to accommodate themselves to those of another, do not always produce understandable results. For dramatic purposes the most authentic dialect in the world is of no value if words and meanings are not clear. When a Japanese employs his articulatory habits on English words, one of several things can happen. First, the word he utters may convey no meaning at all to a listener, even when that word is supported by its context. Second, his formation of the word may be understandable, but only when heard in phrase or sentence context. Last, the word may be quite clear, both in and out of context.

The first of these results is to be avoided, no matter

how authentic the transposition is. Two words, singly and in context, illustrate the point: *sip* [sɪp] in a proper Japanese dialect is pronounced *sheep* [ʃip], both the *s* [s] and *i* [ɪ] undergoing change, and *tea* [ti] is pronounced *tchee* [tʃi]. One of the original words becomes a wholly different word while the other becomes a nonword. Nor, in this instance, is there help from context. *Sip your tea* would be heard as *sheep your tchee* [ʃip yuɑ tʃi]. Some clarity might come from an increase of context, for instance, "Please, do not rush, take the time to *sheep your tchee.*" But even then the use of the authentic key sounds is highly questionable.

On this basis the need for a good ear is apparent. When acquired, it will indicate that certain key sounds must be used only slightly and others, authentic as they might be, not at all. The key sounds of [ʃ], [tʃ], and [tsu] fall in this category; each will be treated in more detail later.

A different kind of a detective problem is involved in those key sounds that require context for clarity. Sometimes, in the crossover from Japanese to English, even simple words are required to sustain marked changes. As a result these words, to be understood, must rely heavily on the inherent sense of phrase or sentence. *Very* provides a typical illustration. When the [v] changes to [b] and the [r] to [l], *bely* results. When spelled, this is a nonword; pronounced, its sound identifies the subject with anatomy. But when the word is used in context, the change has a good chance of being sustained—*bely good* ['bɛlɪ gʊd] is a readily understandable combination of words. It follows that the element of context, when it assures understanding, can aid the dialectician in determining the degree of alteration and emphasis a key sound may sustain.

Fortunately, aid beyond that of context is also available. A great number of words are susceptible of more than one authentic crossover. Again *very* can be used. If only one substitution is made, the word can be pronounced as either *bery* or *vely;* each is correct. Moreover, both are strong and both are understandable. It follows that if a legitimately simple key substitution gives increased assurance of clarity, it should be used. Practice in the problem of selectivity is contained in the work ahead, even though the script and the voice on tape will at times overlook this policy by giving full treatment to some of the more obtuse key sounds.

It is proper that most key sounds be presented for study and practice.[1] Therefore the determination of usability is left to the judgment of each performer, the acquiring and sustaining of which should be a natural consequence of this study.

Perhaps the first characteristic of a Japanese dialect to attract the ear of a dialectician, besides the ever-present [r-l]-[l-r] interchange, is the intrusion of extra vowel sounds—[u], [ə], and [o]—in all speech patterns. The Japanese syllabic constitution usually requires each consonant to have its own vowel; even when two consonants come together, they do not sound as they do in our speech. When a Japanese speaks English he corrects what is to him a linguistic error by unconsciously inserting a vowel between adjacent consonants if they are within a word, or between a terminal and an initial consonant in consecutive words—*cannot* ['kænɑt] becomes *conunot* ['kænunɑt], or *knock down* [nɑk daʊn] sounds as *knocku down* [nɑku daʊn].

Sometimes the intruded sound is barely audible, in which case it will probably be the one most commonly uttered in any language, the schwa vowel [ə], as in *above* [ə'bʌv]. When the intruded vowel is more noticeable it becomes either [u], as in *pool*, or [o], as in *obey*. Guidelines are given later.

Although English-alphabet transcriptions of Japanese appear to contain diphthongs, a Japanese is unaccus-

tomed to the formation of diphthongs as they occur in our language. Accordingly he will tend to do in English what he does in his own speech: make an elongated vowel out of our various vowel combinations. Since double vowels are usual in Japanese—*o-o-kii* is the sound of the word *big*—his tendency will be to treat diphthongs as single sounds, simply lengthening the resultant vowel when necessary. This vocal action, however, is of minor rather than major significance. In actual practice it seldom delays the formation of a vowel or slows down the delivery of phrase or sentence.

As an expected circumstance between contrasting languages, a Japanese speaker makes many sounds not usual to us. If you have heard lines delivered by an actor in either a Noh or Kabuki drama, sounds that to our ears are always highly exaggerated, you will readily recognize this point. Of more pertinence to our study is the fact that we make a certain number of sounds not indigenous to a Japanese. New positions of lips, jaw, and tongue and new articulatory movements demand his attention and practice. The degree of vocal success he achieves determines the strength of his dialect. Naturally, partial success—an accomplishment marked enough to guarantee clarity but not proficient enough to constitute mastery—provides the best basis for a strong dialect. Those crossovers of vocal action that give him the most trouble are the ones we will concentrate on.

In the above connection it should be noted that there is a rapidly growing number of persons whose use of a Japanese dialect would be subtle and slight rather than broad and strong. Americans of Japanese ancestry, fluently bilingual, form the main body of this group. Fewer, but numerous enough to be reckoned with, are those Japanese nationals who have developed English as a second language to an extent close to mastery. Only occasionally will such a person lapse and let an [r-l] interchange or a [b]-for-[v] substitution creep into his speech.

The number of vocal substitutions, especially of consonants, which may be made in a Japanese dialect is unusually large. Ordinarily this would be a fortunate circumstance tending to enrich the dialect. But again the problem of clarity presents itself. To reinforce the illustration given earlier, let us consider the case of the word *river*. Here is a five-letter word which legitimately can take four substitutions: [r] changed to [l], [ɪ] to [i], [v] to [b], and [ɚ] to [ɑ]. When spelled out the word *leeba* results, phonetically ['libɑ] is heard. A challenge

---

[1] Some minor key sounds which are only heard intermittently—[v] for [w], [ŋk] for [ŋ], or [d] for [ð]—have not been included in what is already a very full dialect.

to the dialectician's judgment is posed by the presence of these multiple substitutions. Which will you select and which reject when you must use this word?[2]

A more difficult problem of clarity is presented by the Japanese pronunciation of our syllables [si], [ti], and [tu], as in our words *sea*, *tea*, and *to*. In Japanese, [s] before [i] becomes *sh* [ʃ], so that *cereal* and *system* would be pronounced *shereal* and *sheestem* [ˈʃɪrɪəl, ˈʃɪstɪm].

In like manner [t] before [i] becomes *tch* [tʃ]; therefore *team* and *romantic* change to *cheam* [tʃim] and *romanchic* [romantʃik]. In the same vein [t] before [u] is made into *tsu* [tsu], changing *two* (*to*, *too*) to *tsu* [tsu] and *tooth* [tuθ] to [tsus]. A case can be made that some of the above syllabic alterations would be recognizable singly and in context, but such is the change in *sea*, *tea*, and *to* as well as in *team* and *tooth* that caution must be exercised, indicating again that clarity must sometimes take precedence over fidelity to primary-source pronunciations.

KEY SOUNDS OF A JAPANESE DIALECT

The concentration ahead is on the formation and delivery of those sounds which a Japanese speaking in English has not been able to master. A characteristic that will be noted is the practice of not forming in full several consonant sounds. This effect is caused by a failure of lips and tongue to complete syllabic formation as fully or as emphatically as we do in English. Typical is a [b]-for-[v] substitution in which the bilabial action falls short of bringing the lips together, producing a partial [b] which, like its Mexican counterpart, has a slight sound of [w] included. The symbol for this consonant is [β]. Even more distinctive is the terminal [r-l] exchange. Its partial formation is described in detail later.

As in other dialects, niceties of grammatical construction are often missed. If a playwright is aware of this fact, the actor has only to follow the indications in the script. But if the author has not made such indications, it is quite proper to add this element to your delivery. Omission of definite and indefinite articles, substitution of singulars for plurals and confusion of tenses, with a preference for the present tense, are typical errors that can be put to use.

---

[2] A Kyoto guide solved the problem by using *riba* [ˈribɑ], which in context was quite plain: "Boat wait at *ribaside*."

Vowel Substitutions

1. THE INTRUDED VOWELS: [u], [ə], AND [o].

a. [u] AND [ə]. Because the syllabic structure of his language is ingrained in his speech, a Japanese will habitually insert a vowel, [u] or [ə], between consecutive consonants in a word. Sometimes the intruding sound will be strong, in other instances barely noticeable; [u] is the strong, [ə] the weak vowel. Examples: *absolutely* [abusoˈrutəri], *department* [dəˈpatəmənto], *Bangkok* [ˈbaŋukakə].

b. When a word ends in a consonant a slight, moderate or strong vowel sound is added. The tendency, universal in scope, to drop terminal sounds creates the usual inconsistency. If the sound is slight, the schwa vowel [ə] is used, as in *noon* [nunə]. When it is moderate or strong, especially after a plosive (except *t* or *d*), the [u], as in *pool*, is sounded: *dog* [dɔgu], bark [baku].

c. If one word ends with a consonant and the next begins with another, either [u] or [ə] is inserted between the two: *dog bark* [dɔgu baku], *back down* [baku daʊnə], some books [sʌmə buksə].

d. After the plosives [t] and [d], when either is in a terminal position or when the next word begins with a consonant, an [o] is added: *boat* [boto], *boat go* [boto go], *friend* [frɛndo], *friend come* [frɛndo kʌmə].

2. [i] FOR [ɪ].

As in Romance languages and Russian, the Japanese dialect substitutes an [i] as in *eat*, for [ɪ] as in *it*. Not as consistently used as in French or Italian, the change is still marked enough to warrant emphasis. The substitution tends not to occur when the vowel *i* is in the initial position, hence *in* [ɪn] not [in], and *imperial* [ɪmˈpɪrɪlr] not [imˈpɪrɪlr]. In an internal position, however, the change is often heard: *river* [ˈrivɑ], *nip* [nipə], *live* [livə], *little* [ˈlitə].

3. [ɑ] FOR [æ], [a], AND [ə].

[ɑ], as in *father*, has a more extensive use in a Japanese dialect than it does in American speech. The substitution is not consistent; not every [æ] as in *at* and [a] as in *ask* are transposed into the broader [ɑ] form, but enough are so changed to call attention to the practice: *brand* [brænd] becomes [brɑnd], *ask* [ask] becomes [ɑsk], and *sofa* [ˈsofə] becomes [ˈsofɑ].

4. [ɑ] FOR [ɚ].

[ɑ] is substituted for the unaccented terminal *er* [ɚ], and the change is emphatic. In this instance the tendency to drop a final sound does not hold; more often than not the substituted [ɑ] is pronounced with some vigor. *Mother* ['mʌðɚ] becomes ['mʌzɑ], *batter* ['bætɚ] changes to ['bɑtɑ], and *worker* ['wɝkɚ] to ['wʌkɑ].

Diphthongal Changes

Since a Japanese is unpracticed in our formation of diphthongs his tendency is to make our two blended vowels into one long one, especially if he has but little English. As his proficiency in English speech grows his attempts at sounding the diphthong will be marked by partial rather than full enunciation. The latter case is more likely to be a noticeable effect when listening to primary-source sounds, however, than a practical effect to be incorporated into the dialect.

Consonant Substitutions

1. [r], [r-l], [l-r], AND [lr].

The [r] is subject to more different kinds of treatment in all dialects than any other consonant in the English alphabet. It is not neglected here. Actually, it receives more rigorous treatment and is subjected to greater alteration in Japanese than in any other dialect. Here are the various things that happen to it.

a. [ɹ]. When placed after a vowel and before a consonant, [r] is not pronounced: *work* [wʌk], *person* ['pʌsn], *garden* ['gɑdn].

b. [r] TAPPED. When an [r] is neither dropped nor changed into [l] it is pronounced with a tapped (but not trilled) effect, an action in which the tongue tip, taking the customary position near the upper gum ridge as for a normal [r] sound, then makes a quick tap, sometimes two. The action is identical whether a natural [r] or an [r] for [l] is involved. *Rock* is the same as *lock* when the latter is made to sound like *rock*. *Like* is *rike*, *black* becomes *brack*, and *explain* changes to *exprain*, each [r] being tapped.

c. [r-l] AND [l-r]. An interchange either way between [r] and [l] is the most emphatic and most recognizable vocal action in a Japanese (and Chinese) dialect. But the simple statement that every [r] becomes an [l] and

vice versa is not correct. These two consonants do interchange and the alteration is clearly noticeable when either is in an initial position: *right* and *room* into *light* and *loom*, and *like* and *lake* into *rike* and *rake*. (Note that the four substitutions created three other words each with a meaning in its own right, so that if these changes were made, the speaker must be sure that sentence context makes his meaning clear.)

A study of primary sources indicates that [l] might become [r] a little more often than the reverse in the speech of one who is fairly fluent. When [r] is substituted there is a danger, or an opportunity, of comic implications: *lound* and *lound* (*round* and *round*), *Moon Liver*, *Lambling Lose*.

Medial [r] and [l] can also be interchanged in the same way as indicated above.

d. [lr] is a designation of [r] substituted for medial or terminal [l]. [r] is substituted for a medial or terminal [l] (*l* or *ll*) in a distinctive manner previously heard only in lower middle-class English and Cockney speech. The unique feature of this exchange is that the crossover is not complete, neither a full [l] nor a full [r] is sounded. The [r] predominates, however, it being the last sound formed. To achieve the proper effect begin to make an [l], with the tip of the tongue extended toward the alveolar or upper gum ridge. Then, while the tip is extended but before it touches the ridge, form and enunciate an [r]. The resultant mixture of these two consonants produces the desired effect. Proficiency is required because of the extensive use of this unique combination.

Since there is no phonetic designation for this sound, we will adapt [lr] to the purpose. *Well* [wɛl] becomes [wɛlr], *all* [ɔl] changes to [ɔlr], and *full* [fʊl] is heard as [fʊlr]. Some phoneticians simplify the [lr] combination by substituting the diphthong [ɪə] for it. This easier sound is correct but less full and distinctive.

2. [s] FOR [θ] AND [z] FOR [ð].

People of several different languages have difficulty in forming the sound of the English *th*, both the voiceless [θ] and the voiced [ð]. The basic reason for the difficulty is that those languages have no sound that requires the placement of the tongue forward of and against the bottom part of the upper front teeth. Since this placement is one of the more extreme actions in which the tongue is involved, those to whom the motion does not come naturally generally fail to force the tongue far enough forward, leaving it in the position that produces either a voiceless [s] or a voiced [z].

The Japanese, having no *th* sound, freely substitute [s] for [θ], and [z] for [ð]. Consequently *thoughtful* and *theatre* become *soughtful* and *seatre*, while *these*, *those* and *other* change to *zese, zose* and *ozer.*

3. [h] FOR [f].

The fricative [f] is not native to the Japanese language. It does appear in words borrowed from English such as *fork—fooku.* In a consonantal substitution not often encountered, the Japanese form the lips in such a way as to make [h] instead of [f]. When they try to form [f] the action draws the lips into a position closer to the one we use for *wh* [hw], which is the placement you should effect to produce the required [h]-for-[f] substitution. If the result of this action is not clear, however, clarity can be obtained by initiating the [h] and then partially forming the [f] itself. Listen to the word *family* in the word drill that follows.

There is a major exception to the above requirement. The sacred mountain, Fuji, is known to all and pronounced by all just as it is spelled in English. Accordingly, [fu] is an exception. Otherwise such words as *fourteen, fifty, effort,* and *coffee* are pronounced ['hɔtin], ['hɪftɪ], ['ɛhɔtə], and ['kohi].

4. [β] FOR [v].

Like the voiceless fricative [f], the voiced [v] also receives a substitution. A not quite full [b] replaces it. The sound [β] that results when the lips do not quite meet as they normally would is the sound required. It might be called a Mexican [b]. *Very* as *bery* and *river* as *riber*, with the [b] not fully formed, illustrate the substitution. Do not be surprised if the sound of [w] sometimes replaces the [β].

5. [si], [ti], AND [tu].

As was explained earlier, a limited use of the following substitutions is recommended.

a. [s] BEFORE [i]. When placed before the vowel [i], as in *eat*, [s] becomes *sh* [ʃ]. *Sip*, pronounced with [i] instead of [ɪ], becomes *sheep* [ʃip], *sea* becomes *she* [ʃi], and *kissing* ['kɪsŋ] changes to ['kiʃŋə].

b. [t] BEFORE [i]. Following the same pattern as [si]

above, [t] before [i] is pronounced as *ch* [tʃ], so that *tip* becomes *tcheep* [tʃip] and *ticket* changes to *tcheeket* ['tʃikɛtə].

c. [t] BEFORE [u]. Somewhat like [ti] above, [t] before [u], as in *tool*, has an [s] inserted between consonant and vowel. The result is *tsu* [tsu]. With this addition, clarity of meaning becomes a problem: *two* is *tsu, tool* is *tsur,* and *tooth* is *tsus.*

Additional Characteristics

1. INTAKE OF BREATH.

An audible intake of breath during pauses between or in the middle of sentences is an established characteristic of both Japanese speech and dialect. A foreigner, hearing the sibilant rush of air for the first time, is inclined to think that this phenomenon is the result of nervousness, or at least a nervous reaction to the presence of strangers. Japanese linguists, however, say that the external action of drawing in air is motivated by an inner mental process of thinking, of considering, or of collecting thoughts. As such it corresponds to our use of *hm-m-m-m.*

A sibilant action of some distinction, this vocal characteristic can serve a dialectician well when judiciously employed. But overuse or undue stress in utterance can easily turn a unique character trait into a blatant caricature.

To produce the proper sound, narrowly part and extend the lips sideways as you draw air in over the teeth. A soft rather than a harsh sibilance is desired.

2. [ɑ-hɑ-hɑ-hɑ-hɑ].

Another vocal characteristic of some interest is heard when a Japanese listener, to show his attention and his interest, interjects a series of *a* [ɑ] and *ha* [hɑ] sounds in response to the speech of another. The utterance may be short and quick—*a-ha!*—or be extended to a series of *a-ha-ha-ha*—with five to a dozen repetitions. Basically this burst of vocal explosions is intended to say, "I understand, I'm following you," but it also includes an habitual attitude of politeness.

Overused, the expression is bound to detract; such is its strength that overuse is easy. Restraint, however, can put to good use a distinctive addition to a Japanese dialect.

3. AH, SO.

Although the phrase *ah, so* is overworked, especially by those who pick it up as a kidding colloquialism, it has a legitimate use. Functioning in much the same manner and for the same reason as *a-ha-ha-ha-ha*, it can either be heard by itself or as part of a longer phrase, *ah, so, desuca* ['dɛsəkə]. The middle vowel [ə] is so slightly uttered as barely to be heard; sometimes it is not formed at all.

KEY-SOUND WORD DRILL

The material in this section is to be practiced in coordination with the Japanese Dialect tape. The voice on the tape will pause after each word so that you may repeat it immediately, checking your pronunciation against that of the speaker. You are also given space for making notes. The slow tempo and exaggerated enunciation are deliberate, distorted so that you may clearly hear the full sound and discern the muscular action which accompanies it.

(*Voice:* Jerry Blunt.)

Vowel Substitutions

1. [u], [ə], AND [o].

    a. THE INTERNAL [u] OR [ə]. Absolutely, France, taxi, bathtub, attractive, wilful.

    b. THE TERMINAL [u] OR [ə]. Dog, bark, trap, girl, fork.

    c. [u] OR [ə] BETWEEN TERMINAL AND INITIAL CONSONANTS. Tank full, tall man, stop quick, girl go, cup coffee.

    d. [o] OR [ə] BETWEEN MEDIAL OR AFTER TERMINAL [t] AND [d]. Hot dog, notebook, football, bat, last, friend, glad.

2. [i] FOR [ɪ]. River, big, think, Italy, sister.

3. [ɑ] FOR [æ], [a], OR [ə]. Accident, brand, and, ask, back, apple, cinema, sofa.

4. [ɑ] FOR [ɚ]. Mother, batter, later, latter.

Consonant Substitutions

1. [r], [r-l], [l-r], AND [lr].

    a. [ɾ]. Work, porter, surprise, card, large, perform.

    b. TAPPED [r]. Are, careful, really, love, please, hello, elephant.

    c. [r-l]. Round and round, Moon River, Rambling Rose, already, rice, precious, strike, dry cleaning.

    d. [l-r]. Lots of luck, Los Angeles, look, island, glad, people, silent, Helen.

    e. [lr]. Well, all, careful, girl, yellow, bill, sell, silk.

2. [s] FOR *th* [θ]. Thing, thought, theatre, north, health.

    [z] FOR *th* [ð]. The, these, this, father, clothe, breathe.

3. [h] FOR [f]. Family, fourteen, fellow, fiddle, coffee, effort, officer.

4. [b] FOR [v], WHICH IS [β]. Very, vacation, victor, have, average, television, elevator.

5. [si] TO [ʃi], [ti] TO [tʃi], AND [tu] TO [tsu]. As will be noted upon pronunciation, clarity will indicate a lim-

ited use of the following items. For the sake of practice several words whose use is questionable have been included.

a. [s] BEFORE [i] TO [ʃ]. System, cigarette, seemingly, cigar.

b. [t] BEFORE [i] TO [tʃ]. Tea, team, ticket, romantic, Argentine.

c. [t] BEFORE [u] TO [ts]. Two, tulip, tooth, tonight.

Additional Characteristics

1. INTAKE OF BREATH. *S-s-s-s-s-s; s-s-s-s-s-s-s.*

2. A-HA-HA. A-HA-HA-HA-HA.

3. AH, SO. *Ah, so, des-u-ca.*

KEY SOUNDS IN SENTENCE CONTEXT

(*Voice:* Lloyd Kino.)

Vowel Substitutions

1. [u], [ə] AND [o].
   a. THE INTERNAL [u] OR [ə]. The taxi was absolutely attractive. / The passport was from Spain and France.

   b. THE TERMINAL [u] OR [ə]. The girl had a cup, a fork, a book, and a ball. / I think the dog will bark at every ship.

   c. [u] OR [ə] BETWEEN TERMINAL AND INITIAL CON-SONANTS. The tall man placed his bookmark between the pages. / At the Imperial Hotel the doorman got the lady a cup of coffee.

   d. The terminal [o]. The last boat left the river bank. / Oh, Dad hid his head.

2. [i] FOR [ɪ]. The big fish did not live in the river. / His sister thinks she will win.

3. [ɑ] for [æ], [a] and [ə]. The Sahara cinema was brand new. / The ant sat with his sack on the sofa.

4. [ɑ] FOR [ɝ]. Mother gave butter to the batter. / Later the latter came after.

Consonant Substitutions

1. [ɾ], [r-l], [l-r], AND [lr].
   a. [ɾ]. The marshal's sparkplug was covered with carbon. / That person will not barter his cart.

   b. TAPPED [r]. Please say hello all around the island. / The elephant's forelegs were absolutely too long.[3]

   c. [r-l]. We already sang *Moon River* and *Rambling Rose.* / The crown lost much prestige because of the big ransom.

---

[3] A tapped rather than a trilled [r] is recommended.

d. [l-r]. Lots of luck in Los Angeles. / All clouds float above the lovely little lake. / Please listen, Lillian, the people call hello.

e. [lr]. Tell the girl in the yellow dress to be careful. / Well, well, well, do you think all the people will come?

2. [s] FOR *th* [θ]. The author never thought any such thing. / The athlete went north to the theatre.

[z] FOR *th* [ð]. The mother will gather the clothes. / I would rather have this thing than that thing.

3. [h] FOR [f]. It is a felony to drink coffee after the curfew. / Few people have flat feet.

4. [b] FOR [v] MAKING [β]. The television is never in the elevator. / Every victory has an average value.

5. [si] TO [ʃi], [ti] TO [tʃi], AND [tu] TO [tsu].
a. [s] BEFORE [i] BECOMES [ʃ]. His sister did not like cigarettes or cigars.

b. [t] BEFORE [i] BECOMES [tʃ]. The romantic actor was very distinguished.

c. [t] BEFORE [u] BECOMES [ts]. The two tulips will not bloom tonight.

Additional Characteristics

1. INTAKE OF BREATH. I think the massage girl will arrive at the Okura Hotel at possibly eleven o'clock. / Please, where is the signal to call the bellboy or the room maid?

2. A-HA-HA-HA. Now, please listen closely. (*A-ha*) The porter will take your bag for you to the taxi. (*A-ha-ha*) Then you will buy tickets for train to Hakone where you stay Fujiya Hotel. (*Ah, so, desuca*)

READING FOR FLUENCY

For purposes of clarity and to demonstrate the full scope of the dialect, a slower than normal tempo is used.

Baseball in Japan

(*Voice:* Lloyd Kino.)

The game of baseball is as popular in Japan as in the United States, and it is played exactly the same way. To the eye of the casual observer what differences there are seem superficial. For example, the officials are greeted politely and not with raucous boos, and before the game begins the teams line up and bow to the umpires who just as formally return the bow. Again, when the two team managers present the batting order to the plate umpire each bows to him and he repeats their action. However, this ceremonial movement does not mean that manager-umpire relationship is founded on friendly feelings. On the contrary, the leader and the whole team can be very unhappy about a "wrong call."

Each team takes the field to warm up while the fans are coming into the stands. When everything is ready, the plate umpire calls "Play ball!" Then the pitcher goes to the mound, the catcher squats behind home plate, the first, second, third basemen and the shortstop are spaced in the infield while the three outfielders are in their places on the outfield grass. After that, the batter steps into the batting box where he alertly waits for the pitcher to throw the ball. After each delivery the umpire waves his arms and calls "Strike one!" "Ball two!" "Strike three, you out!" or "Ball four, base-on-balls."

Japan has its big leagues. There are two of them, the Central and Pacific, and each includes six teams. Tokyo has two clubs, the Giants and Orions. It is plain that the American influence is strong for there are such other team names as Nankai Hawks, Hanshin Tigers, Chu-nichi Dragons, Taiyo Whales, Hiroshima Carps, and Sankei Atoms. Each team has a large following in this most popular of sports.

The Merchant of Venice, *Shakespeare;* Act I, Scene 1

(The following material was selected for practice, not presentation. To unaccustomed ears, Shakespeare is sometimes difficult to understand even in English. When his work is taken out of context and spoken in dialect, his words can be incomprehensible. However, because of the strength and juxtaposition of key sounds and the physical flexibility required for fluent delivery, this passage has served many a student very well indeed. For this reason it is included here.)

(*Voice:* Jerry Blunt)

GRATIANO: Oh, let me play the fool:

With mirth and laughter let old wrinkles come,

And let my liver rather heat with wine

Than my heart cool with mortifying groans.

Why should a man, whose blood is warm within,

Sit like his grandsire cut in alabaster?

Sleep when he wakes and creep into the jaundice

By being peevish? I tell thee what, Antonio—

I love thee, and it is my love that speaks—

Oh, there are a sort of men whose visages

Do cream and mantle like a standing pond,

And do a wilful stillness entertain,

With purpose to be dressed in an opinion

Of wisdom, gravity, profound conceit,

As who should say, "I am Sir Oracle,

And when I ope my lips let no dog bark."

INDIVIDUAL-PRACTICE EXERCISES

Key-Sound Word Drill

1. The following words are scrambled in a mixture of vowel and consonant substitutions. When determining proper pronunciation, be sure that the degree of dialectal change does not impair understanding.

In all the exercises of this section space has been left below each line for phonetic symbols and other markings.

pillow	sip	highway	good time
they	though	younger	busiest street
rambling	foolish	rival	put back
month	demonstrate	carbon	brought down
cigar	Shanghai	sack	nearest town
dish	fourteen	organize	lets see
hand	hall	seem tame	peanut sack
taxi	late	roof paper	head cold
fork	ransom	since then	paper bag

2. The following key sounds have been placed beside each other so that you may practice the change of lip, tongue and jaw positions necessary for the making of the proper sounds.

Never; book; round; had—strike; elevator; yellow; feather—taxi; polite; television; system—romantic; north; dog; large—stop sign; paper box; left march; lifetime—barracuda; cigarette; evening; distinguish—listen; youthful; sick; passport—fight; believe; health; spark—ah, so, desuca; bathtub; Vera; glad—stillness; sister; believe; effort—ships; lantern; think; people—have; oak stick; elephant; hotcake—attractive; Los Angeles; dry; illusion—tenth; them; think; thorn—weather; dwell; few; place—overcome; wilful; please; tulip—overcoat; first; ant; did—riverside; tankful; carp; careful—surprise; English; already; gather—family; proper; hello; victor.

Key Sounds in Sentence Context

To have a big ticket is a felony.

Please drink your cup of coffee in silence.

The sailor ordered a little fried rice.

Football, boxing, and sumo are all violent games.

Only fourteen aesthetic officers were left.

France is absolutely a very big place.

Long Island is really very little.

Lily will work hard this voyage.

All brown barracuda are large fish.

Mother and father sat together on the sofa.

The big river runs into the lovely little lake.

Japan has very fast and efficient trains.

Ten thousand people climbed Mt. Fuji last Saturday.

The ancient road runs by the sea from Tokyo to Kyoto.

Nikko has very many magnificent shrines and beautiful cedar trees.

Toba is the beautiful place where cultured pearls are grown.

Nara is the famous home of the tame deer.

Round and round the mulberry bush.

The little girl looked long at the big doll.

It will not help to ridicule Helen.

SIGHT READING AND FLUENCY PRACTICE

Japan

The island country of Japan is a beautiful place. Not only is there an abundance of natural beauty, the people themselves are most sensitive in this respect and have created many palaces, temples, parks and gardens of great attractiveness.

Nikko has its famous shrines and its equally famous cedar trees. Kyoto, ancient capitol of Japan, treasures its unmatched temples, among which is Ryoanji [rio'ɑndʒi] with its little lake, its moss garden, and its famous rock garden, a place of serene beauty where every year thousands come to sit in silent meditation on the steps of the Zen temple.

Not far distant from Kyoto is the still older city of Nara. Miles of parkland house the herds of deer that move as freely as the many visitors over the grass and in the temple courtyards.

Toba, located on a spectacular stretch of coast, is the home of the Mikimoto pearl culture. There hundreds of oyster racks are planted in the offshore water to produce the thousands of gems so prized for their distinctive lustre. The new hotel that is located on a rocky headland affords a spectacular view of the coastline.

Appreciation of beauty is not the sole property of the trained architects, decorators, and landscape artists of Japan. So ingrained is this attitude that even in the crowded cities little and large garden plots are planned and planted wherever possible. And traveling through the countryside, on one of the many fast and efficient trains that are the main source of travel from one area to another, one can see how even the stacks of cut grain and reeds are laid out to dry in patterns that please the eye.

Nowhere can more beautiful children be seen. The fact that all faces are round, that all hair is black and cut in the same traditional way, and that the features are always framed by the same kind of round hat in no sense detracts from the appeal of these well-trained youngsters. Dressed in western style or in the native kimono, the very young accompany their parents in a decorous manner. Later, as school children in grammar, junior or senior high schools, they travel their country in guided groups ranging from five to fifty, even to a hundred or more, to visit famous places both near and far.

The Traveler

(On this exercise, try making such grammatical changes as you think proper: for instance, omit articles and leave off plurals.)

The average traveler arriving in Japan from the United States will probably have two strong but quite different reactions. One will be a response to the fact that there are a very large number of things that are familiar. For example, the airport, if the visitor is flying, or the pier, if he is traveling by sea, will look just like the airports and the docksides at home. Then, on the streets in any large place, the private cars, the trucks, and the public taxis will move in traffic patterns similar to the ones he drives in at home; even the "*kamikaze* taxi driver," so famous in Tokyo, is not unknown to him. After all, he probably has had his share of freeway driving. The big buildings, with elevators and all modern appliances, also will be very familiar. So, too, will be the western style of dress of a large part of the population. And of course, since so many people have studied English as a second language, he will hear it spoken in many locations, surprisingly well in very many instances.

Not so familiar, and all the more attractive for that reason, are the evidences on every street of the native dress. Colorful and comfortable, the kimono looks as pleasing on the male figure as on the female. And of course the little boys and girls look very fine indeed.

Japanese politeness also varies greatly from the more casual manners of the Westerner. With both hands placed on the upper legs, the torso of the Japanese person bows from the waist with a fullness of movement that expresses regard for more than the outward forms of politeness. Smiles of considerable width and length often are an important part of the greeting.

And then there are the sounds. Here truly there is a radical difference. For mixed in with the sounds of most vocal exchanges—it makes no matter whether they are in Japanese or English—are the distinctive and often attractive expressions so typically native. First, one will probably hear the very commonplace "Ah, so," or the longer "Ah, so, *des-u-ca*." For example, if one friend is speaking to another, the following might be heard.

"I had a long letter from Mr. Sato last week——"

"Ah, so."

"——and he said he will arrive at the Imperial Hotel on Friday, the fourteenth."

"Ah, so, *des-u-ca*."

Or perhaps, if one person were asked a question, this answer might be heard.

"Oh, (intake of breath) I think the ball game between the Orions and the Carps will begin at exactly (intake of breath) four o'clock."

And still a third vocal habit is heard when one Japanese person signifies his polite attention by exclamations like those in the following.

"What do you think, I have just learned that the students of the English Club at Yamaguchi University will present Arthur Miller's *Death of a Salesman* in February."

"Ah, ha-ha."

"They have planned the first rehearsals so that visitors are welcome."

"Ah, ha-ha-ha-ha."

"Will you want to come with me?"

"Oh, (intake of breath) I certainly think so. I have long wanted to meet those particular students. Thank you very much. See you later. So long."

IV

NEW YORK—BROOKLYN

New York City has all the dialectal variation expected in so large and complex a metropolitan population. Consequently no one pattern of speech can be designated as truly representative of the whole area; there is no such thing as a comprehensive New York dialect. This fact causes the dramatic dialectician to seek specific indications as to what kind of New York speech he is to deal with: the speech of the foreign-born, such as Italian, Yiddish, Puerto Rican; or regional speech of Americans from New England, the rural Midwest, or the South; or the sounds of educated Americans speaking Standard speech; or substandard local speech —for these are the principal ingredients of vocal communication in the greater New York area.

There is a distinct individuality to each of these groups. It should be no surprise to the dialectician that diverse foreign-language blocks have maintained identity, some more, some less, within a communicative field that also features a class speech side by side with representations from various American geographical areas. The result over the years has not been an amalgam in equal or unequal proportions of all these contributing language factors. Members of the Yiddish language community have not altered the speech of salesmen or secretaries from Oklahoma, no matter how long the latter have been at work in the big city. Nor has the Puerto Rican dialect affected the communicative patterns of those of Italian descent any more than New England speech has influenced the Puerto Rican. The diverse forms—foreign, native to the city, Ameri-

can regional, Standard American—still exist; class, education, cultural and linguistic backgrounds predominate as speech determinants. And they predominate in spite of the fact that size of population, proximity of residential areas to work areas, and a speech traffic as constantly flowing and as constantly mixed as is vehicular traffic would seem to militate against precisely set local speech patterns. Yet the patterns are there, each one generally holding its own against intrusion from neighbors.

If there is one distinctive form of vocal expression more shared today than any other, it is one that causes no problem for the average actor. What can loosely be called Standard American—a bulk form of speech now reaching from coast to coast among the educated, the users of dictionaries—exists as noticeably in New York as it does in St. Louis, Salt Lake City, or San Francisco. In this connection it should be noted that what would seemingly be the most pervasive effect on the speech of each new generation, the language of the home, has consistently given way before a pressure for conformity to the language of a community. In a noticeably strong pattern, second-generation Americans have everywhere sought to identify with the new rather than to maintain continuity with the old; the communicative forms of the classroom and schoolyard have triumphed over those of kitchen and parlor. This evolutionary process may be less strong in neighborhoods where language groups exist in solid blocks; but a pervasive hope for educational, economic, and social success in the American way still influences the young to want to sound like friend rather than like family, if there is a difference.

The above indicates that the dramatic dialectician, when studying some roles local to New York City, would have to seek a basis for his dialect in sources external to the area, such as the foreign accents of Yiddish or Italian, or the regional speech of Down East or rural Wyoming. In one notable instance, however, he would not. In the greater metropolitan area of New York there exists one of the most unusual speech forms in America: Brooklynese.

The Brooklyn dialect is distinctive for its uniqueness of pronunciation, the variety of its syntax, and the strength of its idiom. According to one authority, Brooklynese probably is the most set-apart speech, in fact and in popular awareness of that fact, of all American dialects.[1] The scope of this regional speech is as extensive as it is pervasive. While "there is no evidence . . . that any purely geographical variation in speech patterns really occurs within the city, certain pronunciations may have a higher frequency in one neighborhood than another"; and the Brooklyn accent, which "is merely uncultivated New Yorkese, *may be heard in all the boroughs, and in Jersey City and Hoboken as well*."[2] (Italics mine.) Accordingly when an indigenous New York speech is wanted to represent large masses of persons average or below average in education and occupation throughout the city, writers have turned to the use of Brooklynese. For that reason, we study it here.

Both foreign and native influences can be noted in the Brooklyn dialect. Racial backgrounds, for example, are represented by a number of Irish, Italian, and Yiddish sounds and mannerisms. Irish is heard in the pronunciation of such words as *father*, *car*, *time* and *like*, while Italian is noted in a multitude of slurred syllables of the kind that makes "What do you want" sound like "Wha-da-ya-wan'," and Yiddish manifests itself by the addition of a [g] or a [k] to *ing* [ɪŋ], causing *running* to be pronounced *running-ga* [ˈrʌnɪŋg] or *running-k* [ˈrʌnɪŋk].

Native influences are noted in a particular style of speech and a distinctive manner of delivery. It is the writer's responsibility to set down the style, ours to achieve the delivery. Both style and delivery are motivated by the environmental forces indigenous to the area. In this respect Brooklynese finds a counterpart in that metropolitan section of London which houses the Cockney. Although neither dialect influences the other in the slightest degree, both respond with like reactions to like conditions. As is true of Cockney, the Brooklyn dialect features marked vitality in delivery. Sustained tonal energy reflects the vigor of a life that must strive for space and livelihood under most competitive circumstances. Also like the Cockney, the average speaker of Brooklynese is loquacious. Vocal verbosity, almost childlike in its insistence to be heard, is a characteristic of many practitioners of the dialect, though not of all by any means, for it is as possible for an individual to be quiet and withdrawn in Brooklyn as anywhere else. However, a general impression of compulsive talking does exist, enough so that one may feel quite safe in making use when needed of this particular idiosyncrasy.

Brooklyn speech, again like its Cockney counterpart, is unusually expressive. A need to make one's wants and feelings known in an environment so crowded as to be insensitive to slight utterances motivates a more than usual stretch of vocal elements. In another statement that reflects the average person rather than the distinct individual, it can be said that seldom is there doubt as to how a speaker of Brooklynese thinks and feels on any subject. Such revelation can be accomplished only by the use of more than average variety in pitch, tempo, and force patterns. Accordingly, the range of pitch should extend well over the three- to five-note spread of the usual conversational average, while tempo, seldom tending toward slow, should be used in a medium-to-fast pace balanced by a considerable variety of stop and go. Force is used to make the emphatic statements which permeate even the average Brooklyn speech, with much employment of stress on accented syllables. Further, it is in the evolving of such patterns as these that the possibility of an argumentative tone exists; this is another characteristic sufficiently well established to be used in safety by the dialectician.

In contrast to the variable use of pitch, tempo, and force, the element of quality, the last of the four tonal elements in every voice, may be more restricted. The reason could lie in part in the fact that there is a tendency toward nasality in the area; sufficient evidence can be heard on almost any street to support this statement. The reasons for the prevalence of this condition are many, most of which lie outside the scope of this study; it is pertinent only to suggest that an argumentative whine may be a vocal mannerism passed down from pre-

---

[1] Allan Forbes Hubbell, *The Pronunciation of English in New York City* (New York: Columbia University Press, 1950).
[2] Hubbell, p. 11.

vious generations, but in the matter of delivery this suggestion should be regarded as an indication of a possibility, not as an admonition for compliance.

Like so many other dialects in the English-speaking world today, Brooklynese is losing both strength and scope. Popular education, increased ease of travel, and the mass media of communication everywhere have a debilitating effect upon the individuality of regional speech. Loss of distinctiveness in both syntax and pronunciation results. But since the dialectician as often as not must deal with the scene that was as much as with the one that is, the presentation here is made in full strength and with full coverage. The only exceptions to this statement are found in those instances in which certain key sounds, like the glottal stop [ʔ] and the intrusive [r], are discussed because of their validity but not recommended for use for reason of their better employment elsewhere.

KEY SOUNDS OF BROOKLYNESE

Two major characteristics, opposite in kind, condition the formation of syllables in Brooklynese. The first is the practice of making diphthongs out of many vowels —a gliding or slurring process which denotes communal unconcern for preciseness of speech, perhaps even an unconscious flouting of the authority of social class and classroom. The results are shown below.

The second characteristic demonstrates a reverse process. In it syllables are eliminated as words are shortened to the barest essentials of sound: *and* to *an'*, *him* to *'um*, *because* to *'cause*, *happen* to *hap'm* and *something* to *sum'pum* to give a few of many possible illustrations. The process should be immediately recognizable—all of us in every area daily follow the same pattern, if not always to the same extent. Muscular laziness and a natural unconcern for the niceties of enunciation in the easy give and take of ordinary conversation motivate this practice; it is one of our strongest communicative habits. In Brooklynese the process is responsible in part for the large number of colloquialisms which permeate the speech of the area. Much use can be made of this characteristic by the dialectician.

In contrast, there is another feature of the Brooklyn dialect which must, though valid, be handled cautiously and used sparingly, if at all. Indeed, the recommendation here is that this feature either be eliminated entirely or employed unobtrusively. The item in question is a glottal stop. Always a distinctive feature, this valvular action in the larynx is so strongly identified with the British Isles dialects of Cockney and Scotch that employment in Brooklynese runs high danger of missuggestion. The dialectician, trained to full strength and relishing the use of any unique sound, will do well to restrain himself in this instance.

In this connection a wiser course, one that loses nothing in validity, is to substitute a [d] for a [t] and thus legitimately avoid conflict with the glottal stop action. On this plan, *bottle* ['bɑtl] would be pronounced *boddle* ['bɑdl] rather than the *bot'le* ['bɔʔl] of Cockney or Scotch.

Another distinctive but inconsistent feature, the intrusive [r], is also more usually identified with another area and class. The addition of [r], unwritten but sounded, after a terminal vowel—*idea* pronounced as *idear* [aɪ'diɚ]—can be heard in any lingual cross section of New York speech. But it is a vocal action most readily identified with a quite different class and with other localities outside the metropolitan area, so much so its use in Brooklynese could call unwanted attention to itself. As with the glottal stop, the recommendation is for little or no use of this vocal characteristic—the loss will scarcely be noticed in an already full-bodied dialect.

Vowel Substitutions

1. [ɛ] AND [æ] OR [ɛə] AND [æə]. A major feature of Brooklynese is the strength and variety with which the "short *a*" is pronounced. The flatness of sound associated with the dialect arises from a vocal action that places many an *a* forward in the very front of the mouth. The resultant sound may be that of [ɛ] as in *eh*, [æ] as in *at*, or an in-between sound that variously slides from one to the other. In a further characteristic action either the [ɛ] or [æ] as often as not may be stretched into the diphthongs [ɛə] or [æə].

Allan Forbes Hubbell, who was quoted earlier, notes the inconsistency that is present in the treatment of this front vowel when he states: "Many New Yorkers— and this is probably the commonest pattern of all, especially on the intermediate levels of metropolitan speech —pronounce [ɛə, ɛ, æə, æ] in words like *glad, stand, jazz,* in an extremely haphazard fashion." Another authority, C. M. Wise, says "the casual student of substandard New York speech is passably safe in rendering almost any 'short *a*' as [ɛə].[3]

---

[3] C. M. Wise, *Applied Phonetics* (Englewood Cliffs, New Jersey: Prentice-Hall, Inc., 1957), p. 283.

This recognized inconsistency offers a degree of freedom to the dialectician, making it a proper practice to favor now one and now the other of these vowels, according to whichever comes easiest in context. But whatever the variation, the pronunciation of the vowels [ε] or [æ] or the diphthongs [εə] or [æə] is to be strong; failure in this respect will seriously weaken the dialect.

2. [a] FOR [ɑ]. As another indication of the flattening process, the sound of the back vowel [ɑ] as in *father* is pushed forward to the middle position of [a], as in an Eastern pronunciation of *ask* [ask] (not [æsk]). The substitution is made in all three syllabic positions—initial, medial and terminal. Thus it is a duplication of a major key sound of the Irish dialect, which probably was its source. Accordingly *opera* ['ɑpərə] becomes *op'ra* ['aprə], *father* ['fɑðə] changes to ['faðə], and *Utah* ['jutɑ] to ['juta].

3. [ʌ] OR [ə] FOR [ɝ] OR [ɚ]. When *er* [ɝ] is the vowel sound in single-syllable words it is replaced in Brooklynese by [ʌ] (*up*): *her* [hɝ] is replaced by [hʌ]. When the same vowel is terminal in a multisyllable word, the unstressed [ə] is used to represent the changed sound: *helper* ['hɛlpɚ] becomes ['hɛlpə]. Obviously this substitution is not restricted to a Brooklyn dialect but can be heard in uncultivated or unconcerned speech in many areas.

4. [εr]. When an [εr] syllable is in a terminal position the [r] is dropped and the [ε] is extended to [ε:]. In this case *there* [ðεr] becomes [ðε:]. The elongation of the vowel, which is sustained for about as long as it takes to produce the original [r] syllable, is the key to the sound. In some cases the schwa vowel [ə] might replace the dropped [r], but when this occurs the result can sound quite Southern. Since [ε:] is sufficient in itself, the addition of [ə] is neither recommended nor given here.

Diphthongal Changes

1. [æʊ] FOR [aʊ]. Again the practice of pushing a sound forward to make it shorter and flatter can be heard when [aʊ] as in *town* [taʊn] is changed to [tæʊn]. Similar in vowel formation to a Cockney practice, this diphthongal change is often nasalized, as it is in Cockney. Some nasalization is necessary; too much is to be avoided, otherwise merely a nastiness is projected.

2. [ɒɪ] FOR [aɪ]. A Brooklyn dialect alters the standard pronunciation of such a word as *mind* [maɪnd] to the fuller and rounder sound of [mɒɪnd]. Here again is a relation to the Irish dialect. The [ɒ] vowel, you may recall, is produced by a formation which lies halfway between the [ɑ] of *father* and the [ɔ] of *ought;* outside of Eastern New England, [ɒ] is seldom heard and consequently is not easily formed by many. Still, the sound is needed, if for no other reason than that [ɑ] is not strong enough and [ɔ] is too strong.

3. [ɔɪ] FOR [ɝ]. The substitution of [ɔɪ], as in *loin*, for *er* [ɝ], as in the stressed syllable of *bird* [bɝd], is *the* sound most strongly identified in popular consciousness with a Brooklyn accent. To establish identity with Brooklynese, all one has to do, anywhere in the land, is to utter the words *Toity-toid Street* ['tɔɪtɪ-tɔɪd strit] and the link is made. In a consistent substitution [ɔɪ] replaces [ɝ] in all words, except when [ɝ] is the terminal sound. Thus *bird* [bɝd], *girl* [gɝl], and *work* [wɝk] change into the well known *boid* [bɔɪd], *goil* [gɔɪl], and *woik* [wɔɪk].

Fortunately for the dialectician, few key-sound substitutions in any dialect are as easily made and as easily sustained. With a little practice either ear or eye should readily detect the instances in which an alteration is to be made, and the articulators, already accustomed to the pronunciation of [ɔɪ] in such words as *oil* [ɔɪl], will readily make the change.

4. [ɝ] FOR [ɔɪ]. In a curious switch, an exact reversal is made of the substitution explained immediately above —a not uncommon phenomenon which you will encounter several times in these studies. So specific is the alteration, the word *loin* [lɔɪn] becomes *lern* [lɝn], *oil* [ɔɪl] changes to *erl* [ɝl], and *joint* [jɔɪnt] to *jernt* [jɝnt].

As in the item above, this one is also readily identified with a Brooklyn dialect. Its use, however, is not nearly as consistent, a point of some importance, for not all [ɔɪ] diphthongs take the [ɝ] substitution. Indeed, fewer rather than more are involved; among other things [ɝ] never occurs in a final syllable. For example, *oyster, choice, joint,* and *spoil* have the change, but *boys, Lloyd, royal, toys, voice, deploys, envoys,* and many others do not.

Furthermore, the [ɝ] for [ɔɪ] substitution is not as up to date as the others we are dealing with. For some reason or other this key sound has not sustained itself as well as others and consequently is heard less; perhaps its inconsistency is one of the reasons. Whatever the cause, its use or nonuse now becomes a matter of time. In earlier decades it would be heard more, in the later ones less, with World War II a reasonably accurate dividing line.

5. [ɪə] FOR [ɪr]. The result of Brooklynese unconcern for precise enunciation, a slurred pronunciation of *hear* [hɪr] becomes *he-a* [hɪə], creating one of the stronger key sounds of the dialect.

[ʊə] FOR [ʊr]. Paralleling the above item, [ə] is likewise substituted for [r] when joined with [ʊ], as in *put*. Thus *your* [jʊr] becomes *yu-a* [jʊə] and *sure* [ʃʊr] is pronounced *schu-a* [ʃʊə]. The word list for this substitution of a diphthong for a vowel-consonant combination is limited.

6. [oɪ] FOR [ɔɪ]. A subtle rather than a broad change characterizes this substitution. The muscular formation and the placement of [ɔ] as in *ought*, to [o] as in *go*, is very close. Consequently a slight but noticeable change occurs when, in Brooklynese, *boy* [bɔɪ] is pronounced [boɪ]. The alteration takes place in stressed syllables before a vowel, *royal* becoming ['roɪəl] instead of the standard ['rɔɪəl], and in final open syllables as when *destroy* [dɪ'strɔɪ] is pronounced [dɪ'stroɪ]. There is a hint of Irish in this substitution.

7. [ɔ:wɔ] OR [ɔə] FOR [ɔ]. This is one of the most distinctive key sounds in the Brooklyn dialect. It is also the most complex. Always strong, the amount of strength varies from speaker to speaker, all the way from the more involved [ɔ:wɔ] to the simpler [ɔə]. The vowel [ɔ] as in *ought* is the point of departure. To record the Brooklynese substitution at its fullest it is necessary to use the English phonetic symbol of [ɔ:] as employed by Jones in his *Pronouncing Dictionary*. [ɔ:] represents a back vowel sound more rounded and hollow than any usual American sound, consequently its formation requires a more extreme muscular action than we are used to. A reference to the sound of [ɔ:] on the tapes for the phonetic alphabet, or Standard English, would be helpful here.

From the initial [ɔ:], when this substitution is given full strength, the sound glides through the position that ordinarily produces the consonant *w* [w]. However, the sound of the *w* [w] is as much suggested as heard in the vocal progression to either [ɔ] of *ought* or *o* [o] of *go*, with [ɔ] preferred. Put together as an habitual action, the sound should be full but not slow; the diphthong is strong enough as it is without additional emphasis accruing from the element of time. Accordingly *talk* [tɔk] becomes [tɔ:wɔk] and *cause* [kɔz] is pronounced [kɔ:wɔz].

When this substitution is given with least strength the original [ɔ] vowel receives the addition of [ə], so that *talk* [tɔk] becomes [tɔək]. This last effect does little to strengthen the dialect, creating a minor-key sound rather than a major one. However, in the tempo of ordinary conversation it is heard quite often. The first of these two variations is the one featured on the accompanying tape.

Consonant Substitutions

1. [r].

a. [ɤ]. [r] is eliminated when it is in a final position or after a vowel and before a consonant. Thus *war* [wɔr] is [wɔ], and *warm* [wɔrm] is [wɔm]. Like pronunciations of *gear*, *star*, and *storm* offer further examples. Care should be taken that when the [r] is dropped it is not replaced by the schwa vowel, the unaccented [ə].

b. THE INTRUSIVE [r]. A recognizable characteristic of Eastern speech is the addition of [r] after a terminal vowel, especially if the next word begins with another vowel. The word *idea* [aɪ'diə] pronounced as *idear* [aɪ'diɝ] quickly identifies the practice. Because it is much more firmly established in cultivated speech, at least in the minds of those not native to the area, and strongly identified with such personalities as Presidents Roosevelt and Kennedy, the intrusive [r] is not recommended for use in Brooklynese stage dialect, even though it can be heard in primary sources.

2. [ɓ] AND [ɗ]. Again unconcern and lack of precision are manifest in the practice of dropping [b] and [d] when either is in a middle position in a multisyllable word. *Probably* ['prabəblɪ] pronounced *pro'bly* ['prablɪ] and *fundamental* [fʌndə'mɛntl] pronounced *fun'amental* [fʌnə'mɛntl] illustrate the practice. It will be recognized that this diction can be heard in many other areas as well as in Brooklyn.

3. [d] FOR [t] OR [tt]. A marked but subtle feature of Brooklynese is the substitution of [d] for [t] or [tt]. This is in addition to the more commonplace practice in many dialects of substituting [d] for *th* [ð], which is the subject of the next item below.

In the making of syllables, [d] is more easily formed than [t], consequently it replaces [t] whenever there is a tendency to slur—and slurring is a consistent characteristic of Brooklynese. *Beautiful, British,* and *pretty* pronounced respectively as *beaudiful, Bridish,* and *priddy* illustrate the practice, one that is also heard elsewhere.

4. [d] FOR [ð], and [t] for [θ]. A substitution of the plosives [d] and [t] for the fricatives [ð] and [θ] is another major characteristic of the dialect, one that has long been associated in the popular consciousness with the speech of the Brooklyn area. *The, them, other*, and *mother* pronounced [də], [dɛm], ['ʌdə], and ['mʌdə] represent a substitution of [d] for [ð], while *think, author*, and *with* given as [tɪŋk], [ɔtə], and [wɪt] illustrate the substitution of [t] for [θ].

5. [m] FOR [n] OR [ŋ]. A speaker of Brooklynese has no more claim to this vocalization than thousands of other Americans across the land. That fact, however, does not preclude the use here of this particular idiosyncrasy. The effect is recognized when *seven* and *standpoint* are pronounced *sev'm* and *stam'point*, or when *leaving* and *slipping* are given as *leav'm* and *slip'm*. This practice is also treated later in An Additional Characteristic, in which the dropping and eliding of syllables of all kinds are included in one process.

6. [n] FOR [ŋ]. In what is one of the most common malpractices in American speech, the g of ng [ŋ] is dropped, shortening the present-participle ending *ing* [ɪŋ] to *in'* [ɪn]. Examples: *runnin', eatin'*, and *talkin'*. If the sounds are further degenerated, as they often are, and the schwa vowel [ə] replaces the [ɪ] vowel of *ing* [ɪŋ], then the uncultivated sound of *run-un'* ['rʌnən], *ea-tun'* ['itən], and *talk-un'* ['tɔ:wəkən] will be heard.

7. [ŋ] TO [ŋg] OR [ŋk]. When a foreign linguistic background is present, principally Yiddish or Slavic, a Brooklyn dialect can show the effect by the addition of [g] or [k] to *ing* [ɪŋ]. In this event the g of *ng* is not dropped as in item 6 above but receives a regular pronunciation to which is added [g] or [k]. The result, though occasionally soft, generally is striking, so much so that unless there is a specific need to indicate particular foreign influences, the practice is better left unused. No examples are given on the accompanying sound track.

8. [j] FOR [hj]. A simple case of physical slackness causes the pronunciation of *hu* [hju] to be shortened to *u* [ju]. Consequently *human* ['hjumən] becomes *'uman* ['jumən], and *humor, 'umor* ['jumɝ].

9. [w] FOR [hw]. In a like action, the h of *wh* [hw] is also dropped. This simplification is commonplace throughout the country and can be heard wherever thoughtlessness and laziness pervade speech patterns. By this action all *wh* [hw] sounds are altered: *when*

[hwɛn] to *w'en* [wɛn], *what* [hwɑt] to *w'at* [wɑt], and the like.

An Additional Characteristic

Dropped and elided syllables. The practice of dropping and eliding syllables in words and phrases is so pervasive in a Brooklyn dialect it must be treated as a major characteristic, one that stands boldly forth in its own right. Few other regional speech patterns, even the most bucolic, can equal Brooklynese in this respect. Not only does this element demonstrate an unconcern for proper speech habits, it also shows a distinct attitude toward those forms of authority whose function it is to set standards of manners and practices for others to follow. Interestingly enough, this attitude is not necessarily one of disrespect, as would ordinarily be supposed, but rather one of self-sufficiency or self-certainty, as though to say "You have your rules, I have mine, and mine are just as good as yours." The same attitude is found in the vocal delivery of a Cockney, and for precisely the same reasons.

In each case the result comes from a lack of complete articulatory action. Consonants and vowels are dropped or incompletely formed in words and phrases to the extent that an auditor is required by habit to supply the exactness the speaker lacks. In other words, a full sound must be assumed from a partial or suggested sound. As a result, contractions of many kinds occur, the speaker, with accustomed ease, tying the remaining syllables together over the gap of the unpronounced syllables.

The dropping or eliding of so many different vowel and consonant combinations is a process quite native to most of us, at least by ear if not by practice, a process that began in the street and schoolyard even if it did not do so in the home. So usual is it that examples can be readily understood without benefit of the multiple listings required to denote each category.

The following instances indicate the frequency and extent of this vocal characteristic; a̸lmost, pi̸cture, ques̸tion, pad̸dle, chic̸ken, temp̸e̸rature, got t̸hem, let's go, giv̸e me, wha̸t i̸s going on, help̸e̸d ̸him, jus̸t b̸ecause, t̸hat's w̸h̸y, an̸d so ̸on.

In addition to the above, it should not be overlooked that the usual American mispronunciations exist in Brooklyn to the same extent they do elsewhere: *git, jist, kin, wuz, ta* for *to, ya* or *youse* for *you*, and many more.

KEY-SOUND WORD DRILL

Space is left beneath each line for your writing of symbols or notes.

(*Voice:* Larry Moss.)

Vowel Substitutions

1. [ɛ] AND [æ] OR [ɛə] AND [æə]. And, hand, answer, Nebraska, laugh, yea, disaster.

2. [a] FOR [ɑ]. Father, opera, car, hard, obstinate, spa.

3. [ʌ] OR [ə] FOR [ɜ] OR [ɝ]. Her, blur, stir, Dodger, further, letter, talker, feller.

4. [ɛ:] FOR [ɛr]. There, where, care, fare.

Diphthongal Changes

1. [æU] FOR [aU]. Town, now, round, about, bound.

2. [ɒI] FOR [aI]. Mind, find, wide, ride, why.

3. [ɔI] FOR [ɜ]. Thirty-third, bird, girl, work, jerk, person, permanent, certainly, world, curl.

4. [ɝ] FOR [ɔI]. Oil, joint, choice, oyster, ointment.

5. [Iə] FOR [Ir]. Hear, fear, clear, near.

   [Uə] FOR [Ur]. Your, sure, endure, pure.

6. [oI] FOR [ɔI]. Boy, join, noise, royal, enjoy, exploit.

7. [ɔ:wə] OR [ɔə] FOR [ɔ]. Talk, off, horse, because, normal, moth, caught, across.

Consonant Substitutions

1. [r̸]. War, warm, far, farm, gear, star, year.

2. [b̸] AND [d̸]. Probably, submarine, hundred, wonderful, fundamental.

3. [d] FOR [t] OR [tt]. Beautiful, British, writer, batter, pretty.

4. [d] FOR [ð]. The, these, this, brother, father, feather, rather.

   [t] FOR [θ]. Thank, think, thing, earth, north, truth.

5. [m] FOR [n] OR [ŋ]. Seven, open, cabin, oven, bye and bye, slipping, leaving.

6. [n] FOR [ŋ]. Running, throwing, talking, ending.

7. [j] FOR [hj]. Human, Hugh, humid, humor.

8. [w] FOR [hw]. What, when, why, white, whine.

An Additional Characteristic

DROPPED AND ELIDED SYLLABLES. And, because, that's, him, her, something, twenty, chicken, temperature, let's go, come here, want to, going to, out of, clean them.

KEY SOUNDS IN SENTENCE CONTEXT
Vowel Substitutions

1. [ɛ] AND [æ] OR [ɛə] AND [æə]. Grandpa and grandma answered the letter from Nebraska. / The batter hit

a three-bagger that fell on the grass. / Yea, imagine, Sam and Annie was laughing.

2. [a] FOR [ɑ]. Father drove the car into the yard. / The bar to the ark was obstinate.

3. [ʌ] OR [ə] FOR [ɜ] OR [ɚ]. Her purpose was to further stir the batter. / The taller sailor was the main talker.

4. [ɛ:] FOR [ɛr]. There was little care for the fare. / The bear did not dare leave his lair.

Diphthongal Changes

1. [æʊ] FOR [aʊ]. How about right now? / Myrtle was bound to get around town.

2. [ʋɪ] FOR [aɪ]. You'll find what you like on the ride. / The high path is wide and dry.

3. [ɔɪ] FOR [ɜ]. The girl works on 33rd Street. / This jerk is certainly a permanent person.

4. [ɚ] FOR [ɔɪ]. You got to put oil on that joint. / Today the oysters are choice.

5. [ɪə] FOR [ɪr]. Come here without fear.

[ʊə] FOR [ʊr]. You're sure the water is pure?

6. [oɪ] FOR [ɔɪ]. The boy will enjoy the exploit. / The toy coin came from the royal purse.

7. [ɔ:wə] OR [ɔə] FOR [ɔ]. I talk because it's normal to talk. / Get off the horse at the corner. / The moth was caught in the storm.

Consonant Substitutions

1. [ɼ]. They don't care if they are far from the war. / What is the form of the fare this year?

2. [b̶] AND [d̶]. The submarine is probably a hundred yards from here. / I'm sending you a bottle of wonderful fundamentals.

3. [d] FOR [t] OR [tt]. That British writer wrote about the turtle. / Those batters look pretty little.

4. [d] FOR [ð]. This feather belongs to father. / Ain't you bothered by the rather hot weather?

[t] FOR [θ]. To tell the truth, I thought that North was there. / Why on earth didn't you think to tell the truth?

5 AND 6. [m] FOR [n] OR [ŋ]; [n] FOR [ŋ]. Seven persons were running to open the cabin. / They'll be throw-

ing things from this standpoint bye and bye.

7 AND 8. [j] FOR [hj]; [w] FOR [hw]. What humans don't

suffer in humid weather! / Why you going to humili-

ate Hugh with white?

An Additional Characteristic

Don't you want to come here with the chickens so

that I can clean them?

Boy, that's really something when the temperature

gets all the way up to a hundred and twenty.

READING FOR FLUENCY
The Boys

(*Voice:* Patricia Madison.)

Come spring, summer, or autumn, in these times of

the almighty machine, some guys stand on the street

corner and talk and talk and talk. That's all they got to

do these days, because the chances are they are out of

work. A job ain't easy to come by, especially now when

everything is automated in a manner of speaking. A

person has to have a special kind of training, and that

ain't always easy to get, not if you already done your

high school time and should be considered to have

finished your education. So what else is there for a fellow

to do when he is waiting for something to turn up?

And talking is easy. There is all manner of subjects

for conversation—football and baseball and how the

various teams are making out—how the pitchers are

doing and if they are rotating proper and taking their

turns on the mound, and what their earned-run average

is, and how lousy they are at the plate with a bat in

their hands. And then there are the hitters, which is a

matter of daily concern, if for no other reason than that

the percentages are always changing and it takes a

sharp person to keep up with all the statistics, and if

there is one thing a fellow has got to know it is who is

leading the leagues in hitting, also who is getting the

home runs and the extra-base hits. And there is always

speculation as to whether so-and-so can stand up to the

pace or is he going to start slipping and go into a slump,

and stuff like that.

If it happens that the weather gets too hot, everybody

gets off the corner and goes into Maxie's for a beer. Then maybe they start talking about world affairs, which is a subject of immediate concern to all of us, and somebody remembers what it was like from the standpoint of being in the army and being stationed abroad. As like as not, even if he didn't get around none too much, he lets on like he did, seeing important people and talking with them and stuff like that, so he acts like he has all the answers for sure. In which case what else can the other guys do but clam up and listen. Unless of course there is some joker there that reads all the papers and thinks maybe he knows all the answers too.

In which circumstance, as like as not, the various parties are going to get real talkative, and the more words they let fly the more personal they are liable to get, until bye and bye they might get to throwing something besides words, like punches for instance. Then look out, because Maxie is sure to call in the law—what else can he do in circumstances like that? In which case

things are probably going to get back to normal pretty quick. There might even be a beer on the house.

Much Ado about Nothing, *Shakespeare;* Act II, Scene 1

(*Voice:* Larry Moss.)

BENEDICT: O! she misused me past the endurance of a block: an oak but with one green leaf on it, would have answered her: my very visor began to assume life and scold with her. She told me, not thinking I had been myself, that I was the prince's jester; that I was duller than a great thaw; huddling jest upon jest with such impossible conveyance upon me, that I stood like a man at a mark, with a whole army shooting at me. She speaks poniards, and every word stabs: if her breath were as terrible as her terminations, there were no living near her; she would infect to the north star. I would not marry her, though she were endowed with all that Adam had left him before he transgressed: she would have made Hercules have turned spit, yea, and have cleft his club to make the fire too. Come, talk not of her; you should find her the infernal Ate in good apparel. I would to God some scholar would conjure her, for certainly, while she is here, a man may live as quiet in hell as in a sanctuary; and people sin upon purpose because they would go thither; so, indeed, all disquiet, horror, and perturbation follow her.

Talking and Speaking

(*Voice:* Patricia Madison.)

Talking is one thing, but speaking is another, and there certainly is a world of difference between them. Talking is just talking, see, like between a certain two persons who have nothing else to do and are just sitting on the stoop passing the time of day. In which case whatever comes to mind is the immediate subject for their conversation—it can be about this or that, it don't make much matter what.

But speaking is different. It's like you was talking to a lot of people and what you was going to say was important. Then you've got to look out for your words and be sure you get the right ones so that you are expressing yourself proper. You make the right choice and you get yourself a point, as easy as spreading oil on water. Then you can get down to fundamentals and what you say will probably sound wonderful. But if you want to speak good, you certainly better rehearse, for sure as anything in the world you are going to be nervous.

Everybody talks, but certain persons speak better than others. For instance, Hugh, who is pretty good, always sounds better than Herbert, and that's the truth, though there ain't much the matter with the latter. And then there is Gertrude, who certainly is better than either of the others. Gertrude is actually a very serious person. She is so good she is never unprepared, even in an emergency. So when it comes to talking in front of the public, Gertrude is one of the finest speakers I know—for the money, she is my choice.

INDIVIDUAL-PRACTICE EXERCISES

Key-Sound Word Drill

1. The following words are scrambled in a mixture of vowel, diphthong, and consonant substitutions. In all the exercises of this section space has been left below each line for phonetic symbols or other markings.

				Key Sounds in Sentence Context
am	coin	humane	out and out	
yard	cause	where	taller	This person or that makes no matter.
burr	storm	happen	north	The brother stood around with his friend.
count	bear	person	lingerie	No wonder Max got the chicken for nothing.
time	clamber	scatter	tide	After crossing Madison, Myrtle stood on the corner.
circumstance	turtle	thought	joint	The Pasha stood firm in Persia.
point	those	certainly	loyal	They fear that the earl will come near here.
sneer	standpoint	kind of	corner	Madge and Dad are going to go to Jersey City.
allure	catching	you	bad	I'm going to New York because I want to.

2. The following key sounds have been placed beside each other so that you may practice the change of lip, tongue and jaw positions necessary for the making of the proper sounds.

bad; all; bounce; oil—badge; third; bath; church—

rafter; curb; gather; something—work; answer; be-

cause; further—store; person; wide; nothing—annoy;

wonderful; rehearse; grass—human; sneer; turpentine;

slipping—anger; forth; mother; north—youngster; yes;

personal; told—master; other; here; circle—probably;

kitty; catholic; hue—beautiful; earnest; round; farm—

service; oyster; boy; you—cold cream; let me; let's go;

what's the matter—why; batter; twenty; shirts—

imagine; her; seven; leaving—fine, fellow; learn; choice.

Person after person went to the new oil station.

The Dodgers probably will win another banner this year.

They lost thirteen footballs all told.

It certainly is a pleasure to talk to Norma.

Her brother is leaving seven keys to open the cabin.

Are you going to clean the car after all?

Grandpa is going to cut the grass by the grandstand.

Sam thought the theatre was north of there.

What in the world happened in Nebraska?

Herman worked very hard to earn his dinner.

Many dolls do nothing but talk and talk.

Yes, he certainly gave us a clear answer all right.

This is the joint where they serve very special oysters.

SIGHT READING AND FLUENCY PRACTICE
The Poster

"Come here, come here, and you shall hear, all about the wonderful world of words!" That's what the pretty poster said, all lettered out in purple and black colors. It was stuck up on the wall where everyone passing could see it for certain.

And it spoke the truth, you know. Words are wonderful, among the most wonderful things man ever created on this earth, that's for sure. And fundamental, too, for both writing and talking, probably as fundamental as anything you are ever going to come across. No matter what you are doing, whether you are working as a writer or just using them in ordinary ways, like when two fellows are just talking in what they term normal conversation, words are still the choice of most people for expressing themselves proper.

And that's exactly the point the pretty poster was making. It was telling the *what*, *when* and *why* of a certain lecture that was going to be given. And everybody was welcome, boys and girls, fathers and mothers, grandpaws and grandmaws, just about anybody who was interested. Whoever wanted to hear what this particular person was going to say should certainly feel free to come to the hall. But those individuals who wanted to be sure of getting a choice seat had better get there plenty early, otherwise they might find themselves standing at the back of the room with their hats in their hands and no proper place to park their persons.

Thursday night, at eight-thirty, on North Thirty-third Street, that's what the little poster said. And right after that information the question was asked, "What do words mean to you?" Which in a manner of speaking is what they call a teaser, the purpose of which is to stimulate the minds of that class of persons who have no fear of mental activity. Then there was a picture of all kinds of people standing and listening to about twenty different kinds of talk coming from twenty different places, like loudspeakers, car radios, telephone receivers, transistors and lots of other gear like that. All of which was indicating, in a manner of speaking, that the average person like you and I are being bombarded on all sides by a never ending stream of words, to use a poetic expression. Which is the truth. And being so, the question is raised, at least in the minds of all thinking persons, as to exactly how they get along in a wordy world.

All of which sets the perceptive reader up for the stimulating series of phrases quoted in the beginning of this article—"Come here, come here, and you shall hear, all about the wonderful world of words."

Harold's Birthday Party

Harold, who lived in Brooklyn, was going to be thirteen, and the date for his birthday was drawing near. So naturally there was talk between his parents about a party. At first his father and mother thought that they might fix up something as a surprise affair. But then they knew Harold would certainly be thinking about what might happen, which meant that probably

a surprise party just wouldn't work at all, there wasn't a chance of pulling anything off, not with a bright kid like they had. So they came out in the open and broached the subject to him. Well, the result was that the kid was certainly pleased, and happy too, because his parents were so thoughtful.

Once the proposition was presented for public discussion, as you might say, the first consideration was, who was going to get invited to the party. Harold's mother naturally thought the polite thing was to give an invitation to most of the kids in his room at school. But both Harold and his father were against that. This party was for fun, said the latter, and that meant just having the kids with which Harold was on friendly terms. In a way, that narrowed the field considerably, if for no other reason than that Harold was a very active little person, and positive, too, especially about who he did and didn't like—of course it was this last circumstance which was the main factor in cutting down on the size of the gathering. Still there would be more than enough persons present to make all the noise required on such festive occasions.

So a list was made. There was little Herman Meyers and big Joe Catoni, Herb Krakowski and Tony Lombardi, Mike Murphy and Lester Parker. About Georgie Kramer there was some question. If he was asked, what about his sisters, Thelma and Bertha? Living over in the Bronx like he did, at 131 St. and Grand Concourse, either Georgie's father or his big brother would have to bring him over, and the point was, would whoever was doing the bringing want Georgie to lug his two sisters along?

Harold and his family were talking some time about this, when suddenly Harold got very positive, like he could, and said he didn't want any girls, no girls at all, and certainly not any of Georgie's female relatives, that was for sure. So that took care of that. Besides, Harold added, if they were going to ask his own cousin, Jerome, which they ought to do, there was sure to be a fight, because Georgie Kramer and Jerome didn't get along any too well together.

Thus it was resolved, the list should be kept small and kind of intimate, so that everybody could have fun, and so that there would be enough to eat, and every single kid could have all he wanted—if he got sick later, that would be his own concern.

What to eat, that was the next question. Well, right off Harold had the answer. Hamburgers and frankfurters were his choice, there wasn't anything better, and that was for certain as far as he was concerned. But his mother wasn't so sure. How about something like chicken, she asked—probably those kids hadn't ever had anything as fancy as chicken at a birthday party before. "Fancy-dancy," Harold's father snorted; how on earth were they going to get seven to a dozen kids to sit down for a formal chicken dinner—there wasn't a chance, not if he knew something about kids.

That made it two against one, the burgers and franks won. With 7-Up, lots of potato chips and any kind of salad the mother wanted, and a couple of different flavors of ice cream, like chocolate and pistachio, the menu was set. "Yea," said Harold, "that's cool. An' a candy bar when they are all leaving, just to hold 'em till they get home for supper."

AN AMERICAN
SOUTHERN

No one manner of speech exists for all those who live in the South. There is as much variance in pronunciation and the use of colloquialisms between residents of the Mississippi Delta and the inhabitants of the northern part of that state as there is between the speech of a Texan and a Virginian. Indeed, so diverse are the speech patterns of those who are generally termed "Southerners" that no complete catalogue of pronunciations exists.

In spite of the fact that it is impossible phonetically to assert the existence of a uniform Southern dialect, it still is possible to establish speech patterns on a prototype model for those who would learn a Southern dialect. A body of distinctive characteristics, common to all varieties, provides a broad and truthful basis for the creation of a "standard" Southern speech.

In this respect it should be noted that although certain plays demand a localized speech, *Tobacco Road* for instance, most others do not. No regional patterns are required for the characters in *A Streetcar Named Desire*, *Cat on a Hot Tin Roof*, and *The Little Foxes*— for these and other like pieces, a "standard" Southern speech is sufficient.

Before introducing the key sounds of the Southern dialect, three misconceptions regarding Southern speech should be corrected.

First, there is a mistaken belief that all Southern speech is uniformly slow. The truth of the matter is that tempo of utterance is an individual characteristic. The number of persons in any one Southern locality who

talk rapidly probably equals the number of those who speak slowly; many a Southerner could compete on even terms with a fast-talking Northerner, as news telecasts have repeatedly demonstrated. There are tangible reasons for the assumption that all Southern speech is generically of a deliberate nature. One derives from the area-wide practice of emphasizing diphthongs, an action which increases the length of a word sound. This increase in turn creates a suggestion of slowness— a suggestion we tend to take for actuality. Another reason is an assumption that climatic conditions cause a slowdown of speech activity. This impression is predicated on the unreasoned thought that temperature readings are the same throughout all regions of the South, thus blanketing southern Alabama and northern Virginia, or the Texas Panhandle and the Georgia coast under the same weather and climatic ceiling. It further assumes the same readings for all months of the year, when, in fact, the climate is enervatingly hot for only a limited portion of the time.

Second, a belief, companion to the one above, is that Southern speech can be so slurred that unintelligibility often results. What was said above bears equal application here. In justice it must be stated that slurred speech knows no geographical limitations; Americans everywhere are notorious for the smooth vocal surface they put on most consonants. In this connection it must be remembered that *in the theatre no dialect, not even the finest, is of any value unless it first can be heard and, second, be understood.*

A third misconception is that Southern speech is over-loaded with colloquialisms. "Ya'all," "Suh," "a-tall," "little-ole-bitty," and "Ah'm goan ta carry Cousin Tom ta town," are typical. In point of actual fact, days can be spent in a southern locality without once hearing these or similar expressions. In any case, the employment of such terms is properly the responsibility of the playwright.

KEY SOUNDS OF AN AMERICAN SOUTHERN DIALECT

Vowel Substitutions

1. [ɪ] FOR [ɛ]. A major characteristic of Southern speech is the substitution of the vowel [ɪ], as in *it*, for the [ɛ] as in *end*. The [ɪ] substitution requires that such words as *any, men, enter,* and *general* be reproduced by a more than normal occlusion of the jaws, accompanied by a lateral extension of the lips. To the non-Southern ear, the vowel sound which results from these positions might seem flat and somewhat inclined to nasality. This effect arises from the association of [ɪ] with the nasal consonants [n] and [m] and is no more than a normal result; no extra stress is called for.

2. [ɜ] FOR [ɝ]. One of the best-known characteristics of Southern speech is the elimination, in initial, medial, and terminal positions, of the [r] sound from the vowel *er* [ɝ]. The result is written as [ɜ]. To achieve the new sound, begin the vowel as usual but stop short of forming the [r]. In an initial position the change causes *earn* [ɝn] to become [ɜn] by gliding the vowel sound directly into [n] without the usual tongue action which produces the [r]. An identical result is achieved when the [r] of *er* [ɝ] is not formed in the medial position of *bird* [bɝd], which then is sounded as [bɜd], or in the final position of *blur* [blɝ], which becomes [blɜ].

3. [ə] FOR [ɚ]. When *er* is in a terminal position and unaccented, as it nearly always is in a multisyllable word, in Standard American it receives a change of phonetic symbol, the mark then being [ɚ]. Consequently the last syllable in such words as *further* and *brother* is scored [ɚ]: *further* ['fɝðɚ] and *brother* ['brʌðɚ]. In American Southern, however, even the unaccented *er* [ɚ] drops the [r] part of the sound, replacing it with the unaccented (schwa) vowel [ə]. Thus *further* and *brother* are pronounced ['fɜðə] and ['brʌðə].

4. [a] FOR [aɪ]. Still another substitution is effected when the diphthong [aɪ] is shortened to the vowel [a].

Thus a normal *right* [raɪt] becomes the Southern [rat]. As in item 2 above, the vocal action requires that the first vowel [a] be sounded and sustained directly into the consonant without forming the [ɪ] part of the diphthong. This procedure is in contradiction of the more usual Southern practice of making many single vowels into diphthongs, as later discussions will show.

5. VOWEL EXTENSIONS: [æj] FOR [æ], AND [ɔw] FOR [ɔ]. Two vowels, [æ] and [ɔ], are given extensions by the addition of a glided consonant. The [æ], as in *at*, receives [j]; thus *man* becomes [mæjn]. The [ɔ], as in *ought*, gets the addition of [w], so that *dog* [dɔg] becomes [dɔwg]. When either of these actions is overdone, a matter easy of accomplishment, caricature replaces strength. In this connection, do not confuse the exaggeration you will hear on the tape, which is performed for analytical purposes, with an invitation to caricature the dialect.

Diphthongal Changes

A varied use of the diphthong is one of the most noteworthy features of the Southern dialect. Examples of the extent to which this phenomenon appears are given in the drill work which follows. Embracing two vowel sounds as it does, the diphthong provides the auditory signal which establishes the characteristic Southern drawl, even when speech is delivered at a normal or a rapid pace. In by far the greatest number of cases, one vowel, the schwa *uh* [ə], is added to the existing vowel to make up the diphthong. However, in one list of words the vowel [ɪ] as in *it* completes the diphthong.

You will undoubtedly notice, in several instances, that the slide of the diphthong from one vowel to another invites a further addition of the sound of the gliding consonant [j], as in *ya*, between the two. Thus *aunt* [ænt] pronounced in proper Southern as [æənt], would be exaggeratedly extended to [æjənt]. An unwanted suggestion of caricature would again intrude.

Consonant Substitutions

1. [r]. You will find, as you move from dialect to dialect, that the consonant [r] figures more prominently among the key sounds of every dialect, domestic or foreign, than any other consonant or vowel. The Southern dialect offers no exception; here it receives as complete a handling as any consonant can: it is pronounced full

strength in an initial position, and in a few instances with equal force in a medial position; in most medial positions, however, it is slurred, and it is dropped, with or without a substitute, in a terminal position. All handlings are demonstrated in the drill work ahead in what is, for all the seeming complications, a series of relatively simple actions.

2. [n] FOR [ŋ]. A second consonant change requires the elimination of *g* from *ng* [ŋ]. This deletion causes little or no problem; all of us are already fairly expert in the practice.

Special Pronunciations

Lastly, attention must be called to a few distinctive word pronunciations. The *Ah* [a] for *I* and *mah* [ma] for *my* are well known, as is the *Suh* [sʌ] for *Sir*. But equally changed are three additional words, here scored with their new pronunciations: *sentence* ['sɪnɪns], *important* [ɪm'pɔnənt], and *strength* [strɛnθ]. In each of these the change is caused by a failure to enunciate all consonants: in *sentence* the [t] is dropped, in *importance* the [r] and [t] are eliminated while an extra [n] is added, and in *strength* the *g* disappears.

This prototype Southern dialect does not include the distinctive variations which would be found in the area around New Orleans, or in the Brazos section of Texas, or the hill country of Kentucky, or other such places.

It also avoids any of the comic projections which humorists and other performers often mistakenly apply to their use of Southern speech. Although such application is something which society has had to put up with for some time, and which has plagued Irish, German, Italian and other dialects as well, yet there is little need to compound the error by performing an action which often goes well beyond the bounds of correct dialectal usage.

The Southern dialect is most melodious to hear and pleasant to speak. Unless forced into caricature, there are no pronounced pitch or tempo patterns; all tonal elements combine to produce the expressiveness usual in vocal communication everywhere.

KEY-SOUND WORD DRILL

The material in this section is to be practiced in coordination with the Southern Dialect tape. The voice on the tape will pause after each word so that you may repeat it immediately, checking your pronunciation against that of the speaker. The slow tempo and the exaggerated enunciation are deliberate, distorted so that you may more clearly hear the full sound and discern the muscular action which accompanies it. In regular tempo, of course, the sharp edge comes off the exaggeration so that the sounds are as fluent as they are full.

Listen carefully to the pronunciation of each syllable. Check the required position of tongue, jaw and lips. Avoid muscular tenseness as you move your articulators in the exact action demanded by each vowel, diphthong and consonant. Space is left below the lines for your phonetic or other notation.

(*Voice:* Jerry Blunt.)

Vowel Substitutions

1. [ɪ] FOR [ɛ]. Any, men, enter, Tennessee, twenty, when, general, tender, temper, Ben.

2. [ɜ] FOR [ɝ]. Early, earn, earnest, bird, dirt, purse, word, blur, her, prefer, were.

3. [ə] FOR [ɚ]. Murder, father, adore, horror, liar.

4. [a] FOR [aɪ]. Right, time, fine, my, life, like.

5. VOWEL EXTENSIONS: *a.* [æj] FOR [æ]. Man, bath, hand, am, and.

b. [ɔw] FOR [ɔ]. Dog, hog, law, bought, fought, Paul.

Diphthongal Changes

1. [æə]. Add, after, ask, aunt, basket, laughter, path, glass.

2. [ɔə]. Ought, all, author, call, jaw, saw, court, short.

3. [ɪə]. If, ill, is, inside, itch, dish, kick.

4. [ʊə]. Book, could, cushion, stood.

5. [ɑə]. Ark, rock, scarf, yard, ah.

6. [ɛə]. Ebb, edit, egg, bed, deck, head, met, tell, well, west.

7. [aə]. Liar, fire, hire, higher.

8. [eɪ]. Take, neighbor, age, babe, face, may, stray.

Consonant Substitutions

1. [ɾ]. SOFTEN OR ELIMINATE WHEN IN A MEDIAL POSITION: barrier, scarce, marshal, distortion, environment, worth—Mary [mɛɪ], Harry [hɛɪ], berry [bɛɪ], BUT NOTE THAT THESE LAST MIGHT ALSO BECOME Mary ['mɛrɪ], Harry ['hɛrɪ], berry ['bɛrɪ].

   DROP FINAL [ɾ]. Bar, star, car.

   DROP FINAL [ɾ], SUBSTITUTE [ə]. Door, floor, where, there, bear.

2. [n] FOR [ŋ]. Falling, running, thinking, going (SOMETIMES *goan* ['goən]).

Special Pronunciations

Sentence, important, strength, my, I, Sir.

KEY SOUNDS IN SENTENCE CONTEXT

The numbers below correspond with those used in the previous section.

(*Voice:* Beth Ann Drew.)

Vowel Substitutions

1. [ɪ] FOR [ɛ]. The sense of these sentences is not important. / When did those men enter that part of Tennessee? / He lost his temper in front of his general.

2. [ɜ] FOR [ɝ]. The early birds were a blur in the sky. / Sir, I prefer not to say a word about that old purse.

3. [ə] FOR [ɝ]. The murder of his father filled him with horror. / I adore the four gentle horses.

4. [a] FOR [aɪ]. I had a right fine time at the party. / He might not like ripe pears.

5. [æj] FOR [æ]. The man put his hand in the bath. / I am, and I am not going to go over there, so there!

   [ɔw] FOR [ɔ]. When the dog bit the hog he broke the law. / Paul and Saul fought to a draw.

Diphthongal Changes

1. [æə]. Ask your aunt if she will take the glass from the basket. / He sat down after the laughter was over.

2. [ɔə]. You all ought to law that author in court. /

There was a short call at the auction.

3. [ɪə]. Did you put the dish inside the tent?

4. [ʊə]. Would you please stand the book where it

should be?

5. [ɑə]. I think the ark hit the rock in the yard.

6. [ɛə]. Well, I said I was going to put my bed at the

edge of the entrance.

7. [aə]. The liar said the tire was on fire.

8. [eɪ]. I aim to take my neighbor to the face of the

cliff. / At his age he may stray away.

Consonant Substitutions

1. [ɤ]. Mary had scarcely met Harry at the barrier (*repeat*) when the marshal appeared to perform his part

of the ceremony. / The bar on the door had fallen to

the floor and it lay there under the chair.

2. [n] FOR [ŋ]. I have been running and stumbling and

falling all over.

Special Pronunciations

I have not got the strength to enunciate this impor-

tant sentence.

READING FOR FLUENCY

The Bells, *Edgar Allan Poe*

(*Voice:* Jerry Blunt.)

Hear the sledges with the bells,

Silver bells!

What a world of merriment their melody foretells!

How they tinkle, tinkle, tinkle,

In the icy air of night!

While the stars that oversprinkle

All the heavens, seem to twinkle

With a crystalline delight;

Keeping time, time, time,

In a sort of Runic rhyme,

To the tintinnabulation that so musically wells

From the bells, bells, bells, bells,

Bells, bells, bells——

Hear the loud alarum bells,

Brazen bells!

What a tale of terror, now, their turbulency tells!

In the startled ear of night

How they scream out their affright!

Too much horrified to speak,

They can only shriek, shriek

    Out of tune,

In a clamorous appealing to the mercy of the fire,

In the mad expostulation with the deaf and frantic fire

    Leaping higher, higher, higher,

    With a desperate desire,

And a resolute endeavor

Now,—now to sit or never

By the side of the pale-faced moon.

From **The Compleat Housewife** [1]

(*Voice:* Beth Ann Drew.)

Take a Quart of middling oysters, and wash them in their own Liquor; then strain them through a Flannel, and put them on the Fire to warm; take three quarters of a Pint of Gravy and put to the Oysters, with a Blade of Mace, a little white Pepper, a little Horse-raddish and a Piece of lean Bacon, and half a Lemon; then stew them leisurely. Take three Penny Loaves, and pick out the Crumbs clean; then take a Pound of But-

ter, and set on the Fire in a Sauce-pan that will hold the Loaves, and when it is melted, take it off the Fire; then pour off the Clear, and set it on the Fire again with the Loaves in it, turn them about till you find them crisp, then put a Pound of Butter in a Frying-pan, and with a Dredging Box dust it with Flour. Then mix that and the Oysters together; and when stewed enough take out the Bacon, and put the Oysters into the Loaves; then put them into a Dish with Slices of Lemon; and when you have thickened the Liquor, squeeze in Lemon to your own taste.

Hamlet, *Shakespeare;* Act IV, Scene 1

(*Voice:* Jerry Blunt.)

HAMLET: How all occasions do inform against me

    And spur my dull revenge! What is a man,

    If his chief good and market of his time

    Be but to sleep and feed? A beast, no more.

    Sure he that made us with such large discourse,

    Looking before and after, gave us not

    That capability and godlike reason

    To fust in us unus'd. Now, whether it be

[1] London, 1739. E. Smith.

Bestial oblivion, or some craven scruple

Of thinking too precisely on th' event

(A thought, which, quarter'd, hath but one part

    wisdom,

And ever three parts coward) I do not know

Why yet I live to say "This thing's to do,"

Sith I have cause and will and strength and means

To do't. Examples gross as earth exhort me:

Witness this army of such mass and charge,

Led by a delicate and tender prince,

Whose spirit with divine ambition puff'd

Makes mouths at the invisible event,

Exposing what is mortal and unsure

To all that fortune, death and danger dare,

Even for an egg-shell. . . .

INDIVIDUAL-PRACTICE EXERCISES

Space is left below each line for written transcriptions.

Key-Sound Word Drill

Any; mirth; right; law—dog; enter; ought; ask—

take; after; straw; bed—tire; earn; twenty; glass—Paul;

ought; cushion; add—age; horror; itch; fine—my; book.

when; bought—her; hand; fought; fire—laughter; gen-

eral; tack; am—neighbor; man; murder; court—tell;

like; Mary; where—falling; edge; basket; were—Ben;

stood; right; there—did; Harry; hand; draw—going;

where; all; path; might; come—well; worth; chair; in;

bath—men; thought; stray; cur; stood; on; floor—ten-

der; right; adore; age; ark; is—scarf; hand; well; prefer;

end; fought.

Key Sounds in Sentence Context

The gentleman gave ten dollars to his favorite

charity.

The father adored the daughter and was very tender

with her.

The early bird saw the worm in the dirt.

The purse was worth a sight more than the general

paid for it.

The men from Tennessee might live to a ripe old age.

Harry is going to give it to you.

The man put the ham in the bath water.

I prefer the dog which Paul bought.

My aunt brought her gentle brother to the law court.

Mary did not want to edit the author's book.

A little old dog sat inside the fence on the edge of the yard.

Take the glass and the dish to the other neighbor.

The car sat for four hours before the door.

Larry caught the chair which he thought was falling into the fire.

Carrie was wearing her pretty corsage to the important gathering.

He scarcely had the strength to put the heavy bar under the tire.

Tell Claude he ought not to call Ben a liar.

Where laughter is heard, someone is having a right good time.

I can't (sometimes "cain't") help thinking that the eggs in the basket ought to have been better.

I met her at the edge of the bigger courtyard and took her hand before leading her down the path to the right of the building.

SIGHT READING AND FLUENCY PRACTICE
The Raven, *Edgar Allan Poe*

Once upon a midnight dreary, while I pondered weak

and weary,

Over many a quaint and curious volume of forgotten

lore—

While I nodded, nearly napping, suddenly there came

a tapping,

As of someone gently rapping, tapping at my chamber

door.

" 'Tis some visitor," I muttered, "tapping at my cham-

ber door—

Only this and nothing more."

Ah, distinctly I remember, it was in the bleak De-

cember,

And each separate dying ember wrought its ghost upon

the floor,

Eagerly I wished the morrow;—vainly I had sought to

borrow

From my books surcease from sorrow—sorrow for the

lost Lenore—

Nameless here for evermore.

"Prophet!" said I, "thing of evil!—prophet, still, if bird

or devil!—

Whether Tempter sent, or whether tempest tossed thee

here ashore,

Desolate yet all undaunted, on this desert land en-

chanted—

On this home by Horror haunted—tell me truly, I im-

plore—

Is there—*is* there balm in Gilead?—tell me—tell me, I

implore!"

Quoth the Raven, "Nevermore."

Sketches and Eccentricities of Col. David Crockett, *David Crockett*

. . . I was *rooting* my way to the fire, not in a good

humour, when some fellow staggered up towards me,

and cried out, "Hurrah for Adams!" Said I, "Stranger

you had better hurrah for hell, and praise your own

country."

Said he, "And who are you?"

"I'm that same David Crockett, fresh from the back-

woods, half-horse, half-alligator, a little touched with

the snapping-turtle; can wade the Mississippi, leap the

Ohio, ride upon a streak of lightning, and slip without a

scratch down a honey locust; can whip my weight in

wildcats,—and if any gentleman pleases, for a ten-dollar

bill, he may throw in a panther,—hug a bear too close

for comfort, and eat any man opposed to Jackson."

Harvest and Kitchen, *Anonymous*

When corn on the cob and sliced tomatoes begin to

lose some of their early first admirers, the challenge is

on. The homemakers' harvest starts with the first radish

in the spring, gains momentum as the months roll by,

and by late summer the garden actually seems to be

"sassing" us back with its teeming vegetables and fruits.

Corn, tomatoes, beans, carrots, squash, and other vege-

tables invite us to good eating; peaches, plums, pears,

and berries second the invitation. Whether she is mak-

ing the best of garden sass, or taking advantage of good

buys in the market, the lady of the house has her

kitchen humming in late August.

A Pioneer Theatre, *Sol Smith*[2]

[Sol Smith describes a production of *Pizarro* played by a limited company in Cincinnati in 1820.] "For my own part, I was the Spanish army entire! . . . Between whiles I had to officiate as High Priest of the Sun; then lose both my eyes and feel my way, guided by a little boy through the heat of battle, to tell the audience what was going on behind the scene: afterward . . . I was placed as a sentinel over Alonzo! Besides, I was obliged to find the sleeping child, fight a blow or two with Rolla, fire off three guns at him while crossing the bridge, beat the alarm drum, and do at least two thirds of the shouting! . . . As for Sam Drake, when he was killed in the last scene he had to fall far enough off stage to be able to play slow music as the curtain descended."

[In 1830 Old Sol, as he was then called, leased the Natchez theatre with a small company in order to "catch the stars" as they came up river from New Orleans. At the end of the first week the receipts were one hundred and fifty dollars short of expenses. To save the season from a loss Smith decided to operate two theatres, fifty miles apart, at the same time.]

Splitting his company he sent the lesser half on to Port Gibson "where they opened the theatre, and continued to perform three nights in the week for nearly five weeks, at the same time the Natchez concern was in operation four nights in the week!" But even with this device the two theatres could not draw above expenses. Since Old Sol was the great drawing card, he decided to play in both places, opening in Port Gibson as Captain Copp in *Charles II*. Following is an extract from his Journal.

"Wednesday. Rose at break of day, horse at door. Swallowed a cup of coffee while the boy was tying on leggins. Reached Washington at eight, changed horses at nine, again at ten, and at eleven. At twelve arrived at Port Gibson. Attended rehearsal, settled business with stage manager. Dined at four, laid down and endeavored to sleep at five. Up again at six, was rubbed

[2] Sol Smith, *Theatrical Management in the West and South for Thirty Years* (New York: Harper and Brothers, 1868), pp. 23, 64.

down and washed and dressed at seven. Acted *Three Singles* and *Splash*. To bed at eleven-thirty.

"Thursday. Rose and breakfasted at nine. At ten attended rehearsal for pieces for the next day. At one, leggins tied on, braved the mud for a fifty-mile ride, rain falling all the way. Arrived at Natchez at half-past six. Rubbed down and took supper. Acted *Ezekiel Homespun* and *Delph* to a poor house. To bed, stiff as steelyards, at twelve.

"Friday. Cast pieces, counted tickets, attended rehearsal until one. To horse again for Port Gibson, arrived at seven. No time to eat dinner or supper! Acted in *The Magpie and Maid* and *No Song No Supper*, in which latter piece I managed to get a few mouthfuls of cold roasted mutton and some dry bread, they being the first food tasted this day!"

[Sol traveled fifty miles every day in the week except Sunday and acted every night for nearly a month—but his profits balanced his losses.]

The Bluegrass Region of Kentucky, *James Lane Allen*

But after business was over, time hung idly on their hands; and being vigorous men, hardened by work in forest and field, trained in foot and limb to fleetness and endurance, and fired with admiration of physical prowess, like riotous school-boys out on a half-holiday, they fell to playing. All through the first quarter of the century, and for a longer time, county court day in Kentucky was, at least in many parts of the State, the occasion for holding athletic games. The men, young or in the sinewy manhood of more than middle age, assembled once a month at the county-seats to witness and take part in the feats of muscle and courage. They wrestled, threw the sledge, heaved the bar, divided and played at fives, had foot-races for themselves, and quarter-races for their horses. By-and-by, as these contests became a more prominent feature of the day, they would pit against each other the champions of different neighborhoods. It would become widely known beforehand that next county court day "the bully" in one end of the county would whip "the bully" in the other end; so when court day came, and the justices came, and the bullies came, what was the county to do but come also?

VI

*

STANDARD ENGLISH

*

In England and throughout the British Isles, the way a person speaks—his syllabic pronunciation as well as the rhythm and melody of his speech—is perhaps more revealing of geography and education and social standing than in any other country in the Western world.

Every national language has its regional dialects, with forms of urban and rural, educated and uneducated speech. Few if any, however, have as many conditioning factors, both natural and man-made, as Standard English. To the student of dialects, this circumstance makes recognition simpler but accomplishment more difficult.

Fortunately, to American ears the difference is clearly marked between the speech of the upper-echelon civil servant and the Cockney of Bethnal Green, between the resident of Edinburgh and the man who lives in O'Casey's Dublin. Equally fortunate for the dialect student is the fact that out of the multiple dialects of England, one form of dialectal utterance has been given semiofficial sanction by the phonetician, and quasiofficial standing by the general public, with the result that it is accepted as standard by most Britons.

Being standard does not mean that this particular form of vocal utterance is absolutely uniform in pronunciation, rate, and melodic patterns—no speech in the world has achieved that questionable distinction. As early as 1755, Dr. Samuel Johnson noted in his epoch-making Dictionary that it was impossible to model pronunciation "after the example of the best company because they differ so much among themselves." And more recently, in a facetious mood, a Brit-

ish phonetician remarked that the term "King's English" had to be changed because there had been so many monarchs who couldn't speak it. Even more emphatically, Eric Partridge says in reference to uniformity of pronunciation, "Yet look at the reverse of this deceptively engraved, misleadingly worded coin of the realm of speech and you will find that, despite all the prohibitions of the law-givers, all the regulations of the planners, all the *don'ts* of teachers, . . . pronunciation, although appreciably more uniform in 1951 than in 1900, is, regarded dispassionately, far more varied, divergent, irregular than regular, convergent, uniform." [1]

This diatribe to the contrary, it must be recognized that a usable form of English speech, called by the sturdy title of Standard English, does exist, and that it is conveniently conditioned, organized, and catalogued for the ready reference and practice of the actor dialectician.

Standard English is the dialect of the educated Englishman, the result of social and school traditions of pronunciation. It is the speech of the British Broadcasting Corporation and the majority of characters in the plays of such playwrights as Shaw and Coward. Basically, it is a South-of-England dialect which has its center in London and which is taught, and consequently sustained, in all the major public schools (private institutions in an American sense) in the land.

The dialect has many names. Daniel Jones, a pioneer

---

[1] Eric Partridge and John W. Clark, *British and American English since 1900* (London: Andrew Dakers, Ltd., 1957), p. 187.

English phonetician, termed it Received Pronunciation, and scored it phonetically in his *English Pronouncing Dictionary*, a work that is still the standard authority on the subject. H. C. Wyld, an Oxford phonetician and professor of literature, called it Received Standard Dialect. Others have termed it Modified Standard Dialect, Public School English, Well-bred English, Upper-class English, and Good English.

Eric Partridge explains the somewhat puzzling use of the term "received" when, in speaking of what he terms the four main standard pronunciations for English, that is, Public School Standard (sometimes called Southern English), Scots Standard, Irish Standard, and American Standard, "each is *received* . . . within its own area or sphere of influence and tolerated (more or less) outside."

A. C. Gimson of the Phonetics Department of the University College of London explains further that: "the term 'Received Pronunciation' is applied to that type of accent, originally the local educated speech of London and the south-east of England, which is accepted by the BBC and most people of this country as an unofficial standard. During the 19th century this accent was used by the upper classes in all parts of the country, and therefore, had class connotations, which today are less marked than they were. It is true that the BBC announcers have been taken as models of this type of pronunciation, though since the war, some of the earlier uniformity has been lost."

Whatever its name, this particular dialect is the unquestioned representative of educated, upper-class speech in England. To a speech-conscious nation it represents the acme of social and cultural vocal communication, whether one is born to it or educated into it.

The users of other regional dialects, such as Yorkshire or Lancashire, will maintain that theirs are just as ancient, legitimate, and honorable as Standard English, and can with some justification claim an equal or superior distinctiveness of utterance. But there is no question that the Received Pronunciation of Daniel Jones is the established model of educated, upper-class, social, diplomatic, and cultured speech throughout the British Isles.

With such factors as increased education, increased mobility (begun with the evacuation of children during World War II), and increased mass communication, there is no doubt that Standard English will be spoken by more and more Englishmen in the years ahead; perhaps, as Partridge says, not uttered with an exact uniformity, but spoken as a recognizable Standard none the less.

AFFECTED ENGLISH

A warning should be given about a particular use of Standard English. Such is the nature of this speech, being associated with conscious social patterns, that when it is employed in an improper manner, a note of affectation results. It is true that a Briton's heightened social awareness can and does often create what sounds like a note of self-consciousness to many American ears.

But then Standard English is self-conscious. The habitual user is as aware of his speech as he is of his posture or his social deportment; it is an awareness as ingrained as courtesy in a person who has always practiced that social grace. When a speech with this characteristic is used inappropriately, its basic nature is changed from what it is to what it was never intended to be, and falseness or affectation results. In addition, erratic ideas about the extent to which all Englishmen use such *passé* expressions as "By Jove," "Hip-hip," and "I say, old chap," indicate a lack of practical knowledge.

Something should be said about the tendency of some American actors to attempt a Standard English pronunciation whenever they read an English author, especially Shakespeare. Unless the other members of the company do the same, the result is a mixed speech, part English, part American. Consistency within a company is desirable, and an entire American group, properly trained, can act Shaw or Coward with distinction and propriety in the accents of Standard English; indeed, such an achievement is the aim of this chapter. But to "put on" Standard English on a hit-or-miss basis is malpractice on any stage and with any author.

KEY SOUNDS OF STANDARD ENGLISH

The difference between Standard English and Standard American, broad as this latter term might be, is marked in the minds and ears of Standard English and Standard American speakers. On paper these two forms of speech are not nearly so differentiated—some eight principal alterations separate the two. If an American speaker can maintain with strength and consistency these limited changes, he will speak Standard English well and properly.

Vowel Substitutions

1. THE "BROAD *a*" [ɑ]. To the American actor, no other element of Standard English is more characteristic and more puzzling than the vowel sound represented by the "broad *a*" [ɑ]. The English employ it to a much greater extent than we do in the United States. And to us it is not always clear just when it should be sounded. Fortunately, there are rules, both complex and simple, conditioning its use.

We will use the simpler set, secure in the knowledge that if we do commit an error, the latitude of variance in every dialect lets us be sure that someone, somewhere has already established a precedent.

A. C. Gimson, Reader in Phonetics at the University College of London, states in reply to a letter of inquiry: "As for the 'Received' use of [ɑ] in words like 'after, master, bath, grant' (as compared with [æ] or [a] in other types of British English), it can only be said that earlier short [a] was generally lengthened and retracted to [ɑ] before [f, ɵ, s] or nasal consonant + (plus another) consonant in the London region at the end of the 18th century. But a number of exceptions occur—e.g. 'grass, dance' with [ɑ] but 'crass, romance' with [æ]." To those last two we might add the word "damn," [dæm], not [dɑm].

A fairly similar statement is given by Larsen and Walker in their *Pronunciation, A Practical Guide to American Standards;* they say that the "broad *a*" [ɑ] is used before "*f, nc, nt, ss,* and *th.*"

In supplement to this statement of rules, it can be added that continued practice will aid the student considerably in developing a commonsense judgment as to when a "broad *a*" [ɑ] is or is not to be used. The following examples illustrate the point. The list is from Stuart Robinson's *The Development of Modern English.*

Broad *a*	Medium or short *a* [a] or [æ]
class, pass, grass	mass, gas
dance	entrance (*verb*)
example, sample	lamp, ample
plaster	plastic

To this list should be added the seeming inconsistencies of *can't* [kɑnt] but *can* [kæn], *aunt* [ɑnt] but *ant* [ænt], and *tomato* [tə'mɑtou] but *potato* [pə'tetou].

Such commonplace words as *land, man, has, hand* never receive the broad *a*, while the second syllable of Lancaster and the third of *circumstance* may be pronounced either as broad or short. The use of the accompanying Standard English tape should do much to clarify this problem.

2. [ɔ:]. This vowel, which is a distinguishing characteristic of Standard English, is not formed in American speech. The phonetic symbol [ɔ], as in the word *ought*, is the closest representation we have of this key sound. Yet [ɔ] is not sufficient in itself to mark the change. The new vowel is made by dropping the jaw and placing the tongue as if to say [ɔ], then closing the lips in a restricted circle at the same time the upper throat is slightly enlarged and tensed. If this action is taken as [ɔ] is pronounced, a full but somewhat hollow sound results.

The letters *a* and *o* are the ones most used to carry this particular sound, as in *all, law, ought, awful* and *pause.*

3. [ɪ] for a terminal *y, ly* and *lly.* The vowel [ɪ] as in *it* is used as a terminal sound for the letters *y, ly* and *lly* in Standard English as it is in Standard American. It becomes a key sound only because the English give it stronger emphasis. Where we tend to swallow the final syllable so that it almost disappears, they give a stress which, although never as marked as a primary accent, is strong enough to be heard. When applying the necessary stress, which should not be strong enough to call attention to itself, care must be taken that the vowel sound of [ɛ] (*yet*) does not intrude, otherwise affectation can result.

The final syllable of such words as *many, policy, necessity, very,* and *lovely, cleverly, really, frightfully* take the additional emphasis this key sound requires.

Diphthongal Changes

1. [ʌou] FOR [ou]. Treating the triphthong *uh-oh-oo* [ʌou] as a diphthong is part of an attempt to get American ears to distinguish the difference between Standard American [ou] and the Standard English pronunciation of the identical symbol. The word *go* [gou] can be written the same phonetically in both of these "Standards," but there is no question that a difference of sound exists. [ʌou] is our representation of that sound.

This might be termed the "so don't go" diphthong for the reason that all three words contain the same vowel combination. To achieve the sound, add a barely perceptible *uh* [ʌ] before the regular pronunciation of

[ou], making the result compact rather than drawn out.

The diphthong is distinctive and has wide use. Beware of exaggeration. If the syllable becomes too orally flat, it will take on the characteristic of a Cockney exclamation.

2. [rɪ] FOR [ɛrɪ]. Standard English speakers do not give a secondary accent to those polysyllables which end in *ary, ery, ory*. Instead, the final syllable is unaccented and shortened. The result is that our pronunciation of *ary, ery* and *ory* [ɛrɪ, orɪ] must be changed into the simpler [rɪ], as in *writ*, letting the [ɛ] or [o] vowel remain unsounded. Typical Standard English words carrying this sound are: *secretary* ['sɛkrətrɪ], *cemetery* ['sɛmɪtrɪ], *necessary* ['nɛsɪsrɪ], and the familiar *laboratory* [lə'bɔrətrɪ], with its change of stress.

3. [ju]. This key sound is made by few Americans. Because it can easily be overdone, it requires careful control in formation. The [j] sound itself has the value that *y* [j] has in *yet* [jɛt]. To the [j] is added the vowel [u] as in *pool* to form a diphthonglike combination. *You* [ju] results. Representative words which take this key sound are: *duke* [djuk], *duplicity* [dju'plɪsɪtɪ], *new* [nju], and *Tuesday* ['tjuzdɪ].

Consonant Substitutions

1. [r]. In Standard English, as in other dialects, [r] has a variable use.

As an initial sound, as in *round* or *rush*, it is always pronounced. Otherwise, the rule is that [r] is dropped before consonants or when in a terminal position. When this last instance occurs, the schwa vowel [ə] is substituted in some cases.

Naturally the other side of the above rule is that [r] is sounded when followed by a vowel; this last holds true when [r], even if terminal, is followed by a word whose first syllable is a vowel, especially if the two are linked in fluent speech. A caution must be made, however, that even if the [r] is sounded because followed by a vowel, the pronunciation is never as strong as the hard [r] of most American speech—above all, never is it given the harshness of some rural or Midwestern pronunciations.

In an important variant, when [r] is located between two vowels, it is delivered with a single tongue tap. This is the action which produces the familiar English pronunciation of *very* and *sorry*. One tongue tap against the upper gum ridge is sufficient; if more is done, the affectation of a fully rolled or trilled [r] results.

Here are examples of the variable use of [r]:

a. DROPPED BEFORE A CONSONANT: obse̶rve, ma̶rshal, pe̶rfo̶rm, spa̶rk.

b. NOT SOUNDED WHEN TERMINAL: her [h₃], fur [f₃], car [kɑ].

c. NOT SOUNDED WHEN TERMINAL, BUT REPLACED BY THE SCHWA VOWEL: year [jɪə], there [ðɛə], after ['ɑftə], remember [rɪ'mɛmbə], dear [dɪə].

d. TERMINAL [r] PRONOUNCED WHEN FOLLOWED BY AN OPENING VOWEL: the *star is* bright (note, however, that if the plural were used, *stars are*, the [s] causes the [r] to be dropped); they will *pair off*, she *wore a* robe; *nor I; for it*.

e. SINGLE TAPPED WHEN BETWEEN TWO VOWELS: very, sorry, character, mirror, variant.

Special Pronunciations

Certain Standard English Words, with the same spellings and meanings as their American counterparts, require different pronunciations. Here is a partial list:

schedule ['ʃɛdjul]
privacy ['prɪvəsɪ]
issue ['ɪsju] *not* ['ɪsʃu]
tissue ['tɪsju]
figure ['fɪgə]
patent ['petɛnt]
clerk [klɑk]
Derby ['dɑbɪ]

laboratory [lə'bɔrətrɪ]
process ['prosɛs]
nephew ['nɛvju]
garage ['gærɑʒ]
patriot ['pætrɪət]
glacier ['glæsjə]
hostile ['hɔstaɪl]

The words *been* [bin], *again* ['əgeɪn], *either* ['aɪðə] and *neither* ['naɪðə], may or may not receive the pronunciation indicated by the accompanying phonetic symbols. Daniel Jones in his *English Pronouncing Dictionary* favors the above usage, but also lists as legitimate variants the pronunciations which are more familiar to American ears. Perhaps not more than half the users of Standard English employ the favored Jones pronunciation. This variation would seem to allow a freedom of choice to the dialect student. The suggestion is made, however, that since a speaker of non-Standard English needs all the help he can get to strengthen his speech, he employ the pronunciations indicated above.

Pitch Patterns

In Standard English, and all other English dialect forms, marked variety in the use of the tonal element of pitch is a noticeable characteristic. The increased range of pitch results in greater expressiveness, a fact of which most American speakers seem unaware.

To accomplish an increase of tonal inflection, the dialect student must free himself, both mentally and physically, from the restrictions of his usual pitch patterns; to do this often necessitates the breaking of long-held habits. The increase of scope to be achieved, however, does not require any change in the thoughts and feelings which prompt his speech. There should not be a sound of any "put on" pitch inflection in the new patterns.

KEY-SOUND WORD DRILL

The study and practice of this section is to be coordinated with the Standard English tape. There will be a pause after each word so that you may repeat it immediately, checking your pronunciation against that of the speaker. Try for exact formation of the lip, jaw, and tongue positions on each sound, especially the new ones.

Space has been left below each line for scoring phonetic or other symbols.

(*Voice:* Jerry Blunt.)

Vowel Substitutions

1. [ɑ]. Ask, answer, after, half, past, bath, demand, disaster, master, command, castle, vantage, France, example.

2. [ɔ:]. All, law, ought, off, abroad, horse, George, force, remorse, pause, thought, talk, stall, Paul, wall.

3. [ɪ]. Ability, necessity, policy, many, berry, funny, lovely, really, cautiously, carefully, hilly.

Diphthongal Changes

1. [ʌou] FOR [ou]. So, don't, go, told, over, holy, omit, most, moment, tone.

2. [rɪ] FOR [ɛrɪ]. Secretary, necessary, evolutionary, cemetery, laboratory, satisfactory.

3. [ju]. Duke, duplicity, new, Tuesday, duty, student.

Consonant Substitutions

1. [r].

   a. DROPPED BEFORE CONSONANT: observe, short, word, bird, Portia, hard.

   b. TERMINAL NOT SOUNDED: car, far, her, slur, are.

   c. TERMINAL NOT SOUNDED, REPLACED BY [ə]: year, there, here, after, empire, prefer, matter, letter, your.

   d. TERMINAL, BUT FOLLOWED BY OPENING VOWEL: star is, pair off, wore a, nor I, for it, slur at, farther on.

   e. SINGLE TAPPED BETWEEN TWO VOWELS: very, sorry, character, mirror, variant, Mary, paragraph.

Special Pronunciations

Privacy, issue, figure, patent, clerk, Derby, laboratory, hostile, process, nephew, schedule, been, again, either, neither.

KEY SOUNDS IN SENTENCE CONTEXT
Vowel Substitutions

1. [ɑ]. Father passed down the primrose path. / The pastor asked that the answer be given by half-past

four. / I can't get the ant off the basket, but Auntie can.

2. [ɔ:] FOR [ɔ]. All who fear the law ought not to be caught. / After the pause Paul felt remorse for his daughter left at the resort in Albany. / They saw that the water ought not to stain the wall in the loft.

3. [ɪ] FOR *y, ly, lly*. The lovely lady had many friendly calls on Friday. / It was really awfully silly of Mary to marry Harry. / Obstinacy in diplomacy is not always the best policy.

Diphthongal Changes

1. [ʌou] FOR [ou]. He was told to row over the river. / She did not know she possessed the old and holy stone. / Don't omit to hold the most cones at the last moment.

2. [rɪ] FOR [ɛrɪ]. My secretary has not been revolutionary for the last half century. / It is not necessary to go to the elementary conservatory.

3. [ju]. The new duke came on Tuesday. / The duplicity was due to the student's stupidity.

Consonant Substitutions

1. [r].

   a. Portia spoke some short words to the parson. Neither the orchestra nor the organ were heard o Friday.

   b. The car struck the bar with a fearful jar.

   c. We were there year after year. / The letter wa sent here and there about the Empire.

   d. They will all pair off farther on. / Roger or Mar will go for it.

   e. Harry was very sorry about the lost terrier. Every variant was a cause for worry to Harriet.

Special Pronunciations

Every schedule has been set by a special process.

We must either settle the issue about the patent i the laboratory or go over it again and again.

The nephew followed the figure of the clerk at th Derby.

London Place Names

(*Voice:* Patricia Lewis.)

Royal Albert Hall; Old Bailey; St. Paul's; Bow Bells;

Soho; Berkeley Square; Grosvenor Square; Leicester Square; Haymarket Theatre; Bayswater Road; The Tower; Thames River.

READING FOR FLUENCY

The slow tempo is intentional.

Hamlet, *Shakespeare;* Act III, Scene 1

(*Voice:* Patricia Lewis.)

OPHELIA. O what a noble mind is here o'erthrown!

The courtier's, soldier's, scholar's, eye, tongue, sword;

The expectancy and rose of the fair state,

The glass of fashion and the mould of form,

The observ'd of all observers, quite, quite down!

And I, of ladies most deject and wretched,

That suck'd the honey of his music vows,

Now see that noble and most sovereign reason,

Like sweet bells jangled, out of tune and harsh;

That unmatch'd form and feature of blown youth

Blasted with ecstasy. O woe is me,

To have seen what I have seen, see what I see!

As a B.B.C. Broadcast Might Sound

The next voice is that of John Snagge, former Head of Presentations, the British Broadcasting Company, London. These two paragraphs stress vocal content rather than thought content. The author acknowledges with thanks Mr. Snagge's personal permission to use his voice in performance of the following passages.

After all the facts have been gathered and brought together year by year, it will be absolutely necessary to go over all of them in the most thorough manner, as it were, otherwise it will not be possible for any or all of us to come to any satisfactory conclusion.

A war of one sort or another has been going on for years. Perhaps we, that is to say all of us in America and England and all of Europe as well, do not exactly like the idea at all, but there it is. One power seems very intent upon the overthrow of another government by diplomacy, if at all possible, and if not by diplomacy, then by brutal force. Everywhere one goes the first demand is for an out-and-out support of current ideas. Normal activities are everywhere imposed upon. I daresay all opportunities are carefully looked over so that not a single chance will be missed. Oh, if only things could be as they were.

Mr. and Mrs. Bancroft, *Sir Squire Bancroft* (Volume 2)

(*Voice:* John Snagge.)

Naturally enough I think it may be expected that I should here express some views on this then important subject, and tell what led me to the bold measure of daring to abolish the pit, more especially from the Haymarket Theatre, which had been long known to boast, and truly enough, the possession of the best and most comfortable pit ever to be found in a playhouse, from the reason that it did not go under the dress circle.

To begin, it is perhaps necessary to remind young play-goers that the pit in the old days occupied the entire floor of the theatre, extending to the orchestra, and as the charge for admission in the leading houses was three shillings and six-pence, the pit quite earned its title of being "the backbone of the theatre." The dress circle and private boxes were the resort of the better classes, the wealthy, or the fastidious. The modern stall was then unknown. Gradually this luxury was introduced. Row by row, very insidiously, the cushioned chairs encroached upon the narrow benches, which,

year after year, were removed further and further from the stage, until at last, in many theatres, all that was left of the old-fashioned pit was a dark, low-ceilinged place hidden away under the dress circle, which, by contrast with its former proud state, seemed but a kind of cellar or reminder of the black-hole of Calcutta.

That thousands of earnest play-goers would far rather sit there in heat and discomfort than go up aloft to better accommodation I don't doubt for a moment, nor do I for another moment deny that I should very likely find myself of the party under their circumstances; but that seems to me outside the question. Matters had entirely changed. The pit had long lost, in most West End theatres, the possibility of being the support it used to prove, owing to the managers of them having, row by row, robbed it of its power, and made the stalls instead their "backbone." This grew to be eminently the case with our management, which could not have endured without high-priced admission.

INDIVIDUAL-PRACTICE EXERCISES

Key-Sound Word Drill

These key sounds are placed beside each other so that you may exercise on the change of lip, tongue, and jaw positions necessary for the making of the proper sounds.

Master; year; go—aunt; there; row—disaster; fear; dough—up; all; over—law; luggage; lost—no; lovely; pause—can't; does; awful; here; old—doesn't; all; facts; go; wrong; there—can't; can; aunt; ant—class; mass; grass; gas—dance; entrance (*verb*)—example; lamp; sample; ample—demand; hand; command; am.

Key Sounds in Sentence Context

The appearance of a pause should not go there.

To avert disaster, the master asked the aunt not to walk on the grass.

He spoke softly, charging the old fellow with an awful error.

Harry discovered that he had not been so clever after all.

The law declares that all lost luggage must be called for immediately.

The lovely girl walked up the garden path with no show of fear at all.

Year after year the same frightful demands were made over and over again.

In the country it is almost necessary to go first here, then there, and, finally, everywhere.

So there you are. Where have you been all afternoon?

Cast no bread upon the water for fear of breaking the law.

Special English Words with American Equivalents

petrol—gasoline	pram—baby carriage
lorry—truck	nanny—nurse
windscreen—windshield	wireless—radio
bonnet—hood	telly—television
boot—trunk	to let—for rent
spanner—wrench	Ltd.—Inc.
lift—elevator	tram—bus
tube—subway	first storey—second floor

SIGHT READING AND FLUENCY PRACTICE

Love for Love, *William Congreve;* Act I, Scene 2

MRS. FRAIL. You are the most mistaken in the world; there is no creature perfectly civil but a husband.

For in a little time he grows only rude to his wife, and that is the highest good breeding, for it begets his civility to other people. Well, I'll tell you news; but I suppose you hear your brother Benjamin is landed. And my brother Foresight's daughter is come out of the country—I assure you there's a match talked of by the old people. Well, if he be but as great a sea-beast as she is a land monster, we shall have a most amphibious breed. The progeny will be all otters; he has been bred at sea, and she has never been out of the country.

VALENTINE. Pox take 'em! Their conjunction bodes me no good, I'm sure.

MRS. FRAIL. Now you talk of conjunction, my brother Foresight has cast both their nativities, and prognosticates an admiral and an eminent justice of the peace to be the issue male of their two bodies. 'Tis the most superstitious old fool! he would have persuaded me, that this was an unlucky day, and would not let me come abroad; but I invented a dream, and sent him to Artemidorus for interpretation, and so stole out to see you. Well, and what will you give me now? Come, I must have something.

Ode on a Grecian Urn, *John Keats* (Portion)

Heard melodies are sweet, but those unheard

   Are sweeter; therefore, ye soft pipes, play on;

Not to the sensual ear, but, more endear'd,

   Pipe to the spirit ditties of no tone:

Fair youth, beneath the trees, thou canst not leave

   Thy song, nor ever can those trees be bare;

    Bold Lover, never, never canst thou kiss,

Though winning near the goal—yet, do not grieve;

   She cannot fade, though thou hast not thy bliss,

    Forever wilt thou love, and she be fair!

Mr. and Mrs. Bancroft, *Sir Squire Bancroft* (Volume 2)

From a tiny square hole in my dressing-room I could see all that went on behind the scenes, and could hear everything that was said on the stage; while Mr. Bancroft was going through that terrible ordeal, my profile might have been seen at the aforesaid square aperture very much resembling a postage stamp. The tumult became so awful that at last I rushed downstairs and walked about wringing my hands, and wondering how it would all end. If the malcontents could but have seen me, I am sure they would have ceased. I at length resolved that if the uproar lasted another three minutes I would myself address the audience, and ask them to listen to me for the sake of "Auld Lang Syne," and to say that after so long a service I ought to be permitted to dictate to them, so to speak, and by gentle reasoning bring about a reconciliation between us. But the noise and hooting ended, and my speech was unnecessary; my next ordeal was that I too should be received with groans and hisses, and I was cold with fear; but my reception when I made my appearance was so great, the welcome so hearty and prolonged, that, combined with all the nervous excitement, it gave me courage, and I acted better than I had done for some time. The night was one of the most awful I can remember; a short time before the doors were opened I went round the beautiful theatre, and could scarcely see the decorations through the black veil; the elements indeed were far from propitious, and, of course, this calamity, for I can call it nothing else, sadly helped to fan the flame of discontent and temper amongst the pittites, and our positions for a time were not to be envied.

VII

*

COCKNEY

*

The story of the Cockney dialect is the story of a place and a people. Less restricted in area and influence than is ordinarily thought, Cockney speech yet is indigenous to one city, London, and to a limited number of places within that city. Simeon Potter, in *Our Language*, says: "Slang and dialect meet and mingle in London cockney, that racy, spontaneous, picturesque, witty, and friendly English spoken not only by Londoners 'born within the sound of Bow Bells' . . . but by millions of other Londoners living within a forty-mile radius of the 'mother of Cities'."

Born in one place, growing and changing through the generations and the centuries, yet clinging always to the same place, the Cockney dialect in its history reflects the history of its users: a story of a people who, against all manner of natural and man-made odds, would not die.

Cockney is a class, one that has at times included many higher-level groups, but which has usually been appraised, generation in and generation out, as the lowest section of the many lower-class groupings of London. Cockney is also a district. Crowding the banks of the Thames, from whose docks and waterways the Cockney has taken much of his living, and in the near-Thames districts in the heart of the old City, generation after generation of Cockneys grew up within or close to the sound of the bells of the little Bow Church.

The uninviting conditions of the Cockney's home and his home areas, the kinds of work he performed, his often unsavory conduct—these factors encouraged the growth of feelings of superiority in most other persons and groups, attitudes of which the Cockney was always aware. At the same time, the gutsy fact of his existence compelled a grudging respect from those same persons, and of this feeling he was also conscious.

The Cockney dialect was not always a speech set apart. At one time the Cockney's antecedents made up almost the entire citizenry of London. Indeed, when that place became a city rather than a town, the Cockney was there, and it was his presence that effected the change. As early as the sixteenth century, it is recorded that all the people of London spoke the London dialect. In other words "Merchants and first Rate Tradesmen, Lawyers and Physicians, inferior Tradesmen, the Apprentices, Hackney-Coachmen, Carmen, Chairmen, Watermen, Porters, and Servants"—all but the "Nobility and Gentry," used what was to become the Cockney patois.[1]

The speech itself had honorable antecedents. MacKenzie MacBride says in *London Dialects* (1910): "The London dialect is really, especially on the south side of the Thames, a perfectly legitimate and recognizable child of the old Kentish tongue to which we owe our earliest written literature. . . . Covering a small area, it is little known outside, and thus people . . .

---

[1] Julian Franklyn, *The Cockney* (London: Andre Deutsch, 1953), p. 9.

mistake it for a mere foundling of the slums, instead of being, as it is, the tongue of the first written English, of the first English Church, of the first English Scholars, and the first English Schools."

Under the vigorous tutelage of the Tudors, London, with its preponderant middle and lower classes, grew rapidly. It was then, in the 1500's, that the Cockneys began to emerge as a distinct group. Their presence was the result of the inevitable economic sifting that sends some persons up to better living and others down to poorer. The process continued through the years.

Enduring a hard life, marginal at all times, ill-housed, ill-clothed, and poorly fed, the Cockney suffered the vicissitudes of a cold, wet climate, the indifference and scorn of a more fortunate citizenry, and the continual scourging of the plague. His mortality rate was always high. Yet, as a social group, he did not die.

Instead, he became a walking, talking, working, lounging, sly, and artful proof of the Darwinian contention that the weak go under and the tough survive. As a class and as a person he developed a unique character: impudent independence was balanced by cringing subservience. On the one side he was prompted at any and all times to "cock the snook" at his betters, and on the other to scramble and scrounge for the leavings of more affluent citizens. At his best he dominated his own area and roved with a saucy assurance over the rest of the city with pushcart, cab, or car. At his worst, he lived on the survival side of weakness, whining and begging (and worse) his way along, enveloped by a kind of derelict pity.

The product of his environment, he possessed and used a sly, animal cunning. A first-hand knowledge of what weakness was, taught him how to probe and touch the weaknesses of others. In survival he developed both an ability to size up the main chance with swift, shrewd judgment, and the sense of timing necessary to act upon his conclusions.

The conditioning of environment showed in his speech patterns. Climate and undernourishment produced an unpleasant adenoidal twang, a characteristic repeatedly used in the music halls by those who "took him off." A characteristic, further, which he himself accepted as a condition of his distinctiveness. But this was yesterday. Today's affluence, of which the Cockney has an earned share, has caused a change of circumstance. Better working and living conditions, better health and education have altered both his physical characteristics and his speech. On the Thames docks, in the streets and marketplaces, in the shops he owns or has entered, the twang is seldom heard and, probably, soon will be heard no more.

Equally indigenous, although also on the decline, is the Cockney inflectional pitch pattern. As whine or insinuating slide, it reflects his mental alertness, his cunning. As one of the "have-nots" who must work on or around the "haves," his survival has depended at times upon his ability to play upon the feelings of his betters. His "All roight, Guv'ner, anyfink you sai, Guv'ner," will never lose its appeal through lack of inflection.

Variety also characterized Cockney tempo patterns, and for reasons similar to the above. Eyes and hands that have been taught to be quick must be supported by an equally quick tongue. There is little slowness or drawl—unless in the expression of scorn—in a Cockney's speech. Actually, his pronunciation and his speed very often render his words unintelligible to any but his own people, as you can hear on one of the recorded selections which accompany this text. Within a controllable tempo margin, however, the stop and go of Cockney delivery will feature variety rather than its opposite.

Colloquially, Cockney is impregnated with a rich and racy idiom. Few other dialects can match its slangy expressiveness. Strong circumstances have impelled a strong utterance. Witted with the sting of satire and sarcasm, or filled with unreserved admiration, a Cockney's choice of words, used or new-minted by him, seldom leave his hearers in any doubt as to the exact state of his feelings. Nor is the use of his idiom restricted to his own form of speech. "Year in and year out the Cockney dialect has enriched Standard English, not with the frozen words of scholarship and science, but with words rich in personality, words informed by mockery, optimism, cynicism, humor. . . . The language of a costermonger compels attention, but has anybody ever been titillated by the language of a London clerk?" [2]

It is to be expected that such a splendid source of expressive material would be employed beyond the utilitarian use of those native to it. From Shakespeare and Jonson through Dickens and Kipling to Bernard Shaw,

---

[2] William Matthews, *Cockney, Past and Present* (London: George Routledge & Sons, Ltd., 1938), p. xiii.

Cockney speech has served its literary users well. Its very bulk in English dramatic literature makes its mastery a must for an actor who would have much to do with English plays. Even more widespread has been the employment of the Cockney dialect in that most distinctive of British entertainment institutions, the English music hall. Perhaps more than any other action, it was the multitudinous Cockney "turns" that spread the influence of Cockney idiom and pronunciation.

As a distinctive dialect, Cockney has grown and changed just as any other dialect would. Because of its walled-in condition, however, there have been fewer than normal alterations. A comparison of today's pronunciations with older evidences from written Cockney reveals that the principal shifts center around the use of a small group of consonants: *v*, *w*, *h*, *t*, and *d*.

Before the turn of the century an interchange of [v] and [w] was quite common. *Wine* and *vinegar* could be mixed to the extent of *vine* and *winegar*, a switch which was bound to appeal to those who were comically minded. Today the [h] is consistently dropped, but formerly it was almost as consistently added, so that there was an interchange somewhat similar to that of the [v] and [w] above. *Inhabit* could become *hin'abit*, just as Ann Hathaway might be changed to Hann 'Athaway. Likewise, there was an earlier switching of the plosive consonants [t] and [d], suggesting, as did the crossing of [v] and [w], a lingering Teutonic influence. A knowledge of these changes will explain some of the dialect writing which the student of Cockney is sure to come across.

The idiom and pronunciations of Cockney are still changing. The present alteration, however, features a new kind of shift; the direction is toward extinction. The interlocking pressures of modern living are forcing the change, and the drift is toward Standard English. No longer do Bethnal Green, Stepney, Whitechapel, Limehouse, and their likes comprise the only location of the Cockney's home and work. He is working out and moving out, and taking his speech with him. How long that speech will survive as an entity is anyone's guess, but today's tempo of change indicates that the end is not far off.

KEY SOUNDS OF COCKNEY

The Cockney is an Englishman. For all the uniqueness of his socioeconomic standing and the distinctiveness of his speech, he still is a member of that broad body of English-speaking Britons who share a large number of common pronunciations. No matter what the variation—Yorkshire, Cockney, Sussex, Scotch—each dialect is composed of English, as opposed to non-English, sounds. The pervasive use of the vowel [ɑ], the diphthong [ou], and the consonant [r] are examples. Therefore the Cockney's non-Cockney pronunciations are those of most other Englishmen.

Such is the strength of Cockney speech, however, that the statement you just read will not always seem to obtain. Indeed, for all the uniqueness of some dialects in the British Isles, few pronunciations can match the attention-getting qualities of Cockney. In some instances, sounds and melodic patterns alike are so unusually strong they tend to obscure those fundamental pronunciations which form the bulk of Cockney utterance.

As is to be expected, there is not just one Cockney dialect. Subtle and broad changes are evidenced between neighborhoods as well as districts, adding to the dialectician's chances of being right in one place and wrong in another. The different types are epitomized by two, one of which would say *Droory Lane*, and the other *Jeoury Lane*. The standardization the dialectician requires, however, is supplied by the fact that both would say *Line*. On this last basis the following key sounds are presented.

Vowel Substitutions

Since Cockney speech features diphthongs rather than vowels, the number of the latter we have to consider is limited to one. The rest mark a shift from vowel to diphthong.

1. [ɔ:]. The rounding and hollowing of the American [ɔ] as in *ought*, which makes the distinctive [ɔ:] of Standard English, is carried even further in Cockney. So strong is the alteration, Cockney rendition would make *fork* [fɔ:k] scarcely related to our [fork]. A smaller orifice of the rounded lips and a greater hollowing of the upper part of the pharyngeal cavity will produce the requisite sound.

Diphthongal Changes

1. [ʌɪ] FOR [i]. This shift marks one of the more subtle alterations from Standard English (or American). If it is not as forcefully recorded by the ear as some of the more noticeable Cockney sounds, this diphthong is just as important, and just as much used. It is produced by

combining the sound of *uh* [ʌ] as in *up*, with the [ɪ] of *it*, [ʌɪ]. *Me* and *teach* are good words to use to bring this diphthong to mind.

2. [ʌu] FOR [u]. This is another instance in which Cockney does more with a vowel than does Standard English. In this case the *uh* [ʌ] of *up* is combined with the *oo* [u] of *pool*. The alteration is as simple and the sound as easy to make as any you will deal with. *Too* and *who* are good words to remember when recalling this diphthong, but most marked of all is the distinctive *coo!* As much an expression as a word, this last sound *coo!* is repeated often in dramatic literature, and although many Cockneys today scorn it as outmoded slang, its use is still quite prevalent.

3. [aɪ] FOR [eɪ]. The substitution of [aɪ] (*time*) for [eɪ] (*eight*) produces the most noticeable of all Cockney sounds, the one you have heard most often in Cockney speech. "The rine in Spine falls minely on the pline" should be enough to set you onto this key sound.

4. [ɑɪ] FOR [aɪ]. Cockney and Irish are quite similar in this instance, although the latter tends to more strength. If *sign* is almost pronounced *soign* [sɔɪn] the sound is made. *Fine, fight, why* and *Eliza* represent the diphthong in varying connections.

5. [æh] OR [æʌ] FOR [ao]. The sound of this diphthong is flat and oral. The placement is far forward, as when *a-ah* [æ] is said in scorn. *Town* (*tahn*) [tæhn], *about* (*abaht*) [ə'bæht] and *now* (*nah*) [næʌ] are good words to associate with this key sound.

6. [æou] FOR [ou]. A longer, flatter sound is made by a Cockney when he pronounces our standard *ou* [ou], as in *go*.

7. [ɛl-r] OR [ɪl-r] FOR *l* OR *ll*. This is probably the most difficult of Cockney sounds to make. It can also be a controversial one, for its strength and formation is not consistent. It is heard most often on monosyllabic words that stand apart: *well* [wɛl-r] and *Bill* [bɪl-r] exemplify the point; indeed, they are probably the two words in which the sound most often is heard. Bernard Shaw liked the diphthong, although he wrote it *ol*, a transcription with which others have disagreed; some have simplified it to [ɪo]: *well* [wɪo] and *Bill* [bɪo], but this leaves out the sound of a partial [l] and [r] which, even though difficult of formation at first, gives a fullness to the sound that adds to its attractiveness. It is a dialect sound to take account of in more connections than one: both lower middle-class English and Japanese have it.

This key sound might best be made by sounding an *eh* [ɛ] or [ɪ] (*it*) followed by a slurred [l] followed by a partly formed [r], neither [l] nor [r] being fully sounded, but blended together, the whole delivered with no more time than is given to a short diphthong. Physically, the tongue tip stops short of contact with the hard palate for [l], and immediately after, the middle of the tongue does not complete its arch against the soft palate for [r], both actions being performed with the upper pharyngeal cavity hollowed and tensed.

The [ɛl-r] or [ɪl-r] is heard in both internal and final positions. *Health* [hɛl-rə] and *chill* [tʃɪl-r] are examples. The extent to which this particular key sound is put to use is a matter of individual judgment and ability.

Consonant Substitutions

1. [h̷]. Probably the best known characteristic of the Cockney dialect is the dropped [h̷]. Less common today than in times past, the use still has the force of a major practice. Both initial and medial positions are affected, so that *'ome* [h̷om] and *'oo* [h̷u] receive no stronger treatment than *be'ead* [bi'h̷ɛd] and *mo'air* ['moh̷ɛr].

In contradiction of some popular opinions, the addition of an *aich* [h] is now almost antique, although it still is heard occasionally as an unconscious irregularity. The younger generations, now properly schooled to place this voiceless fricative where it belongs, probably will end by eliminating the special treatments of [h] entirely as a key sound in the Cockney dialect. For the time being it is still necessary for actors to "drop aiches."

2. [n] FOR [ŋ]. As happens in so many of the dialects spoken on both sides of the Atlantic, the *g* of *ng* [ŋ] is shortened by dropping to *n* [n], so that *running* becomes *runnin'*, and *walking* is decreased to *walkin'*.

3. [k] ADDED TO [ŋ]. In a limited number of cases, most of which center on the word *thing* and its combinations —*nothing, anything*, or the like—the *ng* [ŋ] of *ing* receives the additional hard sound of [k]. Consequently *nothing* ['nʌθɪŋ] is heard as ['nʌθɪŋk] (but see below, section 4). Formerly the [k] ending had a much wider use, and such words as *swearing, playing, wishing*, would receive the [ɪŋk] treatment, but that would be out of place today.

4. [f] FOR [θ]. Again a strong key sound is bounded by a limited use. And again the word most concerned is *thing* and its prefixes. When this marked change is made *thing* [θɪŋ] becomes *fing* [fɪŋ] and *nothing* ['nʌθɪŋ] *nofing* ['nʌfɪŋ].

To closely connect two key sounds, we can take the [k] ending of *ing* just described in the section above and make *nothing* into *nofink* ['nʌfɪnk]. On *thing* and its combinations the added strength is quite acceptable.

5. THE INTRUSIVE [r]. *a.* [r] is heard as an interjection between the vowel and consonant in *af* [ɑf], *as* [ɑz] and *an* [ɑn]. The insertion of [r] is a legitimate but limited intrusion, one that might or might not be used, even one in which a single character might go one way and then the other at different times. At any rate, *laugh, ask* and *can't* may be changed to *larf, arsk* and *carn't.*

b. [r] is also intruded as a terminal sound, much as it is in New England speech. When a word ends in a vowel, especially [ɑ] or [ə], an [r] is formed as the concluding sound. *Idea* [aɪ'diə] pronounced *idear* [aɪ'diɝ] and *China* ['tʃaɪnə] *Chiner* ['tʃaɪnɝ] illustrate a practice which, though legitimate, should be limited in use to just a few instances.

6. THE GLOTTAL STOP [ʔ]. The use of a glottal stop is distinctively Cockney. The action which produces this effect has been described as "a consciously controlled subconscious contraction of the glottis."[3] It is a sudden catch or choke-off of sound which occurs as a replacement for [t], [k], and [p] between vowels. The symbol [ʔ] denotes its presence phonetically. *Little*, pronounced ['lɪʔəl] or *bottle* ['bɔʔəl] demonstrate the internal occurrence of a glottal stop. *Lot of* ['lɔ:ʔɔ:v] or *put his* ['puʔɪz] illustrate its action when two words are handled as one. When [t] is in a final position, which is often, it functions in the same way as indicated above: *got* [gɔʔ] and *not* [nɔʔ]. Practice must make the action of the glottal stop smooth, not sharp-edged.

Cockney Idiom and Slang

Few other dialects have developed more expressive idiom and slang than Cockney. The many idiomatic and slangy sayings create a fortunate circumstance for the dialectician in that the coverage of this aspect of Cockney speech is more properly the work of the writer. Such words and expressions as *O.K., Lunnon* (London), *garn* (disbelief or disagreement), *Gar blimey* (God blind me), *'arf a mo* (moment), *it's not 'arf cold, Guv, yuss* (yes) and *coo* are only starters for a flood of others. Both Matthews' *Cockney, Past and Present* and Franklyn's *The Cockney* have fairly extensive coverages.

[3] Franklyn, *The Cockney*, p. 242.

KEY-SOUND WORD DRILL

The material of this section is to be practiced in coordination with the Cockney Dialect tape. The voice on the tape will pause after each word so that you may repeat it immediately, checking your pronunciation against that of the speaker. Space is left below each line for phonetic or other markings.

(*Voice:* Larry Moss.)

Vowel Substitutions

1. [ɔ:]. Off, fork, walk, forty, important, hospital, sauce, awful.

Diphthongal Changes

1. [ʌɪ] FOR [i]. Me, see, speak, tea, scenes, Japanese, beat, need.

2. [ʌu] FOR [u]. Too, boot, who, boost, coo, prove, cool, through.

3. [aɪ] FOR [eɪ]. Rain, day, place, name, break, obtain, paper, stranger, great, able, representation, Shakespeare.

4. [ɑɪ] FOR [aɪ]. Sign, night, time, I, why, like, life, dry, crime.

5. [æh] FOR [ao]. Town, down, now, bound, about, proud, flower.

6. [æou] FOR [ou]. Go, don't, stone, slow, old, over, staccato.

7. [ɛl-r] OR [ɪl-r] FOR *l* or *ll*. Well, bill, pal, health, still, conceal.

Consonant Substitutions

1. [ʍ]. Home, hide, Henry (or Henery), who, prohibit, rehearse, inhale.

2. [n] FOR [ŋ]. Walking, running, hopping, feeling.

3. [ŋk] FOR [ŋ]. Nothing, something, asking.

4. [f] FOR [θ]. Think, thing, nothing, anything; or [f-k] nothing, something, anything.

5. THE INTRUSIVE [r].

   a. [r] AS INTERJECTION. Laugh, ask, half, nasty, off, can't.

   b. [r] AS TERMINAL. Idea, China, drawing, comma, Shah.

6. THE GLOTTAL STOP [ʔ]. Little, bottle, lot, glottis, pretty, literary, gentleman, citizen, nip, got.

KEY SOUNDS IN SENTENCE CONTEXT

Vowel Substitutions

1. [ɔ:] He's got no fork to eat the sauce. / Paul thought they took an awful fall.

Diphthongal Changes

1. [ʌɪ]. The bee did not like my tea. / She beat the tree with a key.

2. [ʌu]. Coo, it's too cool to put the glue through. / Who gave the boot to the youth?

3. [aɪ]. It was a great shame the paper got lost in the rain. / Shakespeare had able representation in the case.

4. [ɑɪ]. We had a right fine time. / At night Eliza signed the pipe.

5. [æh]. There's a haunted house about town. / About now the mouse has got the flower.

6. [æou]. Don't throw the stone at Jove. / He told the old gentleman to hold the rope.

7. [ɛl-r] OR [ɪl-r]. Well, Bill's a pal. / Health will tell.

Consonant Substitutions

1. [ʍ]. What's so hideous about your home, Henry? / Hey, Harry, hey, listen here to her.

2. [n']. Talking and hitting and hurting. / There's lodging at Newington and Billingsgate.

3. [ŋk]. Something is better than nothing. / Anything you say.

4. [f]. I think you better do nothing. / Something or something, or nothing or nothing.

5. [r]. He gave a nasty laugh. / Ask him to get off the walk, the very idea.

6. [ʔ]. The tittle-tattle paid off for pretty Betty. / You got a lot of nerve to close the glottis.

READING FOR FLUENCY

The first voice you will hear on the Cockney Dialect tape is that of a lorry driver (truck driver), recorded by the BBC on the Thames River docks.[4] It is included here that you may listen to a burst of sound as the primary source material out of which a stage dialect is formed. This is what is being said:

Well, one thing about my job, sir, I really like it.

Here I'm a motor driver—sort of Lord of the Air, you know, driving around no guv'ners (governors), and it's not ('tain't) like working in a factory. You go every-where, see everything, see every industry, all the dif-ferent factories, anything that's made in London you can bet your life that railsman sees in the course of his career, as you might well say. And looking around, one thing that interested me most was I went over (to) St. George's Road, that's over Southwark way, you know, and I went in the factory there, and it was all blind workers making cane baskets, and blimey, I stood there for about half an hour, watching these chaps just sort of feeling touch with their fingers, making these baskets. If you wasn't to—if you didn't know it was a blind factory, you wouldn't know (they) almost had their sight.

That was just one item that always struck me. I've never not really been able to forget that particular point.

Bow Bells, *Whitten*

The slow pace is intentional.

(*Voice:* Patricia Lewis.)

For this Bell, swinging out its music at all hours of the day, came to seem the voice of London herself, to symbolize her hopes and promises, to be her distinguishing feature; until at last, if you were born within the sound of Bow Bells you belonged to

---

[4] Used by special permission of Radio Enterprises, the BBC, London.

London, you could claim citizenship of the great City, you were, in fact, a "Cockney."

The term "Cockney" was not at first a term of reproach; it meant, one who dwelt in the land of Cocaigne, that is, the Land of Plenty. Cocaigne was an imaginary town in medieval story, where all the houses were made of cake, and all the streets paved with gold: so London appeared to the rude country-folk a city overflowing with food and riches: therefore they called the townspeople Cockneys.

Katie Conner, *Dacre*

(*Voice:* Larry Moss.)

On my honour, Katie Conner, is the nicest girl you'll meet;

I dote on her—I'm a "gonner"—she's just nice enough to eat.

Near the water first I caught her, in a little fishing town;

But just lately she's turned stately, and my brain's turned upside down.

Sweet Katie Connor, I dote upon her;

Kate, Kate, as sure as fate, you'll have to marry me;

Or else I have a notion of diving in the ocean,

And mashing all the mermaids at the bottom of the sea.

The Cockney Sergeant

(*Voice:* Larry Moss.)

Here now, step lively, you chaps. No lagging, keep your proper place in line. This ain't no bleeding picnic, you know. The Jerries are just up over the hill always waiting for you, and they ain't holding no cup of hot tea in their hands. So just move along proper now. Space yourselves well apart, and take what cover you can find, but make sure you ain't hiding behind another chap's back. When I gives the signal, you are going to hit out on the double, just like you was on the old Wolverhampton football team. And when all them big guns go poppin off 'round about, just you pay no mind to 'em. Just remember you're the best bleeding soldiers this bleeding army ever had, and when we gets through this bleeding push, the king might make generals out of all of you.

Hi, Lilly

(*Voice:* Patricia Lewis.)

Hi, Lilly, look here. No, here, here. That's right, just between the two branches. Can you see me? Righty-o. Now just step easy-like along the path. Mind the bit of ditch. I know it's a bit on the dark side, but who's to help that now? There are some nasty little bushes, but they can't hurt you, not if you look sharp. Take your time, and hold tight to the parcel; mustn't drop it now, not after all we've been through to get it, eh? That's it— easy does it. Come on now, you can hurry a bit more, you're getting quite clear of all that sticky stuff. There that does it, right enough. Now you just take my hand and follow along after. We're safe and sure now, make no mistake about that, nothing to hold us up. Here we go, off at a good pace. We'll soon leave those nasty kids far behind. Tally ho, now, as they say in the pictures.

Something about London

(*Voice:* Larry Moss.)

Well, there's something about London, I don't know what it is. It's hard to say exactly. It's a city you knows, and then again, it's a city you don't. Take the cab driver. It's years he spends learning his trade— months of walking and cycling and riding, all over the bleeding city, just so he can take you where you want to go, and without heading the wrong way down a one-way street—take him, he knows this town, and then again he don't. Too big, that's what, and, well, too many people. All kinds of blokes, from all over, crowding in here. They pack the walks till you got to put up railings to keep 'em off the pavement, like Piccadilly Circus, you know, coming up from Haymarket Street. Well, how you going to know all about them—not half you're not.

It's not just us, gar blimey, it's the whole scoop. A little of this and a lot of that, and you got races and colors all mixed up like bottles sitting in a row in your favorite pub. Who's to know all them? But they're here, they're London. It's the people, the little and the big, the great and the small, that make up a place, I always say.

Well, perhaps I better take that back a bit. There's

places, too—like Tower Bridge and Waterloo Station, and the Strand and High Holborn, and Belgrave Square —where it don't half take your brass to live in one of their fancy flats—St. Paul's and the Houses of Parliament, and the old Roman wall, bit of that's there too. Places are important, make no mistake about that.

And where I live, Stepney, you got to count that in, and Whitechapel and Mile End and Limehouse—those places what had the guts blasted out of 'em in the war. Places that one fellow said had squalid streets, mean houses and great hearts. One night thousands of homes were blasted open, up they went and down they came. Gas mains, water mains, drains, electric cables, telephone cables—all smashed. Hundreds of craters in the roads, in one of 'em a doctor held by his heels and hanging head down to give help to someone pinned down below, and all the while another bloke is using a firebomb to heat water to make tea for all—that was something, right enough.

London, I can't rightly say, there's something about it, you think you know it, and then you don't—hold on, that's not right. Better switch that around—when you just get to thinking you don't, then, blimey, that's when you do.

INDIVIDUAL-PRACTICE EXERCISES
Key-Sound Word Drill

These key sounds are placed beside each other so that you may exercise on the change of lip, tongue and jaw positions necessary for the making of the proper sounds.

Off; me; fine; game—do; beat; down; slow—well; nothing; ought; go; right—cool; night; half; round— can't; little; rain; grow—flower; fork; still; something— be; proud; all; day—bottle; important; nasty; page— told; time; think; teach—don't; make; plain; face—say what's over—all old laws—make demands there—a pound a day—put butter all over—better get going— fine right hook—again he fought—fair, fat, and forty —out and about—naughty but nice—down daisy down—beat pain night and day walking Henry home— literary Japanese applauded Bill last time for nothing.

Key Sounds in Sentence Context

He had his eye on the main chance.

It was his fate to come in last in the great race.

In a way it is not strange at all that fair play happened.

He's got the fork, but I'll give him what for if he takes the pipe.

He doesn't care nothing for nobody, not him.

Waiting all day and I haven't got my pay yet.

Yes, Harry Hawkins is a first-class name.

Walking down the street with a daisy in her hand.

He's taking down verbatim everything you say.

You won't half get cold out there.

What a lot of little bottles you got up there.

The gentleman is a British citizen lodging in Billingsgate.

Gaiety and light-heartedness in the face of adversity.

That ain't nothing to what he might have done.

Coo, the Queen said it was about time to make a change.

Here now, don't go about it that way, change around.

Work apace, work apace—honest labour makes a merry face.

Being my daughter's wedding day, ten thousand pounds I'll give away.

SIGHT READING AND FLUENCY PRACTICE
Speaking Out

There are times when I don't know what the people who run the government are thinking about. You can follow its policies for years and still not know what it is they are up to. Of course I know that it ain't possible for most of us, the average man on the street you might say, to know all the ins and outs of politics. We got to take a lot on faith, for the simple reason that we can't know all that's going on behind the scenes. Who knows what this ambassador said to that ambassador last week, and who is pals with who today, or who is going to have rough and hasty words with who tomorrow. All the same, I'd like it much better if the powers that be would take it into their heads to let us in on something. By right we ought to have some say on such little items as taxes and wages and traffic regulations. Know what I mean? Right.

Music-Hall Songs

Like an hengine he could go,

To 'Ackney, 'Ampstead Eaf, or Bow,

I never shall survive the lorse

Of poor old Jack, my chestnut 'orse.

My name it is Sam Hall, chimney sweep,

My name it is Sam Hall.

I robs both great and small,

But they makes me pay for all,

Damn their eyes.

Daisy, Daisy, give me your answer do!

I'm half crazy, all for the love of you!

It won't be a stylish marriage,

I can't afford a carriage,

But you'll look sweet

Upon the seat

Of a bicycle built for two!

Something about London

First off, if you're going to make the rounds of the town, you got to know what you're up against. It's a mighty big place, and one side of the water or the other, it covers a lot of ground. If it's speed you're after, then the Underground is what you're looking for. Get on the Tube and in no time at all you're at any place you like. But you won't see nothing. Can't have it both ways, can you? If it's the sights of London you came for, then you got to stay above ground.

A lot of people like to start off seeing the Tower and the places round about. Plenty of others begin their sightseeing by coming down St. James Street and walking along the Mall to Buckingham Palace to see the Changing of the Guard, taking a chance that the Queen is home. If that's the way you want to go, you can stroll along Birdcage Walk and come out close to Westminster Abbey. That's a place, something to see there, right enough. Plenty of great ones waiting for you there, and quite a few little ones too; not only the big names got put under, there's others you never heard tell about.

Up the street a bit is Whitehall, and that's right nice. Got the horses standing there, on guard you might say, only they don't do nothing—trained for it, just standing. And the soldiers with their shiny helmets and breastplates, they're the same, sit there without blinking an eye, seems like. They don't mind how many times a tourist takes a picture, they can pop away all day for all the soldiers seem to care.

When you get hungry there's shops all along the way, tucked here and there, some even out of sight and hard to find. Tea any time you like, and cakes if you've a taste for 'em. More hearty food, like steaks and chops, is found in the bigger places. Famous names, too, all over the West End. But Soho, that's the place for eating; anything you want, just name it and there's a place where you can get it. Crowded at night, though, so it's safer to make a reservation, a booking, we call it. Watch out if you're driving a car, no place to park. Like that all over, ain't it? I hear that every big city has got its problems. Cars, coo—we make 'em, but we don't know where to put 'em. All too true, ain't it? Best take a cab—right?

VIII

*

IRISH

*

The Irish dialect presented here has the specific purpose of fulfilling the dialect needs of the modern Irish play. It does not take into account the variety of indigenous speech which exists throughout the island; an exact and complete representation of regional speech gives way to dramatic requirements.

There is no loss in this arbitrary action—Ireland's dramatic authors not only present a good cross section of Irish speech, they do so with great skill and truthfulness.

The material in Irish plays represents the best in modern Irish literature. And the variety is gratifyingly broad. Sean O'Casey's dialogue in *The Plough and the Stars* and *Juno and the Paycock* is authoritative for the speech of the underprivileged of Dublin. With great artistry he identifies idiom in pronunciation with the rhythm and melody patterns which characterize all Irish speech. John Millington Synge does the same thing with a provincial dialect in *The Playboy of the Western World* and *Riders to the Sea*. It is a speech, he asserts in a preface to *Playboy*, which is "as deliciously flavored as a nut or an apple," and so it sounds to our ears. Lady Gregory and William Butler Yeats are literary as well as provincial, each concentrating upon one-act plays, the work of both being largely responsible for the Irish literary revival out of which the present Irish theatre has grown. On the other hand, Paul Vincent Carroll writes the speech of a middle-sized town as he mixes educated with uneducated characters in *The White Steed* and *Shadow and Substance*.

To any reader of Irish dramatic literature it is obvious that Irish playwrights present the various dialect forms of Irish speech at their best and strongest. In contrast, the dialect student who hears an Irish tourist or immigrant, or who travels in Ireland, may listen for some time before he hears what he has come to think of as standard Irish. Throughout the island itself and especially in Dublin such other forms as Standard or middle-class English can be found in abundance. Nor will talk heard on the street or in shops or hotels always come up to the level of vocal delivery one anticipates after listening to such performers as the late Barry Fitzgerald, or one or another of the many fine actors and actresses Ireland has exported. But these facts should in no way detract from the student's determination to achieve the fullness of pronunciation and idiomatic expression which characterizes the best of indigenous Irish speech.

To a trained and appreciative ear there is no more attractive dialect in the English language than Irish. However, it is easier to recognize and respond to the appealing rhythms and melodies of its vocal patterns than it is to explain their presence. There are many times, in written and oral forms, when Irish prose can be very close to poetry. Any attempt to analyze the phenomenon must take into consideration first the people themselves and then their land and climate.

At once a hardy and fanciful and humorous people, the Irish, living close to nature in an environment hardly benign, have developed an elemental sensitivity to both the known and unknown in the forces of nature. The imaginativeness which, in the face of harsh and often cruel climatic conditions, could create leprechauns instead of ogres would more likely see and feel beauty than meanness in both natural and human relationships. A Celtic strain must be taken into account: an earlier Gaelic influence which went deep and stayed long; a mysticism which sought release in dance and song also left its impress on the rhythm and melody of local utterance.

The principal characteristics of an Irish dialect are: (1) the absence of those English pronunciations which are found in nearly all other dialects in the British Isles, the broad sound of [ɑ] and the dropped [ɾ], for example; (2) a unique pronunciation, not found elsewhere in the island areas, of a few vowels and consonants; (3) a change of word order in sentence structure, also found nowhere else; (4) a larger number than usual of idiomatic expressions; and (5) the presence of attractive rhythmic and melodic qualities in many vocal patterns.

A glide in pitch and an elongation of vowel and diphthong sounds are responsible for the last characteristic noted above. In this respect Irish is a self-conscious dialect, one that always affects the ear, a point that such authors as Brendan Behan, Sean O'Casey, and the earlier Synge make abundantly clear. Even when these writers are read silently their words and the fluency of their diction are *heard* by the reader to a greater extent than is usual with most writing in the English language. The effect is increased when the words and phrases are pronounced.

One of the best known characteristics of Irish speech is the richness of its idiom. An abundance of meaningful colloquialisms can be found in both written and oral forms. This is usually true of the language of any people who live close to nature and have a long cultural tradition; the Irish are among the world's best in developing this natural tendency. Their methods of doing so are unique. To the usual number of locally telling expressions they have added changes in both word order and word use, switching words around so as to alter normal sentence structure at the same time they alter the normal forms of the words they use. For the normal statement "He will be coming now," Irish colloquialism would have "It's himself will be coming now." A random speech from Synge's *In the Shadow of the Glen* stands as illustration for thousands of others on this point.

TRAMP. Have no fear, master of the house. What is it I know of the likes of you that I'ld be saying a word or putting out my hand to stay you at all?

The use of *himself* for *him* and the addition of *at all, at all* (*a'tall, a'tall*) at the end of a sentence, the insertion of *do you now* and—, *is it*, or *what are you after* or *I'll be after* or *I'm destroyed entirely, God help me* all add the character to Irish speech that most of us have come to expect. Further acquaintance will not disappoint us.

In this connection it would be well to remember, however, that invention of the single expression or the pat phrase by a non-Irish person or an inexperienced writer is more likely to produce a hackneyed and cliché product than one that has the freshness of Irish authorship.

There are two languages and consequently two kinds of speech in Ireland today; Gaelic and English. Both are legal, both are taught in the schools, and both have a daily use, although not in equal portion. English has by far the greater employment. In both written and oral form Gaelic is completely foreign to the English-oriented individual. Its use is directly associated with the earlier revival and present maintenance of a spirit of nationalism among the people of the free state of Eire [ɛərə]. Its presence, however, has had but little influence upon the speech we characterize as an Irish dialect, consequently it need not concern us now. The dialect we study is simply another variation of the uses and sounds of the English tongue, but as employed by Irishmen rather than Englishmen or Americans.

As a result of the Irish literary revival at the turn of the century numerous collections of folk sayings and stories have been published. A large percentage of them feature tales told in colloquial speech, with spelling that attempts to indicate how the words are pronounced in dialect. Since there is no uniformity of approach to the problem of representing sound by spelling, nor any assurance that the hearers hear the same sounds or hear them correctly, an attractively mixed-up body of material awaits the student dialectician. In this mass of material at least one characteristic is constant—no tale remained untold because the teller feared his use of dialect was too strong. Accordingly, no matter what the degree of variation of colloquialisms, most are represented in full strength.

For additional practice material the plays of the authors named earlier are strongly recommended. For the dialectician no better material is available.

KEY SOUNDS OF AN IRISH DIALECT

To achieve an Irish dialect comparatively few alterations are required of an American dialectician. More
would have to be noted if American-Irish speech of the
New England variety, and especially of some parts of
Massachusetts and New York, were also to be considered, or if account had to be taken of the many
minor dialect differences which exist throughout the
island of Ireland itself. For our purpose such distinctions need only be noted; a mastery of all such dialectal
variations is not within our scope.

The limited number of vocal alterations is due to the
fact that one vowel and a few diphthongs carry unusually heavy loads in Irish speech. The number of consonantal substitutions is also limited. Yet the dialect will
be found to be as forceful and as distinctive as any in
the English language.

In some instances a choice between two pronunciations is offered the dialectician. These will be noted
later when the specific sounds themselves are being
discussed. Also a difference, of which the dialectician
must be aware and in which he must be practiced,
exists between the speech of a Dubliner and anyone
living outside the capital or, to be more exact, between
the speech of a character in an O'Casey play and that
of most of the roles created by the other Irish playwrights. The difference is mainly a matter of two
consonant substitutions and will be presented when
those sounds are discussed.

Vowel Substitutions

The first alteration to be noted is one that is related
to the rhythm of Irish speech. It is a matter of timing
and has to do with the duration of sound. In an Irish
dialect most vowels are elongated beyond American or
English usage. This action not only affects the rhythm
of the speech but is also responsible in part for the
pleasing melodic element which is indigenous to the
dialect.

Both vowels and diphthongs are subject to elongation. To achieve the necessary effect a speaker simply
holds on to a syllable slightly longer than usual. The
accomplishment of this action, which is a matter of
awareness and practice, is encouraged by the text of all
good Irish writing.

A caution must be made against singing the syllables
or trying for a singsong effect in phrasing, for if either of

these things is done the dialect will begin to sound more
Norwegian than Irish.

1. [a]. This vowel, the [a] of *ask*, is probably the most
noticeable and most used sound in an Irish dialect.
Unfortunately it is not found in the speech of most
Americans, only a few Easterners employ it. Therefore
it must be an acquired sound, for it is essential to the
new dialect.

[a] is a middle vowel, halfway between the front
vowel [æ], as in *at*, and the back [ɑ], as in *father*. To
locate the placement of [a] and to establish its sound,
first slide from [æ] to [ɑ] pausing in the middle of the
passage to fix the new vowel in your memory, then
reverse the process by sliding from [ɑ] to [æ]. Next, say
ask [æsk] with an American pronunciation, then *ask*
[ɑsk] as in Standard English, then establish [ask] halfway between the two. This is the vowel an Irishman
uses over and over again. The extent of its employment
is demonstrated by the fact that it acts as a substitute
for three or four other vowel sounds.

To complicate matters for the dialectician, however,
it must be stated that [a] is not a steady sound. The
inconsistencies that develop naturally out of any flow
of vocal sounds are more pronounced in this case than
usual. Although both [æ] and [ɑ] are altered to [a] most
of the time, on occasion a speaker's voice will reverse
the process and slip into one or the other of the variants
([æ] or [ɑ]). This change will be heard on the tape.

[ɑ] ᴛᴏ [a]. Compared to the extent of its use elsewhere
in the British Isles, the broad sound of [ɑ] is little heard
in an Irish dialect. The [a] is substituted for it, the latter
performing the same heavy duty in Irish speech that
the former does in Standard English. When the substitution is made, *ah* [ɑh] becomes [ah], *bar* [bɑr] changes
to [bar], and the terminal syllable in *Utah* ['jutɑ] becomes ['juta].

[ɔ] ᴛᴏ [a]. [ɔ] as in *ought* is also altered to [a], so that
ought is pronounced [at] not [ɔt]. To give an illustration
of this vowel in initial, medial and terminal positions,
all [ɔl] is altered to [al], *ball* [bɔl] is changed to [bal], and
straw [strɔ] becomes [stra]. If for any reason there was a
need to mitigate the strength of the dialect, the speaker
could alter [ɔ] to [ɑ] instead of to the more emphatic [a].
In the far from exact standards which exist in all forms
of human speech, account must always be taken by the
phonetician and dialectician of the variance of sound
that occurs between two individuals whose talk should
be almost alike, and even of the variance which can be

heard (by the not always exact ear of the listener) in the speech of one person. Accordingly, in an Irish dialect [ɔ] can vary in value, changing from [a] to [ɑ] as a matter of choice or chance. In the mouth of a master of the dialect, however, the alteration becomes merely a matter of flexibility in control. Whatever the circumstance, [a] should be expected to carry the major burden.

[ʌ] TO [a]. [ʌ], as in *up*, like the other vowels just considered, and more easily than most, surrenders many of its uses to [a]. Thus *up* [ʌp] becomes [ap], *run* [rʌn] changes to [ran], and *other* ['ʌðəʳ] to ['aðəʳ].

[æ] TO [a]. Only a few [æ] syllables are changed to the vowel value of [a], but some of those few are important because of the frequent use of the words which hold them. Such commonplace terms as *half, past, after, ask, man, aunt, demand, grant,* and *path* are on the list. It should be noted that in Standard English all of these words except one, *man*, would be pronounced with a broad [ɑ]. This gives us a rule of sorts to follow in handling the limited substitutions which occur in Irish speech when [æ] is changed to [a]. The greatest number of pronunciations of the front vowel [æ] still will emphasize only an elongation, however.

2. ELONGATED VOWELS: [i], [e], [a], [u], [o]. In this group [e] and [o] are the most important and receive the greatest emphasis. Not only are they to be elongated when appearing as themselves, they also assume an extra burden when the diphthongs [eɪ] and [ou] are shortened to their length. In these cases *eight* [eɪt] becomes a long [et], and *know* [nou] a long [no]. Further, the [o] should be more rich in tonal value than it normally is; a dropped jaw and rounded lips will produce the fullness required. The elongated vowel is preferred in works that emphasize a literary rather than a colloquial quality.

The degree of elongation any of the above vowels receive is dependent upon the vocal delivery of the character being played. For example, in O'Casey's *The Plough and the Stars*, the character Fluther, especially as created by Barry Fitzgerald, would lengthen his vowels more than the younger character Clitheroe. To the same extent, in Carroll's *The White Steed*, Canon Matt, irascible but lovable, would habitually hold on to his vowels beyond the duration of sound used by the younger and sterner Father Shaughnessy.

In all cases the elongation of these vowels adds to the musicalness of the dialect. Because the characters to be presented on stage seem to ask for it, the increased duration of sound will be more pronounced in the theatre than it is in most instances of everyday use. A demonstration of the elongation of each is given in the Key-Sound Word Drill.

3. [ɛ] TO [ɪ]. In a limited number of cases the vowel [ɛ], as in *ever*, is changed to the sound of [ɪ], as in *it*. Save for the fact that this substitution is both so emphatic and so traditional, the relatively small number of usable instances would make the substitutions quite minor. But *never* ['nɛvəʳ] and *devil* ['dɛvl] are so patently identified in Irish dialect as *niver* [nɪvəʳ] and *divil* ['dɪvl] that failure to make the substitutions would be a noticeable oversight—even though the alteration might be characterized in some cases as more American-Irish than native Irish. The advice here is to employ the substitutions when either more strength or more comic content is required.

4. [ʌ] TO [ʊ]. Also limited and also strong is the substitution for [ʌ], as in *up*, of [ʊ], as in *put*. Actually, the substitution is not that simple, for the sound required goes a little beyond the [ʊ] of *put* in the direction of [u], as in *pool*. The [ʊ] of *put* is given because that vowel is the closer of the two to the desired sound.

Because this substitution is not heard in all variations of the Irish dialect, it is not proper to say that it is mandatory. Definitely identified with the speech of Dublin, it can and should be used in an O'Casey play. Beyond that, the use of the substitution may wisely be limited. Character requirements—uneducated or comic roles, for example—should dictate the use or nonuse of this new vowel. If it is employed, then *Dublin* ['dʌblɪn] becomes ['dʊblɪn] and *jug* [dʒʌg] changes to [dʒʊg].

Diphthongal Changes

The elongation of tone with which we have been dealing receives full emphasis in the formation of diphthongs, even to the extent of making possible triphthongs out of two of the substitutions we have to consider.

1. [aɪ] TO [ʌɪ] (OR POSSIBLY TO [ʌoɪ]). When made, the substitution indicated here produces one of the best known sounds of the dialect. It is immediately recognized when *Mike* [maɪk] is pronounced [mʌɪk]. (To avoid complications, the idea is introduced only parenthetically that to some ears the resultant sound from the above substitution comes out in triphthong form as [ʌoɪ]. When it does so the sound is receiving its fullest possible treatment; there is no doubt that [ʌoɪ] is used by some speakers. However, the [ʌɪ], a simple and proper substitution, is completely adequate.)

A degree of breathiness is associated with the emission of this diphthong, adding a further characteristically Irish element to the sound. A discussion and a caution are offered on the subject of breathiness when it is treated in a later section.

The diphthong is found in initial, medial, and terminal positions.

2. [aʊ] TO [ʌʊ] (OR POSSIBLY TO [ʌɔʊ]). The entire discussion of the section immediately above could be repeated here, the only difference being in the sound of the diphthongs (or triphthongs) themselves. *Out* [aʊt] pronounced [ʌʊt] is an example of the substitution.

3. [ɔɪ] TO [aɪ]. Another distinctly Irish sound is made when *boy* [bɔɪ] is pronounced [baɪ], or *joy* [dʒɔɪ] becomes [dʒaɪ].

Not all [ɔɪ] diphthongs should receive this alteration. When a doubt as to what word is being uttered is in a hearer's mind—as when the word *coy* [kɔɪ] is pronounced as [kaɪ]—or when context does not make the word obvious, the above substitution should not be made.

4. [i] TO [eɪ]. The pure vowel [i], as in *easy* [izɪ], is stretched into the diphthong [eɪ], as in *eight*. *Easy* [eɪzɪ] results from the substitution.

Not by any means is every [i] altered to [eɪ]. Whether the [i] retains its original tonal value and is merely elongated or changed to the above diphthong is a matter for the ear of the dialectician to determine. *Tea* [ti] and *key* [ki] would accept the substitution and be heard as [teɪ] and [keɪ], but *be, flee, he,* or *Marie* would not. Accordingly, care should be taken that this substitution is not overemployed. As distinctive as *meeting* ['mitɪŋ] and *decent* ['disnt] are when pronounced ['meɪtɪn] and ['deɪsnt], a complete substitution of this diphthong would only cause confusion. Multiple possibilities of its use are given in the Key-Sound Word Drill.

5. [oʊ] TO [aʊ]. When the diphthong [oʊ], as in *old*, is not reduced to an elongated [o], as it very often is, it should receive the substitution of [aʊ], causing *old* to be enunciated as *auld* [aʊld]. Since either treatment of the vowel and diphthong is legitimate, context and personal inclinations usually determine which will be used. But when use of [aʊ] might seem too close in tonal value to the Standard English diphthong of [ʌo]—*soap* [sʌop], for example—the use of the pure but elongated vowel is recommended.

Consonant Substitutions

1. [r]. Still holding its place as the most altered consonant from dialect to dialect, [r] receives another and very different treatment in this study. In contrast to the soft [r] of American Southern and Standard English, the uvular [r] of French and German, and the front-trilled [r] of Scotch, the Irish [r] is a hard, solid sound. A strongly vibrating consonant (or semivowel) which is sustained by energetic muscular action of the middle and back of the tongue as well as by a tensing of the walls of the pharyngeal cavity, the Irish [r] is effectively heard in all three syllabic positions—initial, medial, and final—it even resists with moderate success the human tendency to drop or swallow the terminal syllable in a multisyllable word. The word *rear* [rɪr] shows the consonant in first and last positions, *arrive* [ə'raɪv] in the middle.

An additional characteristic of an Irish [r] is the strength of its connection to the preceding vowel of [a]. The [r] not only terminates the sound in no uncertain manner, it also seems to give clarity to the vowel itself. Two words illustrate the point: *horse* [hars], *insert* ['ɪnsart].

The sound of [ɝ], as in *her, bird,* or *father,* also is enunciated in a positive manner, giving strength to the [r] portion of the syllable.

2. [n] FOR [ŋ]. The *g* of *ing* is consistently dropped: *rowin'* ['roɪn] or *meetin'* ['meɪtɪn].

3. [θ] TO [t]. The voiceless fricative *th* [θ] can be pronounced two ways, either as it usually is in Standard American or English—*th*irty, ca*th*edral, wi*th*—or with a [t] substitute—['tɝti] or ['tɛrti], [ka'teɪdrl], [wɪt]. Actually, this substitution is almost identical with a similar practice in a German dialect. In both instances the dialectician learns as a matter of linguistic common sense when not to make the substitution. For example, *thought* [θat] would, and should for middle-class and uneducated persons, change to [tat], but *thatch* should not be so treated.

4. [t] TO [θ] AND [d] TO [ð]. In an exact reversal of the above substitution, in an O'Casey play the voiceless [t] becomes a voiceless *th* [θ], and a voiced [d] changes to the voiced *th* [ð]. The voiceless substitution is easy of management. If *trespassing* is pronounced as though it were spelled *th*respassing and *butter* as bu*th*er, the change is made.

The substitution of a voiced [ð] for [d] requires more physical flexibility. In this case the tongue must execute a familiar action in an unfamiliar place to make *drink* [drɪŋk] become [ðrɪŋk] and *wonder* ['wandɝ] change to ['wanðɝ]. The physical action requires the tip of the tongue to touch the edge or back of the upper front teeth with the sides of the tongue held against the upper molars so that passing air is forced between tongue and teeth. The position is one in which you are thoroughly practiced. The difficulty lies in applying the action to unaccustomed places and to a limited number of words, and those only on initial and medial syllables.

Examples, taken from O'Casey's plays, of both of these substitutions will be presented in the Key-Sound Word Drill. As with most of this author's work, the identity of such characteristics with Dublin speech is pronounced.

Melodic Patterns

The melodic element in Irish speech is the result of an extensive use of variety in pitch, usually by glides rather than steps. There is no set pattern that can be drawn as notes on a musical scale to illustrate how any one phrase is to be delivered. The reason is that a pitch pattern represents the meaning intended, and multiple meanings are possible for every phrase. For illustration, two individuals do not say the same phrase—"Hello, how are you?"—in exactly the same way, nor does one person deliver a phrase exactly the same way every time he uses it. If his meaning is exactly the same, there will be marked similarity between the two deliveries; otherwise the pitch patterns vary subtly or broadly in response to subtle and broad changes of meaning.

It has already been stated that vowels and diphthongs are held longer and enunciated more fully than is usual in most dialects. When a greater variety of pitch—more stretch up and down the vocal scale—is added to elongation, the result is a noticeable increase in the melodic content of the speech. But the added stretch in a pitch pattern is not to be forced or arbitrarily imposed; it must come because a definite thought motivates each line reading, and the purpose of the speaker is to express that thought as clearly as possible. Naturalness in the flow of dialogue as well as clarity of meaning is the result of a properly motivated delivery. On the other hand, artificiality and a singsong delivery are the usual products of pitch patterns that are arbitrarily imposed.

The change of word order in sentence structure as well as the punctuation employed by the major Irish writers both indicate and encourage the rhythms and melodies indigenous to an Irish dialect, making it outstanding among all kinds of regional speech, matched in these respects only by the Welsh and Yiddish. But its fluency must be free and its sounds fully formed.

Breathiness

A condition of breathiness indicates that more air than is needed is being expelled on certain syllables. Breathiness is a pernicious habit most often found in deliveries that are affected or overdramatic. As a rule its use is to be avoided except when an overdramatic or affected character is to be created, one that acts at acting. But an exception to the rule can now be made with propriety, for certain sounds in an Irish dialect require an aspirate quality. When properly produced—that is, when not put on or overdone—the result is pleasing to the ear. The action involved requires that slightly more time than usual be taken for the making of a breathy syllable while more air than usual is permitted to escape, and the sound of the escaping air is slightly heard.

The voiceless consonants [p], [t], [k], [f], [θ], [s], [ʃ], [h] and *wh* [hw] best permit the action which produces breathiness.

A judicious use of the element of breathiness is strongly recommended.

Miscellaneous Pronunciations

A few words which are not part of a larger group require distinctive pronunciations. The word *boy* is typical, for it not only can be given either as [bɔɪ] or [baɪ], but sometimes as *boyo*. By no rule but that of usage, *by* [baɪ] and *my* [maɪ] become colloquialisms when pronounced [bi] and [mi]—"By [bi] the look of it" and "Come here, my [mi] lad."

Variations

Each dialectician must determine for himself answers to the questions of how extreme a dialect should be and which set of variants should be used for which playwrights. To be of some help in this matter, the suggestion is made that for uneducated persons or for strongly provincial characters or for comic roles the full catalogue of vowel, diphthong, and consonant substitutions be used as required by an author's script or as determined by the speaker.

But in those cases in which an author's style emphasizes a beauty of diction or has a marked literary quality, certain restrictions are recommended. For example, in the work of Synge it is suggested that the following characteristics *not* be used: [ɪ] for [ɛ], as in *ever* [ɪvɚ]; [ʊ] for [ʌ], as in *mug* [mʊg]; [aɪ] for [ɔɪ], as in *boy* [baɪ]; [eɪ] for [i], as in *easy* ['eɪzɪ]; [aʊ] for [oʊ], as in *old* [aʊld];

and that the consonants [t], [d], and the two *th*'s [θ] and [ð], keep their usual pronunciations.

Although a decision to eliminate some or all of the items above from the work of such an author as Synge is somewhat arbitrary, it must be granted that an elongation of vowel sounds produces a better effect on the ear than do the alternate substitutions. For example, in Synge *easy* sounds better then *asy*, *boy* better than *by*, and *thirty* better than *tirty*.

KEY-SOUND WORD DRILL

The material of this section is to be practiced in coordination with the Irish Dialect tape. The voice on the tape will pause after each word so that you may repeat it immediately, checking your pronunciation against that of the speaker. Space is left below each line for scoring phonetic or other symbols.

(*Voice:* Jerry Blunt.)

Vowel Substitutions

1. [a].

   a. [ɑ] TO [a]: odd, on, army, heart.

   b. [ɔ] TO [a]: all, ought, off, jaw.

   c. [ʌ] TO [a]: other, up, hunt, ran.[1]

   d. [æ] TO [a]: half, after, man, rather.

2. ELONGATED VOWELS: [i], [e], [æ], [u], [o].

   a. [i]: each, deal, agree.

   b. [e]: able, day, great, safe.

   c. [a]: Adam, am, Pat, Saturday.

   d. [u]: cool, moon, truth, who.

   e. [o]: oak, old, loan, no.

---

[1] *ran* [ran] belongs in the next line.

3. [ɛ] TO [ɪ]: ever, never, devil, seven, again.

4. [ʌ] TO [ʊ]: fun, Dublin, mug, rough.

Diphthongal Changes

1. [aɪ] TO [ʌɪ] (OR [ʌoɪ]): Mike, fine, night, rival.

2. [aʊ] TO [ʌʊ] (or [ʌoʊ]): out, town, now, cloud.

3. [ɔɪ] TO [aɪ]: boy, noise, oil, point, join.

4. [i] TO [eɪ]: easy, keep, decent, meeting, tea, beat, priest.

5. [oʊ] TO [aʊ]: old, cold, told.

Consonant Substitutions

1. [r]: right, circle, horse, father, torch.

2. [ŋ] TO [n]: meeting, boiling, timing, mugging.

3. [θ] TO [t]: thirty, cathedral, thousand.

4. [t] TO [θ]: butter, trespass, water, trying, after.

5. [d] TO [ð]: wonder, drink, dress, draw.

Breathiness

Teams, technical, proper, participate, what, forty, thirsty, certain.

Miscellaneous Pronunciations

You, youse, goodo, boyo, school, whilst, whisht, by, my, other, mother, beyond, with, soldier, police.

KEY SOUNDS IN SENTENCE CONTEXT

Vowel Substitutions

1. [ɑ] TO [a]. What's the matter, it's not an odd thing
about the heart, at all—at all.

   [ɔ] TO [a]. The author thought the law was wrong.

   [ʌ] TO [a]. Another onion will only give youse an
ulcer.

   [æ] TO [a]. All the man wanted was a bath.

2. ELONGATED VOWELS: [i], [e], [a], [u], [o].

   [i]. Each will eat an apple.

   [e]. He's had a great ache all day long.

   [a]. Can't you see, Matt's the lad with the hat.

   [u]. The kangaroo stooped in the cool of the moon.

   [o]. Auld Joe is only going to loan the stone.

3. [ɛ] TO [ɪ]. Devil a one I ever seen. / Rest easy, we'll
go again at twenty to seven.

4. [ʌ] TO [ʊ]. Believe me, it was a rough, tough fight

Diphthongal Changes

1. [aɪ] TO [ʌɪ] (OR [ʌoɪ]). Five is on the right side of time.
/ Mike was a fine Irish lad with a mind of his own.

2. [aʊ] TO [ʌʊ] (OR [ʌoʊ]). Will youse look now, and see
how are the clouds in the south?

3. [ɔɪ] TO [aɪ]. The oil bubbled up to the boiling point.

4. [i] TO [eɪ]. By Jasus, it's easy to keep decent.

5. [oʊ] TO [aʊ]. 'Twas only the old horse that was sold
on the street.

Consonant Substitutions

1. [r]. The other horse ran thirty yards over the grass.

2. [ŋ] TO [n]. With a mug in each hand, they were standing and talking and laughing.

3. [θ] TO [t]. He was thwarted by doubts in theology.

4. [t] TO [θ]. All mysteries will be solved after the demonstration.

5. [d] TO [ð]. I wonder if I should order another drink?

Breathiness

All the technical points were made perfectly clear in
the proper way to the participating teams.

Miscellaneous Pronunciations

By the look of her, that's the mother of the little
chiseler, you know, the boyo from the school beyond
that the police have got their paws on.

Whist, now, another one of you can stand with me

when my hat is raised by the sound of the soldier's signal.

READING FOR FLUENCY
Thucydides, B. Jowett translation

(*Voice:* Jerry Blunt.)

While in this part of the engagement the Lacedaemonians had the victory and routed the Athenian ships, their twenty vessels on the right wing were pursuing the eleven of the Athenians which had escaped from their attack into the open water of the gulf. These fled, and, with the exception of one, arrived at Naupactus before their pursuers. They stopped off at the temple of Apollo, and, turning their beaks outward, prepared to defend themselves in case the enemy followed them to the land. The Peloponnesians soon came up; they were singing a paean of victory as they rowed, and one Leucadian ship far in advance of the rest was chasing the single Athenian ship which had been left behind. There chanced to be anchored in the deep water a merchant vessel, round which the Athenian ship rowed just in time, struck the Leucadian amidships, and sank her. At this sudden and unexpected feat the Peloponnesians were dismayed; they had been carrying on the pursuit in disorder because of their superiority. And some of them, dropping the blades of their oars, halted, intending to await the rest, which was a foolish thing to do when the enemy were so near and ready to attack them. Others, not knowing the coast, ran aground.

When the Athenians saw what was going on their hopes revived, and at a given signal they charged their enemies with a shout. The Lacedaemonians did not long resist, for they had made mistakes and were all in confusion, but fled to Panormus, whence they had put to sea. The Athenians pursued them, took six of their ships which were nearest to them, and recovered their own ships which the Peloponnesians had originally disabled and taken in tow near the shore. The crews of the captured vessels were either slain or made prisoners. Timocrates the Lacedaemonian was on board the Leucadian ship which went down near the merchant vessel; when he saw the ship sinking he killed himself; the body was carried into the harbor of Naupactus. The Athenians then retired and raised a trophy on the place from which they had just sailed out to their victory. They took up the bodies and wrecks which were floating near their own shore, and gave back to the enemy, under a flag of truce, those which belonged to them. The Lacedaemonians also set up a trophy of the victory which they had gained over the ships destroyed by them near the shore; . . . Then, fearing the arrival of the Athenian reinforcements, they sailed away under cover of night to the Crisaean Gulf and to Corinth, all with the exception of the Leucadians. And not long after their retreat the twenty Athenian ships from Crete, which ought to have come to the assistance of Phormio before the battle, arrived at Naupactus. So the summer ended.

Arrah-na-Pogue, *Dion Boucicault;* Act I, Scene 2

The scene of this Irish melodrama of the last century is a cottage and a landscape. The spelling, which is as the author-actor wrote it, poses problems of inconsistency for the dialectician. Obviously Boucicault, who must be classed as a "professional Irishman," wrote very rapidly and with not too much concern for how he indicated sounds on paper. Still, there is value in his work, especially as it represents the kind of material which occasionally comes an actor's way.

(*Voices:* Patricia Madison, Jerry Blunt.)

ARRAH. Let me go, Shaun! D'ye hear me, sir, let me go!

SHAUN. First I'll give ye the coward's blow. Come here, ye vagabond, till I hit ye under the nose wid me mouth!

ARRAH. I'll strike ye back, ye villin! (SHAUN *kisses and releases her.*) Isn't this purty treatment for a lone woman?

SHAUN. Ye'll git no better, now I warn ye! so don't go marryin' me this blissid day with 'shtravagan' expictations; ye'll have to live from hand to mouth, and whin ye're out of timper, I'll sit moy face agin ye—moind that!

ARRAH. Ye're moighty airly, Shaun; didn't ye say that ye had to drive Michael Feeny over from Holywood last night?

SHAUN. Sure enough; but he got down at Glendalough to walk across the hill.

ARRAH. What brings ye here at all? Did ye think anybody was wantin' ye?

SHAUN. 'Iss, indeed, ses I. There's that *colleen dhas* all alone wid the cow to milk and the pigs to feed and the chickens; and the big barn beyant to git clane an' swate by the avenin' for the widding, to-night, and not a haporth of help she'll take from mortial. I'll go and give her a lift.

ARRAH. Will ye now, and afther bein' up all night an on the road betune Holywood and Rathdrum?—sure ye haven't had inny rist at all?

SHAUN. Rist, darlint? what would I want wid rist for the nixt six months to come? Wid the love in me that makes ivery minnit a fortune, sure, rist is only a waste of toime, an' to shut my eyes on the soight av your face before me, is sinful ixtravagince, me darlint.

The Game of Hurley [1]

Well, the way it is, Mr. Rogers, when we'd all come from school, we'd all go in and get the bit of grub or whatever was going, and we'd come out with the most awful looking weapon, and we call it a hurley stick. It was off of small pieces of bars and pieces of poles, everything, there was no recognition of what you could use,

as long as you could use it to hit the ball, that's all that mattered. Well, outside of our house was a big circle, a concrete patch, do you know it, Mr. Rogers? Well, that used to be a favorite place until the law (got) starts to breathe down our necks. Well, there would be about forty (call?) to us, there'd be maybe twenty, thirty, maybe forty would be playing it, and it was darn rough. For any time when we'd try to be respectable we'd only allow thirteen on a side. Now this is all transpired in school. We'd all pick our own teams. On one or two occasions I'd be a captain, or for that again I'd only be just an ordinary player.

But the occasion I'm going to talk about, I was chosen as captain up at the school. When I come down, I picked me boys, and the toughest I could lay me paws on. So we started off on Stanley Road outside the house, on the circle, and we were flying away, goodo—there was, well, as we say over here, there was skin and snots flying that day. And I really mean that. There was lumps taken out of my own head, me back, me side, and I gave what I got back to the rival team, that's all

---

in play here. So the way it ended up very, very sad. It ends up in a general melee, and Mrs. O'Roark's windows were all put in.

So the squad car comes out and we all disappears. So we finishes up our game, it's a place we used to call the Back of the Wall. It's about fifty yards from where we started to play first. And it's a big vacant lot, and there was a desperate amount of potholes on it, it wouldn't be safe to put a horse into it. But that's where we finished up our game, and out of the twenty-six I'm sure twenty went to hospital that night. Oh, that's the truth. I went to the hospital myself, and I got a couple of stitches in me head, I got me hand stitched—

Did you leave your mark on anybody else?

Oh, by God, we did. That was the tradition. Like if you didn't leave your mark, you weren't in the game.

INDIVIDUAL-PRACTICE EXERCISES
Key-Sound Word Drill

These key sounds are placed beside each other so that you may exercise on the change of lip, tongue and jaw positions necessary for the making of the proper sounds.

Like forked lightning—all; easy; old; horses—never; demand; tough; oak—Pat; five; able; go—oil; easy; town; for—father; tea; time; torch—army; cool; mug; circle—butter; believe; noise; down—Mike; sold; pay; path—perform; all; wonders; now—five times forty-two—never; hold; cold; drinks—thirty; awful!; light; devil—cheat; thunder; when; dull—stone; hold; proud; drop—proper; dreams; thwart; five—where; teams; always; go—certain; birds; arrive; after.

Key Sounds in Sentence Context

He swam from the car to the bar.

Ah, father has a great heart after all.

Audrey thought she caught the ball.

Autumn ought not to be awful.

All ushers are not as ugly as umpires.

It's a darn rough run.

Her aunt walked the garden path.

Pat will be in the meeting until half past ten.

Mike's ego won't heal because of his zeal.

Kate can't possibly pay by eight.

It's Adam that can't add.

Is it himself that's snooping after the truth?

Herself don't know if she's going to go.

You can't throw the stone as long as you hold it.

Heaven was never a place for the devil.

Yesterday Pat was sent home again and again.

The subs were not up to playing in Dublin.

The steak was tough, but the sun was fun.

His rival was behind the times.

Have you ever seen the like of the light that night?

Pat's out to the south of town.

No sound came out of his mouth.

The boy joined in the noise.

The oil spoiled the oysters.

They keep the tea for the meeting.

The team walked easy through the decent street.

Hold on, there, you'll do as you are told.

We owe the old man for the foal.

The rose ran right around to the rear.

Don't be talking and laughing during the meeting.

All told thirty thousand made up the total.

He was caught trying to mix butter with water.

We can't undergo another drop of drink.

On what corner will you be standing to catch the thirty dirty thieves?

All the team will participate in a hearty singsong.

SIGHT READING AND FLUENCY PRACTICE
The Riot

Ah, it was a lovely riot, one of the best I ever seen. There was public and private fights going on all over the place. Everyone was having a grand time.

It was Dublin, in the fall of the year, and on a Saturday late afternoon and night, so you see a better time couldn't have been picked. We were just turning into O'Connell Street, having come down from Guinesses' brewery walking along the Liffy, when we saw a great gathering of people, packed close in all across the wide street, and kind of moving around like there was some excitement going.

Well, you can be certain we didn't know what to

make of it. The grinding heel of the English oppressor had been gone long enough for the circumstance to be known to all, or nearly all, so there was little call for another brave battle for home rule and the glorious independence that was coming with it. "What is it, a-tall, a-tall," we said, remarking that the thrust of the traffic had stopped, and that drivers and passengers alike were getting out of the cars and lorries to have a closer decko at the commotion, or whatever it was that was going.

"It's at the foot of Nelson's Pillar," I said. "It is, right enough," she said, "and what are we waiting for?" So with the taste of the malt from the sampling at the brewery making a solid foundation for excitement, or whatever, we pushed forward with all the others on the walk, till we could come up to the action.

"Look at 'em," she says, as we hurried along, "look at the faces on 'em."

I did, at the same time feeling the same look on my own mug. "Proving that independence isn't everything, is it," says I, thinking out loud. And knowing straight off that the figure on the top of the pillar in the center of the long stretch of O'Connell Street was somehow mixed up in the whatever was going.

And I was right. Which accounted for the looks on the faces, like a preliminary call for an Easter Rising. The old bugger Nelson had been posted on his pillar like a Black and Tan lookout for all these years. No true Irish patriot had liked him since the day he got stuck there long ago. And they hadn't liked him any better as time ripened the rebellion that was coming on. But somehow the old boyo had stood his ground and held his place.

Till this Saturday night, that is. As we found out when we come up to all the rest.

"Who is it?" says my wife, craning her neck to look at the top of the tall bronze shaft where a couple of fellows were moving on the platform that circled around old Nelson's feet.

"I don't know who it is," volunteered a big fellow with his hat pushed back and a fall of black hair coming down over a very pleased countenance, "but whoever they are, they're out to do the country some good."

"Rowdies, most likely, set on destruction of public property," said another fellow, and by the look on his and the first one's face as he answered I could see the promissory note for the fighting to come.

Well, at least the last part of what the second fellow said was true. Destruction it was that was the purpose of the four lads gathered at the feet of Nelson on his high perch. There they stood, partly yelling down at the surging crowd three or so stories below and partly looking up at their victim.

"Whatever is it on the back of the one to this side?" asked my wife.

Half a dozen voices tried to tell without knowing much, till one topped all the others. "By God," it said in a tone of quiet excitement, "it's a flame thrower he's got, as sure as Patrick was a saint."

"It is indeed, indeed it is," said several others all at the one time. "But whatever for?" was the next cry.

To which the first replied, and youse could hear awe in his tone, with some pride mixed in, "He's going to melt the old bugger down!"

And so he was, as it turned out. Only——

But just then came a great shout of joy from those on the street in front of the door that opened to the staircase on the inside of the pillar. There stood the police squad that was headed for the top determined to perform their public duty by arresting the four boyos up above. That was the point, there they stood, for they certainly couldn't move onwards and upwards—foiled they were by a thoughtfully jimmied lock in the solid bronze door. Only a Dublin crowd can make that noise, and then only when they are confronted with the delightful sight of officers of the law thwarted in the performance of certain aspects of their lawful duty.

By then everything was getting stopped in the center of town as the good news spread out in all directions. I saw a dozen double-decker buses standing in a line and empty on a side street, where they were waiting for the late Saturday traffic to pick up again. All the stores were closed by managers wanting only an excuse to lock up and get out in the fun. But the pubs were open, and they were doing a rushing business, enough to oil up the wrists and elbow joints for some of the pushing and poking that was to come.

And all the while, up on top, the boyos, being good Irishmen, were warming up the crowd with speeches, getting everybody ready for the great moment to come, when the trigger would be pulled and the great flame would lick out and shoot up and melt old Nelson down till he was only a little puddle on a big shaft. And of course the police, being just as good Irishmen, and knowing well how to play a part proper, moved around and yelled up and pleased the crowd a lot.

Well, that's the way things were when it came time for the waiting hush to fall all over the whole spread of O'Connell Street, disturbed by only a few pockets of turbulence where private parties were starting to row a little early. And there we stood along with all the rest, with our necks stretched out, quiet outside, but with a jumping going on somewhere within. And then it was time.

Now perhaps you read in your newspaper or heard on the telly not long ago about the big explosion that occurred in Dublin, when Nelson's Pillar on O'Connell Street was all blown up, or down? Well, that was true. Ten years or more after the time I'm telling about, Nelson and his big round shaft were destroyed for good and all. And the circumstance was this, which explains in part why Ireland didn't win its independence a half-a-hundred years earlier than it did.

You see, in all the excitement of preparing for the great event of melting poor old Nelson down, somebody forgot to check out the principal piece of equipment. So when the trigger was pulled or the switch was flicked, or whatever, all that came out was a little blue flame not more than big enough to light a good Saturday night cigar. Nelson, it is reported, never batted an eye.

But it was a lovely riot all the same.

*

SCOTS

*

Scots, no matter what the variation, is a local dialect. It is regional speech that has resisted alteration under the influence of television, education, and intercommunity exchanges of the kind that modern traffic now introduces. Where mass communications, education, and travel have caused change, the pronunciation of Scotch individuals or communities tends to take on the leveling characteristics of a generalized Scottish-English speech or, for a more limited few, of Standard English. Such speech is little suited to the needs of a stage dialect.

Fortunately, in rural areas and small towns, in the Highlands as well as in such cohesive industrial cities as Glasgow, the Scottish dialect, though varied, is still as distinctive as any in the British Isles.

Variation, in Scots, is of two kinds. One kind is a matter of degree, the other of differences in pronunciation. In respect to the first, while dialects everywhere range from slight to strong, few can match the swing of Scots from a more-English-than-Scottish accent to a fullness of dialect that not only keeps the form of many words as they were a century ago, but delivers them in a distinctive utterance that challenges the best capabilities of the dialectician. Indeed, the prevalence of older speech forms indicates that in this chapter sounds should be spelled out as well as indicated phonetically.

In most Scottish literature, of the last century or of this, narrative passages are written in straight literary style, but dialogue generally is written in dialect. Since older authors are better known and their works more available, the best practice materials for a dialectician are the stories, poems, and songs of famous former writers.

As regards differences in pronunciation, an arbitrary division indicates that three major dialects are spoken in Scotland today. One is represented by the speech of the capital, Edinburgh. A second is heard in the Highlands, with additional strength in the islands beyond. The third comes from the industrial and shipbuilding complex of Glasgow. In all areas, however, certain usages are the same: the front-trilled [r], for example, is heard in varying degrees of strength; the glottal stop is also uniformly used but varies as to stress. In contrast, in each division there are distinctions: the extensive use of the "broad a" [ɑ] in the Highlands; the French-like *u* (sometimes [ju]) of Glasgow speech.

As in Ireland, a second language is spoken in Scotland. "Hae ye got [gɔʔ] the Gaelic?" is a phrase often heard when local stories or songs are being discussed. Today fewer and fewer person do "have" the older speech. The Celtic strain is responsible for this second language, which has the same roots as the Irish and Welsh varieties, although it is unlike either of the other two. Nor is the use of Gaelic speech or writing as prevalent in Scotland as Eire. Not that a strong sense of nationalism does not exist in Scotland. It does, but not to the extent of building a noncommunicative fence around the people of the land just to establish a feeling of national individuality.

Of the three divisions of the Scottish dialect, the more

universally used and the best understood is the speech of Edinburgh—accordingly that form is emphasized here. In all Scots, however, one characteristic immediately calls attention to itself. It is the presence of the antique word in sound and form. *Ye, aye, wee*, and such contractions as *canna* (*cannot*) recall the speech and writing of yesterday, and induce a sense of continuity not present in most modern dialects.

Perhaps it is not only the force of custom that keeps the evidence of last century still in the dialect, but the hold of story and song as well—Scott and Stevenson, Burns and Barrie unite fidelity to source material with distinctiveness of style in ways a national consensus is proud to claim. Consequently, older forms are still present and used in everyday speech, spoken easily and without self-consciousness.

Experience indicates that certain sounds in Scots are quite difficult of lingual manipulation. These sounds require much practice before they are properly "seated" in the mouth. Otherwise a put-on quality intrudes into the speech. The Scots burr, the extensive "broad *a*" of the Highlands, and the [u] of Glasgow speech are principal instances. All require exact placement of tongue, lips and jaw before mastery is attained. A good Scots demands time and practice, and to retain fluency periodic reviews are necessary.

KEY SOUNDS OF SCOTS

A unique feature of Scots is the variation of spelling and pronunciation in many basic words. It is necessary to match yesterday's words to those of today, showing how each can stand in the other's stead, for there is still an unregulated mixture of the two. Many of yesterday's words have an antique look and sound, nor are they always written and spoken alike. Consequently differences are to be expected, not only in the writings of yesterday, but in the written and spoken words of today as well.

To a reader of Scottish literature many of the words are already familiar: *dee* for *die, mon* for *man*, and *doon* for *down*. An extensive list forms the first part of our Key-Sound Word Drill. In that drill are words that have no sound-alike quality to identify them with their synonyms: *bairn* for *child, kirk* for *church*, and *ben* for *mountain*. These should be known, even though it is more in the province of the writer than the dialectician to instigate their use in sentence context.

Each of the three major dialect divisions has its distinguishing characteristics. The broad form of what we have termed Edinburgh speech employs the least number of older words and is the closest in pronunciation to the sounds and idioms of Standard English or American (modern slang phrases, noticeably those of the young, are no longer the property of any one nation or even of any one community). However, the Edinburgh dialect differs from Standard and middle-class English in that it has many fewer broad [ɑ]'s, [ʌo] diphthongs, [ɔ:] vowels and *ary* [rɪ] contractions. As with all Scots it has the glottal stop [ʔ], but uses it less strongly than the others. The fewer the years of education, the more frequently the g of *ng* [ŋ] is dropped, a dialectal circumstance that holds fairly true throughout the English-speaking world. On a marked decline is the use of an [ɛʳ] pronunciation, *fairst* [fɛʳst] giving way to *first* [fɜst].

A Highland dialect often is the most difficult to understand and to use. At its strongest it can be unintelligible. But it, too, is subject to a process of linguistic erosion that flattens out distinctions. Its most notable feature is an extensive use of the back vowel [ɑ], going far beyond American and well beyond Standard English in its employment of the sound. Only in strong Scots does *had* [hæd] become [hɑd], *man* [mæn] become [mɑn], *hand* change to [hɑnd] and *Mary* [mɛrɪ] to [mɑrɪ]; in some instances the substitution is carried even farther, to the extent that [ɔ:] is used. [u], as in *pool*, is also heard extensively, causing *foot* [fʊt] to be pronounced [fut]. Older words and phrases are retained in Highland and island speech more than elsewhere.

A native of Glasgow is called a Glaswegian. He lives in a highly industrial environment. As might be expected, much of the speech in this area sounds tight and twangy, not altogether pleasant to hear, and consequently not always desirable to reproduce. One Glaswegian actor characterized the native utterance as largely composed of nasal tones, pitched in a high rather than low register, and delivered between reluctant muscles.

Proper though the above characterization might be, it is not wholly true. Some Glaswegian speech is surprisingly soft. Whether or not it is the product of suburbs and outlying areas, as it may be, it is a dialect of sufficient attractiveness to merit study and use. In it the [r] is softer than that heard in other regions and the "broad *a*" [ɑ] is not used as often and as strongly as it is in Highland speech. Further, the Glaswegian is fluent in contractions. Most of all he sounds his [u], as in *pool*, with a difference. Actually he does not use an exact [u], but fits his sound part way between [u] and [ʊ]; in addition, he gives it a Frenchlike placement, so that it is closer to the French sound of [y], as in *une*, than to the [u] the rest of us use. And it is from this last that much of his softness comes. An example of this dialect may be heard on the accompanying tape.

Vowel Substitutions

1. [ɑ]. Except for the Highlander, the average Scotsman uses the back vowel [ɑ], as in *father*, less than his English cousin. Thus *half* [hæf] is not likely to be [hɑf]. But the Hielander uses it more, so that we can say that this sound is both under- and overused as far as speech in the British Isles is concerned. But the broad *a* [ɑ] is not a marked feature of a Scottish dialect.

2. [ɪ] TO [ɛ]. As a continuant of earlier speech, [ɛ] as in *eh* can substitute for [ɪ] as in *it*. Thus *bit* [bɪt] becomes *bet* [bɛt], and *minister* [ˈmɪnɪstɚ], *menister* [ˈmɛnɪstɚ].

3. [ɝ] TO [ɛʳ]. This alteration produces one of the most distinctive sounds in the Scottish dialect. To produce it, the usual sound of [ɝ] as in *her* is changed by first enunciating [ɛ], as in *eh*, then adding a tapped or trilled [r]. The result is that both the [ɛ] and [r] are distinctly heard. Thus *perfect* [ˈpɝfɪkt] becomes *pairfect* [ˈpɛʳfɪkt]. For our purpose (or [ˈpɛʳpəs]) the symbol [ɛʳ] indicates this particular combination of sounds, that is, [ɛ] closely followed by a tapped [r].

4. [ʊ] TO [u]. The upper back vowel [u], as in *pool*, also has a distinctive and heavy use in Scots. It has all of its regular assignments—*use, do, grew*—and additionally is substituted for many [ʊ] vowels—*good, book*—as well as the [au] diphthong, as in *out*. *Good* then becomes *gude* [gud] and *out, oot* [ut].

In many Scottish variations the [u] has the exact value Americans give it. But in some Highland speech and in the Glasgow area it receives a different treatment. The sound is given with lips rounded, jaw dropped, and tongue against the back of the lower teeth. The result is very close to the French [y], as heard in *une* [yn]. Thus *foot* [fʊt], after being changed in regular Scots to [fut], is altered still further by a Glaswegian or a Highlander to the soft sound of [fyt]. This last refinement, although not essential, adds a pleasing and distinctive sound to a Scottish dialect.

5. LIMITED SUBSTITUTIONS. There are several instances in which Scots employs a vowel substitution on a limited number of words, sometimes as few as two. But because these words are either so common—*take*—or so distinctive—*loch*—they should be known.

a. [e] TO [æ]. Two words hold to an older form. *Take* might be pronounced *tak* [tæk], and *make, mak* [mæk].

b. [ɛ] TO [i]. One of the most antique of Scottish sounds occurs when [ɛ], as in *head*, is pronounced with an [i], making *head* [hɛd] *heed* [hid], and *friend* [frɛnd] *freend* [frind]. In a variation, the [i] is also heard when *eye* [aɪ] becomes *een* [in]. The use of this last substitution is limited and is usually best left to the judgment of those who write the dialogue. It is much used by the older authors.

c. [x]. This symbol represents the sound of *ch* as in the Scots word for *lake*, which is *loch* [lɔx]. The exclamation *ach*, or *och*, also carries this Germanlike sound and is still used in ordinary conversation in many parts of the country, especially in the Highlands. The syllable is made by a strong but not too long expulsion of breath on the vowels [ɑ] as in *father*, or [ɔ] as in *ought*, and ended with a very slight tap of the back of the tongue against the uvula.

d. [ç]. Another Germanlike sound is given with as much aspiration as the above, but with the placement forward in the front vowel position of [ɪ], as in *it*. The words *right* and *bright*, both of which might be pronounced in regular fashion with only the variance of a Scotch tapped [r], illustrate this distinctly Scottish sound. Spelled phonetically, they appear as *ri-k-t* [rɪçt] and *bri-k-t* [brɪçt]. Orally, the extra breath, which is necessary for the [ç] sound, is stopped by the closure of [k], which in turn is completed before the [t] is pronounced.

6. [ə]. Scots often injects an extra vowel in a word, especially after an [r]. It is the schwa vowel, the unstressed form of [ʌ], and is written as [ə]. The addition of the extra syllable stretches the word sound. In which case *warm* [wɑrm] becomes *warum* [wɑrəm], and *alarm* [əˈlɑrm], *alarum* [əˈlɑrəm]. While the injection of [ə] is commonplace, it is not used by all; the better educated employ the shorter regular form. The word *film*, pronounced *filum* [fɪləm], however, is in the vocabulary of all.

7. ELONGATED VOWELS: [i], [e], [o]. It is common practice in all Scots for each of these vowels to be held slightly longer than is usual in ordinary conversation.

The [e], as in *eight*, is often extended into the diphthong [eɪ] (a commonplace occurrence in all forms of English speech). The extension is heard in several instances, as when *minister* is neither [ˈmɪnɪstɚ] nor [ˈmɛnɪstɚ] but *mainester* [ˈmeɪnɪstɚ], or when *stone* is *stain* [steɪn].

Diphthongal Changes

1. [aʊ] ᴛᴏ [u]. In modern Scots, a slight elongation of the diphthong [aʊ], as in *out*, differentiates it from a like American sound. But in those instances in which an older pronunciation is used, *out* [aʊt] changes to *oot* [ut]. If a Glaswegian is speaking, the *oot* [ut] can become [yt].

Consonant Substitutions

1. [r]. In yet another manifestation of its versatility, [r] receives a new treatment in Scots: the front tongue tap or trill. This is a national characteristic. Its action produces the Scotch burr. Fully flexible and with practiced ease the tongue taps once or trills two or three times when an [r] is formed. The degree of trill is determined by the nature of the adjacent vowel, or the emphasis each speaker assigns to the sound. Consequently a slight or a strong burr will be heard, but each as fluent as full flexibility allows. More than ordinary time in practice is recommended.

2. [ʔ]. Scots employs the glottal stop, written [ʔ]. Daniel Jones, in his *English Pronouncing Dictionary*, describes a glottal stop as "the plosive consonant formed by bringing the vocal chords together so that when they are separated the air from the lungs escapes suddenly causing audible plosion." *T* and *tt* are the letters most used for this sound. It is heard in medial and terminal syllables, as for instance, *better*, pronounced [ˈbɛʔɚ], or *got* [gɔʔ]. The Cockney also employs a glottal stop.

3. ᴅʀᴏᴘᴘɪɴɢ ᴀ ꜰɪɴᴀʟ ᴄᴏɴꜱᴏɴᴀɴᴛ. In older Scots it is quite usual to eliminate a final consonant on many common words, and on some contractions. In which case *small* becomes *sma'*, and *cannot* is shortened to *canna*. Many of the words in which this action occurs are listed in the Key-Sound Word Drill.

4. [ŋ]. In rural areas and in the speech of a lower middle-class or uneducated person, the *g* of *ng* [ŋ] is dropped, giving [n].

KEY-SOUND WORD DRILL

Word Variations

Space is left below each line for scoring phonetic or other symbols. A pause after each word permits immediate repetition.

(*Voice:* Jerry Blunt.)

yes / aye	fret / fash
oh yes / och aye	father / faither
pretty / bonny	mother / mither *or*
both / baith	maither
brave / braw	good / gud *or* gude
bridge / brig	give / gae *or* gee
brook / burn	go / gang
child / bairn	hands / hons
clothes / claithes	home / hame
church / kirk	hill / brae
cold / cauld	have / hae
come / coom	hat / bonnet
dagger / dirk	Highland / Hieland
dirty / clairty	lake / loch
either *or* either *or* aither	lord / laird
from / frae	many / mony

man / mon

money / siller

more / mair

most / maist

mountain / ben

big *or* much / muckle

no / nae

not / no'

old / ault

one *or* aine *or* yin

over / ower

plaid *or* tartan

poor / puir

run / rin

small / sma' *or* wee

sore / sair

sour / dour *or* dure

so / sae

stone / stain

talk / crack

to / tae

told / tauld *or* telt

up / oop

very / verra

well / weel

what / whit

where / whoore

you / ye *or* ya

Vowel Substitutions

1. [ɑ]. (IN THOSE INSTANCES IN WHICH IT IS USED, THAT IS, HIGHLAND SPEECH.) Aberdeen, any, bashful, hand, man, Mary—and in extreme cases, [ɔ], any, hand, man.

2. [ɪ] TO [ɛ]. Bitter, is, minute, fifty, misfortune, six.

3. [ɝ] TO [ɛʳ]. First, earn, thirsty, search, perfect, observe.

4. [ʊ] TO [u]. Book, good, brook, foot, put.

5. LIMITED SUBSTITUTIONS:

   a. [e] TO [æ]. Make, take.

   b. [ɛ] TO [i]. Friend, head, well.

   c. [aɪ] TO [i]. Die, eye.

   d. [x]. Ach, och, loch.

   e. [ç]. Bright, light, night, right.

6. [ə]. Farm, film, worm, alarm.

7. ELONGATED VOWELS: [i], [e], [o]. Each, cheat, free, great, plaid, oak, hold.

Diphthongal Changes

1. [aʊ] TO [u]. About, down, doubt, house, out.

Consonant Substitutions

1. [r]. Rose, arrive, fear.

2. [ʔ]. Better, glottal, water, pity, likely, got, great, not.

3. DROPPING FINAL CONSONANT. And, all, away, grand, call, small, awful, with, cannot, do not, could not.

4. [n]. Coming, doubting, searching.

KEY SOUNDS IN SENTENCE CONTEXT

Vowel Substitutions

1. [ɑ]. The master was took bad after Aberdeen.

2. [ɪ] ᴛᴏ [ɛ]. It's a pity the minister had that misfortune.

3. [ɜ] ᴛᴏ [ɛʳ]. First let us search for her purse.

4. [ʊ] ᴛᴏ [u]. They heard the good book read by the brook.

5. [e] ᴛᴏ [æ]; [ɛ] ᴛᴏ [i]; [aɪ] ᴛᴏ [i], [x], [ç]. You will not make a good friend if you hit him over the head or in the eye. / Och, aye, the loch was very bright last night.

6. [ə]. The worm lives in the ground on the farm.

Diphthongal Changes

1. [aʊ] ᴛᴏ [u]. The poor wee mouse ran a' around the door.

Consonant Substitutions

1. [r]. Rob Roy was not a man to rise from a hearth in fear.

2. [ʔ]. It's a great pity the loch has not got enough water.

3. Dʀᴏᴘᴘɪɴɢ ꜰɪɴᴀʟ ᴄᴏɴꜱᴏɴᴀɴᴛꜱ. You cannot call all the small bairns away.

4. [n]. Georgie was taking the searching party and they were running along the burn.

Sentences Written in Dialect Form

I'll tak ye oop the brae, Jamie, (*repeat*) an' we'll hae a luk at the auld kirk. (*repeat*) It's a gran' sight, (*repeat*) ye can be sure o' that.

Weel, noo, I hae ma doots aboot the Labor Party, (*repeat*) but we'll see hoo it turns oot.

My, Willie, but yer dirty. (*repeat*) Gee us yer hons; they'll hae to be washed.

Hoo are ye, Maister McDougal?

("*Down*" *given two ways*) Do ye ken, they're pullin' down the ould brig doon at the burn?

Och, aye, it's the pipers of the clan MacClure that are comin' frae the sma' toon.

Angus, will ye no tak a luk at the wee bairn wi' her bonny kilt?

The red stag roams the Hieland moors.

Haggis was served, ho' and tasty, in celebration of the birthday of Bobbie Burns.

Maggie, if ye just poot a new wee flower on yer auld

bonnet, (*repeat*) an' screw ets shape aboot a bet, (*repeat*)

it'll do weel enough.

A' the kilts of yon proud lads and lassies show the

huntin' plaid of the royal Stuart.

READING FOR FLUENCY

**To a Mouse, on Turning Her Up in Her Nest with the
Plough,** *Robert Burns*

(*Voice:* David Crampsey.[1])

Wee, sleekit, cow'rin, tim'rous beastie,

O what a panic's in thy breastie!

Thou need na start awa sae hasty,

Wi' bickering brattle!

I wad be laith to rin an' chase thee

Wi' murd'ring pattle!

I'm truly sorry man's dominion

Has broken Nature's social union,

An' justifies that ill opinion

Which makes thee startle

At me, thy poor earth-born companion,

An' fellow-mortal!

I doubt na, whiles, but thou may thieve;

What then, poor beastie, thou maun live!

A daimen-icker in a thrave

'S a sma' request:

I'll get a blessin' wi' the lave,

And never miss 't!

Thy wee bit housie, too, in ruin!

Its silly wa's the win's are strewin'!

An' naething, now, to big a new ane,

O' foggage green!

An' bleak December's winds ensuin',

Baith snell an' keen!

Thou saw the fields laid bare and waste,

An' weary winter comin' fast,

An' cozie here, beneath the blast,

Thou thought to dwell,

Till crash! the cruel coulter past

Out-thro' thy cell.

---

[1] Reproduced with the personal permission of Mr. Crampsey.

That wee bit heap o' leaves an' stibble

Has cost thee mony a weary nibble!

Now thou's turn'd out, for a' thy trouble,

But house or hald,

To thole the winter's sleety dribble,

An' cranreuch cauld!

But, Mousie, thou art no thy lane,

In proving foresight may be vain:

The best laid schemes o' mice an' men

Gang aft a-gley,

An' lea'e us nought but grief an' pain

For promised joy.

Still thou art blest compar'd wi' me!

The present only toucheth thee:

But oh! I backward cast my e'e

On prospects drear!

An' forward tho' I canna see,

I guess an' fear!

Macbeth, *Shakespeare;* Act I, Scene 5

(*Voice:* Shona McCann; Glasgow.)

The following passage is read in the accents of
modern-day Glasgow speech. In addition to the key

sounds, note the pitch patterns, especially those in
which the pitch is left suspended, rather than uttered in
the descending notes generally used for terminal
thoughts. This unique pitch pattern is heard in conversation as well as in the reading of prepared material.

LADY MACBETH. "They met me in the day of success;

and I have learned by the perfectest report, they

have more in them than mortal knowledge. When I

burned in desire to question them further, they made

themselves air, into which they vanished. Whiles I

stood rapt in the wonder of it, came missives from the

king, who all-hailed me, 'Thane of Cawdor,' by which

title, before, these weird sisters saluted me, and

referred me to the coming on of time with 'Hail, king

that shalt be!' This have I thought good to deliver

thee, my dearest partner of greatness, that thou

mightst not lose the dues of rejoicing by being igno-

rant of what greatness is promised thee. Lay it to thy

heart, and farewell."

Glamis thou art, and Cawdor, and shalt be

What thou art promised. Yet do I fear thy nature;

It is too full o' the milk of human kindness

To catch the nearest way. Thou wouldst be great,

Art not without ambition, but without

The illness should attend it. What thou wouldst

  highly

That wouldst thou holily; wouldst not play false,

And yet wouldst wrongly win.

Thou'dst have, great Glamis, that which cries,

"Thus thou must do, if thou have it,

And that which rather thou dost fear to do

Than wishest should be undone." Hie thee hither,

That I may pour my spirits in thine ear,

And chastise with the valor of my tongue

All that impedes thee from the golden round,

Which Fate and metaphysical aid doth seem

To have thee crown'd withal.

Auld Lang Syne, *Robert Burns*

The next passage is read in a noninterpretive manner and is deliberate in tempo that you might better study the sounds of Glaswegian speech.

(*Voice:* Shona McCann. Glasgow.)

VERSES

We twa hae run about the braes,

And pu'd the gowans fine;

But we've wander'd mony a weary foot

  Sin' auld lang syne.

We twa hae paidled i' the burn,

From morning sun till dine;

But seas between us braid hae roar'd

  Sin' auld lang syne.

And there's a hand, my trusty fiere,[1]

And gie's a hand o' thine;

And we'll tak a right guid-willie waught,

  For auld lang syne.

And surely ye'll be your pint-stowp,

And surely I'll be mine;

And we'll tak a cup o' kindness yet

  For auld lang syne.

CHORUS

Should auld acquaintance be forgot,

And never brought to min'?

Should auld acquaintance be forgot,

  And auld lang syne?

For auld lang syne, my dear.

For auld lang syne,

---

[1] Pronounced [fɪr] or [fɛʳ]; it is easy to hear this word as frère.

We'll tak a cup o' kindness yet,

For auld lang syne.

INDIVIDUAL-PRACTICE EXERCISES

Key-Sound Word Drill

The following key sounds in commonplace words are grouped so as to exercise flexibility and exactness. First apply the dialect to the words as they are written. Next transpose the words and strengthen the dialect to fit the older forms where such forms exist.

Yes; where; you; from—two; clothes; hands; dirty—

brave; good; more; small—very; told; child; about—

church; cow; father; foot—bad; doubt; brook; bridge

—right; perfect; know; is—pity; bright; farm; house—

take; either; bonny; lake—old; first; great; over—aw-

ful; cold; make; do—well; what; hill; up—come; give;

mouse; bitter—grand; man; Mary; had—oh; break;

both; eyes—water; home; many; book—Highland;

look; world; light—cannot; fear; and; stone—minister;

any; free; flower—well; much; six; go—poor; friend;

give; money.

Key Sounds in Sentence Context

Read these sentences in Scots as they are written, working on both exactness of pronunciation and fluency. After that write out the Scotch alternate words in the space provided and practice on them for equal exactness and ease.

EXAMPLE: Take your father from the films. *Tak yer faither frae the filums*.

The church of the Old Light is situated in the little town of Thrums.

The lake is beautiful in the bright moonlight.

Jamie told the little child all about the small mouse.

Angus had his doubts about where to find the bridge.

The milk of the Highland cow is very good.

Do you know how the old lady will make a better pound of butter?

The pretty girl will not come home from the hill.

It's awful cold down by the brook.

Maggie has only the two pair of hands, and that's little enough for the work of the farm.

Jock did not know how to put the cow out of the house.

The minister told the workmen that the hand rail on the foot bridge was not right.

The old people cannot climb the hill from the bottom to the top.

SIGHT READING AND FLUENCY PRACTICE

To a Louse, on Seeing One on a Lady's Bonnet at Church, *Robert Burns* (Portion)

Ha! wh'are ye gaun, ye crowlin' ferlie!

Your impudence protects you sairly:

I canna say but ye strunt rarely,

    Owre gauze and lace;

Tho' faith! I fear ye dine but sparely

    On sic a place.

Ye ugly, creepin', blastit wonner,

Detested, shunn'd by saunt an' sinner!

How dare ye set your fit upon her,

    Sae fine a lady?

Gae somewhere else, and seek your dinner

    On some poor body.

Swith, in some beggar's haffet squattle;

There ye may creep, and sprawl, and sprattel

Wi' ither kindred jumping cattle,

    In shoals and nations;

Where horn nor bane ne'er dare unsettle

    Your thick plantations.

O wad some Pow'r the giftie gie us

To see oursels as others see us!

It wad frae mony a blunder free us,

    And foolish notion:

What airs in dress an' gait wad lea'e us,

    And ev'n devotion!

On Tour in Edinburgh

"Well, here we are now," said the guide, and his voice was thick with a native accent, for he had learned that the more roll he put on an *r* the better the tourist took to his remarks, and the more likelihood of a good tip at the end of the tour. "From here ye can see the whole city—Scotland's capital and her pride, Edinburgh. Yon's Arthur's Seat. You will be told more of that later. Right now, from where we're standing, you are looking at one of the grand thoroughfares of the world. That's Princes Street down below, with the best of modern shops on the one side, and on the other the walks and gardens that make the street famous, all topped with the stirring sight of the Castle itself towering over all.

"Ladies, if it's spending siller you're after, you will do no better than take a good look in all the shops along the street. There is merchandise of all sorts, from wee gifts ye can smuggle home for the bairns you left behind, swimming in all your pools, to onything you've got the money to buy in rich jewels and the like. And there's spirits for those gentlemen that have the good sense to ken there is no better liquor bottled anywhere in the wide world." He turned to two middle-aged men standing to his right, "And don't think you know the taste of it from what you've had at home—dinna ye ken, we're no crazy—what's good we drink oursel'; ye get what's left over.

"If it's claithes you want, take a look at what a master weaver can do with a bit of the finest wool in the world. All home grown. None of that stringy stuff they get off the jock sheep that roam the moors in that country situated somewhat to the south of us, and which the Sassenach will try to sell you at reduced prices. Ours tops them all, that's sure enough. And for those of you fortunate enough to have Scotch blood in your veins, you maun just discover the tartan of your clan. They've books for that, ye know. You can have a kilt made up in either the dress or the hunting plaid, and then wear it when you go to a fancy dress ball, for I'm told it's not proper to wear a kilt on the street in your country, no doubt a custom designed to protect the feelings of those poor folk who canna claim a connection with the land you are now in.

"Now just look at the other side of the street. Never mind the sight of the railroad tracks laid there—do you see how cunning they've covered them up, so that the beauty of the place is not disturbed at all by the presence of a thriving traffic?

"Now just look there at the near end—do you see that monument with the spires piercing the sky? That's the memorial to Sir Walter Scott, the man that taught the English how to write a story. The tower is Gothic they say, and I have no doubt it's true, for you can't keep people from coming to see what our best have done so they can go home and enjoy the same themselves.

"Beyond is the Mound. That's the place where free speech was born, where every man can make his crack about how the world should be run. But he's got to be quick with his thoughts and his tongue, for there's mony who will take him on and try his mettle, and the exchange is right sharp. They say that Lon'on has something like, tucked away in a corner of some public park or other. I'll take you down later and you can hear for yourself how they make their crack.

"Just beside is the National Gallery, where priceless works of art are shown. The Scottish masters are in there, and good works by others, too, if you've time to bide in such a quiet place.

"And now do you see that patch of bright just be-yond? You should ken what that is right enough, for it's been put in photos and films all over the world. You're looking at the famous flower clock of Princes Street. The numbers and the hands are all in growing flowers. And below the ground are all the clock's works, so

cunning the piece keeps perfect time. We maun take a closer look when we get back down below, so save some of your film. It's too bonny a sight to let pass by.

"And off to your left and rising in all its majesty is Edinburgh Castle itself. Just see the strength of it, and beauty, too, but that will come better when we're below looking up. For now just trace the rise by following the course of High Street. See yon palace at the near end? That's Holyrood, rich with the history of this land. There lived Mary Stuart, the most beautiful lass that ever came to be queen. There was dark work done there, too, murders and all the like. Rizzio, Mary's musician, was struck down with a dirk. Lord Huntley it was did it, and Lord Darnley, the Queen's husband, behind it, so they say.

"Aye, there was more than one tragedy there, and many of a different kind. 'Twas there our Bonnie Prince Charlie, after defeating the English for good and all, could not resist the lure of the pretty lassies of Edin-burgh and spent his time dancing in the palace when he should have followed the foe and run them off the land. Too bonnie he was, for himself and for Scotland.

"Holyrood's the Queen's now, her that is Elizabeth the First of Scotland." He paused, and then with a small smile, "We're not too sure about that other one, she that pretended to the throne of England and grabbed it off our Mary.

"But be that as it may, if you will just look to the right of the palace you can see the chapel ruins. The roof and most of the walls are long gone, leaving the arches and the outlines of a window or two. There's nothing like a good ruin for photos. Lets your folk know you've been to one country that's got history behind it.

You are short on ruins, I'm told. Too new. It's a pity. Ruins are good for business.

"Well, enough of Holyrood. Just trace your eye up the street. We'll be going there shortly and then you will know where you are. John Knox's house is along there—he was a bit of a dour one, was John—and then beyond is St. Giles. That's no a kirk, it's a cathedral. It's the home of the Stone of Scone, that bit of rock that's to be sat on or ever the crown will fit.

"And after that, the Esplanade and then the Castle itself. And that's where we're going now. I've cracked enough in this place to give you what you paid for. Tighten your camera straps, and back on the bus."

*

FRENCH

*

A Frenchman will speak English correctly in those instances in which the sounds of his language are like those of the new speech. It is only by the incorrectness of his English utterance that he reveals his nationality, and thus can be said to speak with a French dialect. His incorrectness occurs whenever his native sounds, at odds with the new language, impose themselves by habit upon the foreign speech. Thus, in this dialect, it is necessary to learn to form new sounds and to change the shape and emphasis of others.

To the ears of English-speaking actors and audiences, the incorrectnesses which make up a French dialect both attract and please. They are compounded in part of an engaging vitality, a rhythmic fluency, and a unique syllabic formation.

The different dialects spoken among Frenchmen are as varied as the variation of regional or class speech in any other country. As with each stage dialect studied so far, however, one "standard" dialect can be formed on the basis of the similarities among all forms of native French speech. The principal model the dialectician follows, if one has to be chosen, is that of the educated Frenchman, the one who speaks free of the influence of a regional patois.

In addition to the usual vowel, diphthong, and consonant variations between French and English, a French dialect also features an emphasis upon a nasal quality, not as an individual characteristic, as it is in most instances in the English-speaking world, but as a national trait. As richly resonant as it is nasal, this sound generally pleases the Anglo-American ear. In this respect it contrasts sharply with the nasality of some forms of New England speech, the latter tending to a flatness of utterance which includes but little pharyngeal resonance in its composition.

The nasal consonants [m], [n], and *ng* [ŋ] are featured in the making of this sound. So are two English vowels, the [ɛ] of *yet* and the [ɔ] of *ought*. Each of these, richly rather than flatly resonated in its nasality, can produce a distinctly French sound. Each has its French symbol: [ɛ̃] and [ɔ̃]. Two French words will establish these vowels in your mind: *vin* (wine) [vɛ̃], and *bon* (good) [bɔ̃]. Each vowel undergoes a distinct change of sound because of nasalization, in which sound waves pass through nose as well as mouth, causing [ɛ] (*yet*) to blend with [æ] (*at*), and [ɔ] (*ought*) to merge with [o] (*go*), both taking on additional heavy nasality.

In a French dialect, the first nasal vowel, [ɛ̃], is linked with our prefixes *im* and *in*, both of which would be sounded exactly alike by a French person. Thus English *important* [ɪm'pɔrtənt] becomes [ɛ̃pɔr'tɔ̃], and *increase* ['ɪnkris] becomes [ɛ̃'kris].

The second, [ɔ̃], is often associated with the English word endings *ent*, *ment*, and *ant*, each pronounced in our speech as [ɛnt], [mɛnt], [ænt] and [ənt], but spoken by a Frenchman as [ɔ̃], [mɔ̃], and [ɔ̃]. Some French-English dictionaries give [ɑ̃] instead of [ɔ̃].

In addition to the non-English nasality of the French, three other non-English sounds carry over from native French speech into a French dialect. All require new positional habits for American tongues, jaws, and lips. One is the vowel which is found in the pronunciation of the French word for *street*, *rue*. Its phonetic symbol is [y]: *rue* [ry]. The other, another vowel, is learned from the sound of the French word for *heart*, *coeur*, and its symbol is [œ:]. The third is a dialectician's old friend, the consonant [r], which becomes a uvular or back-trilled [r] in French.

In the section which follows, all three of these non-English sounds will be discussed in detail. The point to be made here is that all three require special emphasis and demand special practice. The advice is to take care in the proper positioning of the articulators involved, as well as to take time in the making of the sounds, both when forming them separately and when inserting them in a context of words. In other words, go slow in your first practice sessions and continue the slowness until the new muscular positions and movements have become habitual. Only then should normal speed be attempted.

KEY SOUNDS OF THE FRENCH DIALECT
Vowel Substitutions

1. [i] FOR [ɪ]. French is one of the Romance languages, and as in each of the others, it substitutes [i] as in *eat* for [ɪ] as in *it*. The exchange is strong, consistent and easily effected. Fortunately it is also easily understood in most instances of its use. There is, however, some possibility of misunderstanding; the sentence "I have a ship" could be taken to mean "I have a sheep."

2. [ā] (*far*) REPLACES [æ] (*at*) BEFORE [n]. Distinctly characteristic only of French is the nasalization of [ā] which is substituted for [æn]. Our *dance* [dæns] becomes [dās], heavily nasalized. The nasalization is not unpleasant; on the contrary the [ā] is more resonated than [æ].

3. [ɛ̃] FOR [ɪ]. [ɪ] as in *it*, when linked to [m] or [n] in a syllable, becomes the strongly nasal [ɛ̃], as in the French word *vin* [vɛ̃]. In contrast to the American pronunciation of the first syllable in *important* and *interior*, the jaw drops and the back of the tongue blocks the sound wave, causing it to pass through the nasal resonating chambers, just as it does when [n] is formed. However, in a French pronunciation, which carries over into a French dialect, neither the [m] or [n] is sounded, leaving the nasal [ɛ̃] to stand by itself: [ɛ̃pɔr'tɔ̃], [ɛ̃tɪrj'œ:r].

4. [ɔ̃] FOR [ɛ] AND [æ] OR [ə]. The strongly nasalized sound of [ɔ̃], a non-English vowel, best demonstrated by the French word for *good*, *bon* [bɔ̃], is formed by the passage of the sound wave through the nasal resonating chambers, just as in the making of the [ɛ̃] vowel described above. This new vowel, [ɔ̃], is most often used as a substitute for [ɛ] in *ment*, for example *government*, and for [æ] or [ə] in *ant*, as in *important*. The result is that the last two letters *nt* are not sounded at all, leaving the nasal vowel [ɔ̃] the terminal sound for the word, as in *government* [guvɛrnə'mɔ̃], or *important* [ɛ̃pɔr'tɔ̃].

5. [a] FOR [e]. The [e] vowel, as in the English word *fame* [fem], changes to the sound of [a], as in the word *ask*. It must be noted that this particular vowel sound, the [a], does not have a country-wide use in America. If you are one of the many who do not employ it, you can best achieve the sound by finding a placement halfway between the front vowel [æ], as in *at*, and the back vowel [ɑ], as in *father*. This makes the usual [æ] of *ask* change to [a].

Uniquely French Sounds

1. [y] FOR [u]. The English [u] as in *pool* may or may not change, depending upon the strength of dialect required, to the distinctly French [y] (no English equivalent), as in the French word for *street*, *rue*. Instructions as to the formation of this vowel, given through the years in all French language classes, are now classic: round the lips as though to say [u] *pool*, but pronounce [i] as in *eat* instead. In the average French dialect this key sound is of minor significance and should be used sparingly; for comic purposes it might be employed more extensively.

2. [œ:]. The sound [œ:] is a French one for which there is no English equivalent. The French word for *heart*, *coeur* [kœ:r], presents the sound in full. Properly employed, this sound becomes one of the most distinctive of all the key sounds in a French dialect; its employment is extensive. Working from an American into a French pronunciation, form [ɛr] as in *air*, but purse the lips, drop the jaw a little, and hollow the pharyngeal cavity slightly as the sound is made. The French word for *actor*, *acteur* [ak'tœ:r], is a good one to use when bringing the sound of this French vowel to mind.

3. French suffixes, three in number, add further distinction to a French dialect. We are already familiar through constant usage with the English suffixes *able* [eɪbl], *ible* [ɪbl] and *tion* [ʃən]. The French equivalents, spoken with a French pronunciation should be used in every instance in which clarity of meaning is sure.

Thus *admirable* ['ædmərəbl] becomes [admi'rɑbl].

Note that the French pronunciation changes the stress, placing it on the last syllable—this is standard. It should also be noted that the number of *able* endings which can be used are limited; *readable, lovable,* and *unmentionable* are cases in point. Three-syllable words are the more susceptible of employment, but each individual case must be measured against a common-sense check.

The *ible* suffix has an even more limited use: probably less than a dozen words are available to the dialectician. The limitation, however, does not affect the strength of this key sound. When it can be used with clarity it carries as much distinction as any. The sounds of *possible* [po'sibl] and *terrible* [tɛ'ribl] are both strong and understandable as both are French words in themselves. But a similar pronunciation of *visible, tangible,* or *invincible* is unusable because of lack of clarity.

The *tion* ending changes with French pronunciation from the [ʃən] or [ʃn] of English to a strong nasal [sijɔ̃] or [sjɔ̃]. *Combination* [kɔ̃binɑsi'jɔ̃] is typical of the frequent use which can be made of this key sound.

Consonant Substitutions

1. [r]. The trilled or uvular [r] is one of the most characteristic of French dialect sounds. The strength of its utterance maintains the reputation of the [r] as the most used and most altered consonant in dialects. The extent to which this key sound can be used, however, is dependent upon the speaker's ability to trill the back of the tongue. Less flexible than the tip, the broad and more thickly muscled back still can trill or tap a sound wave as it is passing by vibrating against and in conjunction with the pendant uvula. The result, when performed on [r], is thoroughly French, quite unlike the front-trilled [r] of the Scotch or Russian dialects, or the rolled [r] of the opera singer.

The French back-trilled [r] is evidenced in all three positions in a word—initial, medial, terminal—although the human tendency to slur or drop the final sound is as normal in the French language as in any other. In no case is the duration of the trill to be any more than slight; for that reason it is sometimes better to think of the [r] as being tapped rather than trilled.

2. [ɧ]. There is no fricative [h] in the French language, consequently the English [h] is not pronounced. This action produces a marked effect, one that strengthens the dialect by its very simplicity. But it is an effect which must be used with care as far as auditor under-

standing is concerned. For example, a command in the French dialect to *hit him* would be delivered as ['it 'im], which might convey to the hearer the idea that cannibalism was being suggested.

The [h] is not sounded in either the initial (*hello* ['a'lo]) or medial (*perhaps* [pɛr''aps]) position.

3. [s] FOR [θ]. The voiceless [θ] is changed to [s]. For those who are not acquainted with the term "voiceless," its use indicates that a syllable is not phonated or sounded, has no vibration arising from action by the vocal folds, but is heard only as air passing through a restricted area between tongue and upper teeth, as illustrated in the word just used, *teeth* [tiθ], or *think* [θɪŋk], which would sound [tis] or [siŋk] in a French dialect.

4. [z] FOR [ð]. The voiced *th* [ð], a phonated sound in which the vocal folds do vibrate while the syllable is formed and held, changes to [z] in French usage. *This* [ðɪs] in English becomes [zis] in a French dialect, and *father* ['faðɚ] changes to [fɑ'zɛr].

5. [ʃ] FOR [tʃ]. The [tʃ] consonant, as in *church* [tʃɝtʃ], may or may not undergo a change to the simpler [ʃ] of *sheep* [ʃip]. The French are conversant with the [tʃ] sound, so its use or nonuse depends upon the degree of dialect strength desired. If employed, the word *church* would be pronounced [ʃɛrtʃ], but note that only the initial, not the final, consonant is changed—this for purposes of clarity.

In French dialect, the English word *chocolate,* which comes from the French *chocolat,* is pronounced [ʃɔkɔla]. The terminal [t], as with all other final consonants in French, is not sounded unless followed by a vowel, which is why *boulevard,* spelled the same in both languages, is pronounced [bul'var] by the French.

6. [ʒ] FOR [dʒ]. In like manner, the [dʒ] sound, as in *judge* [dʒʌdʒ], can be changed to [ʒ], causing that word to be pronounced [ʒʌdʒ]. It can be seen that care must be taken to make certain that auditors understand the word that is so treated. In the case of [ʒʌʒ], if it can be held that the context of a sentence makes the French pronunciation understandable, then the use, full strength, of the dialect is justified. However, if there be a doubt about whether or not the word would be understood, then dialectal strength should be sacrificed.

Altered Stress

Every language has a series of stress patterns which are employed to give a particular meaning to a sentence. (*Example:* "I 'am going downtown.") When a person speaks in a language not his own, it is quite possible that he will apply his native stress patterns to the new speech. The result is an altered emphasis.

In a French dialect the change of stress produces a noticeable result. For illustration, consider two of the many different stresses possible on the one sentence "We were just going." It might be "We 'were just going," or "We were just go'ing," the accent falling on the last syllable of the last word. Often the stress will come on an auxiliary verb, as in "They 'have run into trouble."

Because there is no hard and fast rule to follow in the use of an altered stress, caution must be taken not to overdo the effect. Too much use will do injury to both rhythm and understanding.

French Forms of Address

The French courtesy titles of *Mademoiselle, Madame,* and *Monsieur*—plurals: *Mesdemoiselles, Mesdames,* and *Messieurs*—are as much used as their English counterparts, Miss, Mrs., and Mr. In the French case, however, the pronunciation is quite radically changed from the spelling. Nor is the change an entirely easy one. *Mademoiselle* [madmwaˈzɛl] is not too difficult, but the correct French pronunciation of *Monsieur* [məˈsijə] has always been especially troublesome to American tongues, as French teachers from one end of the country to the other can testify. Since any Frenchman speaking in English but using these words would be expected to give a proper pronunciation to them, it behooves the dialectician to be diligent in his practice. *Madame* [maˈdam] features an altered stress. The plurals of each are: *Mesdemoiselles* [medmwaˈzɛl], *Mesdames* [meˈdam], *Messieurs* [meˈsijə].

KEY-SOUND WORD DRILL

The material of this section is to be practiced in coordination with the French Dialect tape. The accompanying voice pauses after each word for your immediate repetition; check your pronunciation against that of the speaker. Take special care when listening to and then forming those sounds which are distinctly French. Space is left under each line for scoring phonetic or other symbols.

(*Voice:* Jerry Blunt.)

Vowel Substitutions

1. [i] FOR [ɪ]. It, city, inside, big, sister, this, script.

2. [ã] FOR [æn] OR [ɛn]. Dance, difference, distance, silence.

3. [ɛ] FOR [ɪ]. Impediment, imprudent, interior, intrusion, prince. (*repeat*)

4. [ɔ] FOR [ɛ] OR [æ]. Judgment, supplement, infant, discordant.

5. [a] FOR [e]. Famous, blame, dame, rainfall.

Unique French Sounds

1. [y] FOR [u]. Sue, just, judgment, supper.

2. [œ:]. Actor, professor, adore, course, carve, better, harbinger.

3. [abl] FOR [ebl] OR [əbl]. Table, admirable, desirable, formidable.

4. [ibl] FOR [ɪbl]. Impossible, terrible, horrible.

5. [sijɔ] OR [sjɔ] FOR [ʃən]. Attention, permission, pronunciation, question.

Consonant Substitutions

1. [r]. Rose, republic, president, every, horror, mirror.

2. [ɦ]. Hello, here, Henri, behave, inhabit, uphold.

3. [s] FOR [θ]. Thank, thing, author, earth, truth.

4. [z] FOR [ð]. This, there, father, rather.

5. [ʃ] FOR [tʃ]. Church, chocolate, chicken, bachelor, search.

6. [ʒ] FOR [dʒ]. Judge, Jack, George, justice, age, page.

Altered Stress

1. Accoun'table, 'about, for'tunately, nev'er, spite-'ful, dis'appear.

French Forms of Address

Mademoiselle, madame, monsieur—mesdemoiselles, mesdames, messieurs.

KEY SOUNDS IN SENTENCE CONTEXT

Vowel Substitutions

1. [i]. I didn't think this was it. / The big city in the distance is Paris.

2. [ɑ̄]. It is very romantic to dance with Blanche.

3. [ɛ]. The interior of the building was international. / During the period he improvised his interrogation of his prince.

4. [ɔ]. The judgment of the government was to supplement the agreement.

5. [a]. Do not blame Notre Dame for the rainfall.

Uniquely French Sounds

1. [y]. Sue has just had her supper.

2. [œ:]. But of course the actor and the professor will do it. / The fewer the cards the better.

3. [abl]. The offer on the table was admirable. / The atmosphere was too formidable to be comfortable.

4. [ibl]. The accident was terrible. / The opposition's offer was impossible.

5. [sijɔ̃] OR [sjɔ̃]. Admission requires permission. / Attention, *s'il vous plaît*, the lady has a question.

Consonant Substitutions

1. [r]. His friend ran down the red road. / The sight in the mirror filled him with horror.

2. [ɦ]. Hello, Henri, when will you be here? / Her behavior had a very heavy effect on him.

3. [s] FOR [θ]. Thank you for the thought.

4. [z] FOR [ð]. The father said to put this thing there.

5. [ʃ] FOR [tʃ]. The bachelor paid the check for the lunch. / Cheese and chicken do not go together.

6. [ʒ] FOR [dʒ]. The judge got the jump on Jack and George. / The children sold the orange to the agent.

Altered Stress

However you do 'it, it will not mat'ter very much.

Perhaps the traffic will not be 'so slow.

Shared English-French Words

(*Voice:* Betty Lorraine.)

The following recognizable French words are common to both French and English and can be added to those already presented in the previous sections. More words of this kind are in daily use.

amuse	*comédie*	*musique*	*raison*
appartement	*difficulté*	*opéra*	*tragédie*
artiste	*directeur*	*pardon*	*théâtre*
blue	*exemple*	*personne*	*université*
capitale	*fatal*	*public*	*village*
couleur	*minute*	*radio*	*voyage*

Following are French words and phrases which, although not common to both languages, still are recognizable and therefore proper, helpful, and colorful to use.

mon ami—my friend

bon jour—good day

bon soir—good evening

au revoir—good bye

au revoir, Monsieur et Madame (often slurred to: *'voir-msieu-dame*)

merci—thank you

merci bien—thanks very much

oui—yes

garçon—boy, waiter

chérie—dear

beaucoup—very much

comment?—how, what?

comment allez-vous?—how are you?

entrez—come in

savoir faire—ability, tact

n'est-ce pas?—isn't that right?

s'il vous plaît—please

c'est la vie—that's life

faux pas—mistake

Mon Dieu—my God!

rendez-vous

toujours—always

toujours l'amour—always love

voilà—there

cherchez la femme—seek the lady

READING FOR FLUENCY

The pace is deliberately slow to permit checking key sounds; some fluency is sacrificed. This primary-source material was recorded under nonstudio conditions.

(*Voice:* France Rouard.)

Hello, *mes amis*—my friends. I am going to read for you in English as an illustration of the French dialect.

My home was in Paris, France. I lived there for many

years before I came to America. Often I have walked along the famous streets you have no doubt read about: the *Champs Elysées*, the *Rue de la Paix*, the *Boulevard St. Martin*. I have stood in the *Place de l'Opéra*, the *Place de la Concorde*, and I have visited the *Tuileries'* the tomb of *Napoléon*, and the great palace of *Louis Quatorze*, that is, Louis the Fourteenth. If someone were to ask me where the center of the city of Paris was, I would have to say, it is probably to be found in the *Place de la Concorde*. From the *Place de la Concorde*, streets and boulevards go out in all directions. It is not far to the famous church of *Notre Dame*, or to the *Rodin* Museum, or the *Eiffel* Tower. The Seine River flows through the city very close by, and several of the bridges which cross it can be seen from the *Place de la Concorde*. It is in this spot that many of the famous episodes in French history have taken place. So, if you ask me where is the center of the city of Paris, I must say: this is it.

The Lady

(*Voice:* Jerry Blunt.)

She was a very beautiful lady, and she wore her clothes very well, too. When she walked down the *Champs Elysées* in the direction of the *Arc de Triomphe* all the people turn their heads just to look at her. Her dignity is remarkable, *magnifique*. Often she goes without an escort, but of course that is quite all right. I saw her, one morning, crossing a bridge over the Seine River. She was going either to the Tomb of *Napoléon* or to the *Rodin Musée*. There had been a little rainfall, so that the boulevard was clean and shining. Carefully, but with no hesitation, she picked her way through the little pools of water that were still standing on the pavement. She walked as if she were in no hurry at all. Her dress was blue, and the sky was blue, too, and they both looked very beautiful. She stopped to watch some pigeons. They came to her, but she had a little gesture to say there was nothing in her handbag for them. It did not seem to matter. Presently, *un petit garçon*, a little boy came running and scared the pigeons away. She

smiled and walked on.

INDIVIDUAL-PRACTICE EXERCISES
Key-Sound Word Drill

These key sounds are placed beside each other so that you may exercise on the change of lip, tongue, and jaw positions necessary for the making of the proper sounds.

Big; father; thank; there; here—comfortable; church; example; every; actor—adore; George; other; happy; interior—table; chicken; international; too; course—ran; age; dance; script; thirteen—author; formidable; true; salon; rather—infant; romantic; blame; attention; terrible—famous; dish; republic; agreement; who—thought; those; inhale; silence; launched—dominate; pronunciation; agent; desirable; professor—important; horrible; mirror; rainfall; dialect.

Key Sounds in Sentence Context

George's father was both famous and formidable.

Monsieur and Madame Flaubert prefer an apartment at their age.

The radio played music from the opera to amuse the people.

The distance from the capital of the republic is too little.

The large baby poured the chocolate on the chicken.

Bon jour, Mademoiselle Joan et Monsieur François, comment allez-vous?

Pierre had an invitation to dance in the distant city.

The ladies had to change their blue clothing before dinner.

The traffic was so terrible the agents were rather uncomfortable.

Pardon, *Monsieur*, but the color will not fit that person.

Both tragedy and comedy were offered by the university.

The prince and the artist took a voyage as an example to others.

They both think separate thoughts about the dramatic invitation.

Have you heard about the happy accident on the famous boulevard?

The director and the actors have never been in the beautiful theatre.

Thirteen chickens presented a dance exercise in public.

The infant wore a scarf in the government office.

An author gave an orange to a painter in the *Place de la Concorde*.

The *messieurs* and *mesdames* were romantic in the blue moonlight.

It is an honor for the president to read the roll in both the north and the south.

It is fitting for *Monsieur* Jack to adore *Mademoiselle* Angélique.

The country rainfall looked charming in the distance.

Henri placed the agreement on the little table with his other hand.

Perhaps the chair will be more comfortable in the monument.

SIGHT READING AND FLUENCY PRACTICE
Rendez-Vous

There we were, all walking down the boulevard together, and we were all singing the same beautiful song. It was one we had learned long ago at the university when we were much younger. To be able to sing it again, all in unison, made everyone very happy. But then we were sad, too. The ancient government buildings and the old church had changed; the character of that section of the city was very different from what we remembered. Famous landmarks were rubbed out by this and that modern edifice. But still we were together and that was something. At the little river we stopped, standing by the embankment. Then there was silence, and no one made one sound, even, or said anything. Perhaps it was very dramatic, I cannot tell you if it was or if it was not. There was a—how do you say—a stick in my throat, and it was very hard for me to swallow.

Born to Be Late

Hello, *mes amis*—everybody! How are you? I hope you have not been waiting too long for me. I rush and rush, and still I cannot help being late. Isn't it funny, *toujours*—always it is like that with me, never I am on time. With me punctuality is impossible. If I have an appointment to meet the President, even, at a table in a cafe, you can count on it, I will be behind my schedule. My professor tells me that time is important, and he is right—the blame, it is mine. The many things I do embarrass me. I hate to walk over the feet of people in the theatre. Dinner is never hot. The train and the plane go off without me, and I never, never miss the red light in traffic. *Eh bien, c'est la vie*, not everyone was born to be prompt.

The Taming of the Shrew, *Shakespeare;* Act V, Scene 2

KATHERINA: . . . Thy husband is thy lord, thy life, thy

    keeper,

Thy head, thy sovereign; one that cares for thee

And for thy maintenance commits his body

To painful labor both by sea and land,

To watch the night in storms, the day in cold,

Whilst thou li'st warm at home, secure and safe;

And craves no other tribute at thy hands

But love, fair looks, and true obedience;

Too little payment for so great a debt.

Such duty as the subject owes the prince,

Even such a woman oweth to her husband;

And when she is froward, peevish, sullen, sour,

And not obedient to his honest will,

What is she but a foul contending rebel

And graceless traitor to her loving lord?

I am asham'd that women are so simple

To offer war where they should kneel for peace,

Or seek for rule, supremacy, and sway,

When they are bound to serve, love, and obey.

The Taming of the Shrew, *Shakespeare;* Act II, Scene 1

PETRUCHIO: You wrong me, Signior Gremio: give me

    leave.

I am a gentleman of Verona, sir,

That, hearing of her beauty and her wit,

Her affability and bashful modesty,

Her wondrous qualities and mild behavior,

Am bold to show myself a forward guest

Within your house, to make mine eye the witness

Of that report which I so oft have heard.

And, for an entrance to my entertainment,

I do present you with a man of mine,

Cunning in music and the mathematics,

To instruct her fully in those sciences,

Whereof I know she is not ignorant.

Accept of him, or else you do me wrong:

His name is Licio, born in Mantua.

ITALIAN

A dialectician is concerned with two kinds of vocal subject materials, each differing from the other in a very basic way. One is the speech of all those who speak English as a native tongue, every variation being a form of regional speech, a dialect. American Southern, Scots, and Cockney are typical representatives of this category. The other is the speech of all those whose native tongue is not English, who speak English as a second language. Italian, French, and Japanese are three representative members of the latter group.

Variation between different kinds of regional English speech is caused by geographical divisions, climate, and inherited social and economic as well as vocal traditions. Variation in dialect between those of any one foreign tongue who speak English has, in the main, a simpler cause: education, or its lack, is the principal conditioning factor. The Italian, Frenchman, or Japanese who studies English, especially if under an English or American teacher, will strive for pronunciation, grammatical structure, and idiomatic expression as like the instructor's as possible. In this case the principal limiting factors are duration of study, individual aptitude, and strength of influence of the muscular patterns in the native speech. But the tendency of these persons will be to achieve a proper utterance with as little limitation as possible from native habits.

Accordingly, distinction or its lack in a dialect will be in direct proportion to the degree of success in the study of English. The most successful students will

have the least distinctive dialect, and since the attractiveness of a dialect depends upon differences rather than similarities, theirs will also possess the least aural attraction.

Logically, a reversal of the above will work to produce the most distinctive dialect. Such a reversal occurred in the nineteenth-century United States and continued until the advent of World War I. For many decades the great majority of immigrants coming to this country had little or no linguistic preparation for speaking American English, and furthermore had limited opportunities for study after arrival.

An immediate need to obtain work, together with a tendency to group with their own kind, occasioned a quick but limited pragmatic linguistic education. For most of these people an unorganized and untutored acquisition of the new speech was characterized by successful attempts at shortcuts that were sufficient for basic communicative needs; malpronunciations and a multiplicity of idiomatic expressions resulted. The active presence of foreign syllabic formations and stresses thus produced the most distinctive and, interestingly enough, the most attractive dialects.

As a result of this historic process, the concept of most Americans as to what makes an authentic dialect is based upon the speech of the uneducated immigrant rather than that of the educated foreigner. For that reason the best Italian, French, or Japanese dialects are to be heard in this country rather than abroad. Unfortunately for the dialectician, modern education is bringing the process to a stop, a condition that may be regretted by some, but one that cannot be halted.

Of all the dialects to be heard in this country, none has been more typical of the pragmatic learning process than the Italian. Nor have any been more distinctive. It is the volubly rich speech of the self-taught Italian immigrant that we will study, turning for primary-source material to the old rather than the young.

The characteristics that give definition to an Italian dialect are, for our purposes, the same for all Italians, no matter from what part of Italy the individual originally came. Rate of utterance, stress, and a basically similar pronunciation are the same for all, a fact that many native Italians would not want to agree to, but which is a proper fact for a study of this kind. Actually, the Italian language today is still remarkably close to the language of Dante, the first major writer in the popular tongue.

A caution must be issued to the student dialectician. Rapidity in vocal delivery is one of the distinguishing characteristics of Italian speech. But too rapid utterance, especially in the beginning, is detrimental to the acquisition of those new muscular patterns on which proper enunciation depends. Unquestionably, it is best to form syllables as slowly as is necessary to establish the right sounds, and to continue at a like pace until proper habits of enunciation are acquired before picking up speed. Even then, it is better to seem to go fast than actually to do so.

Modern Italian is one of the Romance languages that evolved from the Vulgar or Popular Latin of Rome's Imperial Period. Linguistic processes caused alterations that distinguished each one more and more as time went on, until now each stands a language in its own right.

There are dialect elements in common among all members of the Romance language family, but similarities are only aids, not transferable elements sufficiently strong to make a master in any one of these dialects a master in all. It still is necessary to undertake a separate study in each.

Italian is geographically and textually close to the original Latin source. But the divisive forces of linguistic growth and change through the centuries are of such extent that today the pronunciation, grammatical structure or lack of it, and idiomatic expression of an Italian speaking in English is sufficient enough to distinguish his from a French or Spanish or any other dialect of the Romance language group.

KEY SOUNDS OF AN ITALIAN DIALECT

Variation from usual practices in several particulars is necessary for this study. First, major emphasis must go, not to alteration of vowels and consonants, but to a pattern of speech, one that provides the most distinctive characteristic of the dialect. Second, more division than usual will be made between the limited number of essentials and those sounds of the dialect that may be used at choice. Third, the voice of a primary-source individual, speaking in unplanned reminiscence, will be heard in illustration of a speech that lacks no distinction for all its limited use of vowel and consonant substitutions.

Essential Characteristics

Italian is a language of many subtleties that are or can be reflected in an Italian dialect. Paradoxically, the principal characteristics which give distinction to it are relatively few; a small number of key sounds, fewer than in any other dialect, provide its main strength. Of that number five carry the main burden. Phonetically they are the vowels [ə] and [i], and the consonants [r] and [w], and the [t] and [d] substitutes for *th*. In addition, less emphatic elements are: [u] for [ʊ], a dropped [ʎ], slurred syllables, and errors of syntax.

1. INTERJECTED [ə]. A certain habit of vocal delivery is essential to a full-bodied Italian dialect. It consists of the interjection of a single vowel sound [ə], whose addition provides the outstanding feature of the dialect. [ə] is the unstressed form of the pure vowel [ʌ], as in *up*.

There are only two genders, masculine and feminine, in the Italian language, and each has a vowel ending. Consequently no noun ends in a consonant. Further, a glance at an Italian dictionary shows that an overwhelming majority of all other words also end in vowels rather than consonants. The speaker being habituated to a terminal vowel sound, previous experience forces him to its continued use. But English has many consonant endings. Deprived of what he expects and under pressure of habit, an Italian continues to use what is to him a right action. It is only natural that his interjection employs the most common vowel in his or any other language, the unstressed form of [ʌ], which is [ə].

Since an English word with a vowel ending presents him with no problem, and none is there if the next word begins with a vowel, a speaker is concerned only with those instances in which two consonants come together in a word or sentence, or in which a word ends in a consonant with no other sound following. In those trouble spots, to suit his lifelong habit, an Italian must make a correction. What is simpler than to slip in a vowel where needed, and what vowel other than the one mentioned above, the unstressed [ə]?

The interjection of [ə] also has a psychological motivation. Words to fit a facile expression in a new tongue do not always come readily to mind. As a mechanism to hold attention while searching for the right word, the interjection of [ə] is a commonplace action—used, incidentally, by those native to a language as well as by others foreign to it.

Consequently this distinctive feature appears:

a. As the terminal sound of a single word that ends in a consonant: *wind* [wində].

b. As an interjection between two consonants in a multisyllable word: *midnight* ['midənaItə].

c. As an interjection between words of a sentence when one ends and the next begins with a consonant: *what* [ə] *you want*?

2. DROPPED AND ELIDED SYLLABLES. The second major characteristic of a full-strength dialect is the practice of eliding medial sounds or dropping final sounds or final syllables in a word. As is stated elsewhere, a tendency toward this action is universal. It is emphasized here because the Italian does it more often and more noticeably than any other national; it could almost be said that he does it better, for there is no doubt that his action has an attractive quality, and provided that understandability is not sacrificed, it is to be used often.

Where volubility is a national characteristic, encouraged by freedom of emotional release, and fluency of delivery is more than ordinarily possible because of an emphasis upon vowels, it becomes a natural tendency to neglect the full formation of all sounds. As a result, not only might *wind* become *win'*, or *pretty*, *prit'*, but *trouble* can be shortened *troub'* (*he no tak*[ə] *da troub'*) and *very beautiful* to *ver' beautif*[ə]'.

Unique in this dialect of many dropped syllables is the change in pronunciation that occurs when the *re* in *there* is dropped, an action that causes *there* to be written *the'*, but pronounced *they* [ðe]. Consequently such expressions as "we will go there" are heard in the Italian dialect as "we go the' (*they*)," while "what are you going to do there?" will be delivered as "watta you do the' (*they*)."

Associated with the practice of dropping or cutting off sounds is an equally natural process of eliding letters and syllables. When two like letters or two like sounds come together one is sure to be eliminated and, on occasion, both. *Never regret* will be *nev*[ə] *regret*, while *want to* quite easily becomes *wanna*, the elided sounds so thoroughly welded there is no suggestion of a break in the one word that results. In addition, vocal shortcuts produce such simplifications as *tha'sa* for *that is*, and *a'right* for *all right*.

These major characteristics of dropping or eliding letters and syllables will easily be noted on the accompanying tape.

3. ERRORS OF SYNTAX. Lack of English grammatical habits, not the pressure of former speech habits, is responsible for errors of syntax in an Italian dialect. The results are many and varied:

a. NUMBERS. Singulars are used more often than plurals: *these girl*, *plenty gift*. Occasionally a plural is wrongly employed: *one times*.

b. TENSES. Because English verb forms are difficult, the present tense is overworked: *we eat eight o'clock*, *Tony go yesterday*.

c. PRONOUNS. These noun substitutes often do not agree with their antecedents, or lack proper possessive or objective forms: *this dress, she . . . ; those men, he . . . ; is you belt?, it belong his*.

d. CONTRACTIONS. These typically English grammatical effects—*can't, won't*—give trouble and are simplified by use of the easiest negative: *he no can do it, she not go*.

e. COMPARATIVES. The use of comparative endings—*er* and *est*—in adjectives and adverbs is avoided by an overuse of *more* and *most*: *he run fast, but I run more fast*, and *this family is the most big of all*.

f. PREPOSITIONS. Prepositions are freely omitted: *we go Rome, you sit table*.

4. [i] FOR [I]. As is the case of any untrained or careless person with a Romance-language background, the longer English [i], as in *eat*, is substituted for a shorter [I], as in *it*. This is a consistent practice, and is employed when the syllable is in any position, but especially when initial or medial. Thus *it* [It] becomes [it], and *river* ['rIvə] changes to ['rivə].

5. [u] FOR [U]. Related to the above is the fairly consistent practice of substituting the longer sound of [u], as in *food*, for the shorter [U], as in *foot*. This causes *foot* [fUt] to change to [fut], just as *put* [pUt] becomes [put].

In connection with both paragraphs 4 and 5 above,

it is useful to realize that Italian is a vowel language. Since it is such, speaking Italian or Italian dialect requires more than the usual tension of the muscles of lips, tongue, and jaw. In Italian, vowel openings are quickly attained and firmly held so that the vowel does not waver in quality or pitch and is not slurred. Accordingly all vowels are emphasized, mostly through elongation. At the same time, pure vowels are favored over diphthongs. It was just noted that a shorter [ɪ], as in *it*, gives way to the longer [i], as in *eat*. In the same way the [e] of *eight* will remain so instead of becoming the [eɪ] diphthong favored by Americans.

Aside from the vowels discussed above, Italians speaking English are quite flexible in adaptation to vowel sounds, even to the acquisition of what is to them a new vowel, the [æ] of *at*, which they dexterously work into their catalogue of sounds.

6. CONSONANTS. Several familiar consonantal changes are required in this dialect.

a. [r]. The [r] is trilled with the tip of the tongue.

b. [d] FOR [ð]. Extension of the tongue between the teeth is an unfamiliar muscular action for Italians, so that both the voiced and unvoiced *th*, [ð] and [θ], are difficult of formation and suffer substitution.

[d] replaces the voiced [ð] in all initial positions—*the* [də], *they* [de], *that* [dæt]—but only intermittently for medial placement—*father* ['faðə] or ['fadə], *although* [ɔl'do]. [ð] is not used terminally. A limited use of this substitution is recommended.

c. [t] FOR [θ]. [t] substitutes for the voiceless *th* [θ], and can do so in all positions: *thank* [tæŋk], *youthful* ['jutfəl], *with* [wit].

d. [ℏ]. There is no [h] in Italian; therefore it is not sounded when seen in print or in writing, whether in initial or medial positions: *have* ['æv], *perhaps* [pɛʳ ''æpsə].

In an unusual circumstance, an [h] is occasionally and unknowingly added to the syllabic flow. When two like vowels end one word and begin the next, sometimes when just two vowels are thus related, aspiration is sufficiently strong to produce a distinctive sound of [h]: *the* [h]*episode, to* [h]*us.*

e. [w] FOR *wh* [hw]. The letter *w* exists in Italian only in purely foreign words or names. For all that, there is enough flexibility to cause little trouble in making the new sound. The alteration that does occur is one with which Americans are unfortunately too familiar: the *h* of *wh* is not sounded, causing *where* to be pronounced *wear* and *when, wen.*

Occasional Characteristics

Several quite proper sounds for an Italian dialect are subject to inconsistent use. Both strong and distinctive, they are irregular in appearance. The causes are the usual conditioning speech factors: regional influence, degree of education, and personal mannerisms.

Additionally, the dialect can contain many subtle effects, more than is usual in other dialect forms, occasioned by regional differences found in the native land. The multiplicity and subtlety of these native idiosyncrasies militate against inclusion in such a study as this. Accordingly only the most notable and most used are given below, and they with the understanding that they are for occasional use and not as obligatory sounds.

1. [a] FOR [æ]. [æ] does not appear on an Italian vowel list. The absence does not cause any real difficulty, for both unlettered immigrant and educated person readily add it to speech patterns. What is shown is a tendency to shift the vowel sound backwards in the mouth, changing [æ] to [a]: *Antonio* [æn'tonio] becomes [an'tonio], and *land* [lænd], [land].

2. [ɛʳ] FOR [ɝ]. A trilled *r* seems to ask for a preceding vowel of [ɛ], *eh*, instead of [ɝ], *er*. The need is perceived in Scots, German and Russian, and equally so here. An often used sound, it is heard in *girl* [gɝl] as [gɛʳl], or in *first* [fɝst] as [fɛʳst], or *heard* [hɝd] as ['ɛʳd].

3. [aʊ] FOR [ɔ]. The *au* and *ou* which ordinarily are sounded as [ɔ], *ought*, incline an Italian to read them as the diphthong [aʊ], as in *ouch*. That treatment might (not *must*) be given at times to such words as *pause* [pɔz], or *bought* [bɔt], which become [paʊz] and [baʊt].

4. [e] FOR *and*. The single letter *e*, pronounced [e], as in *a*, the first letter in our alphabet, is the Italian word for *and*. It is to be expected that an Italian will often substitute his word for ours, *and* becoming [e]. Since there is small likelihood of loss of intelligibility, the substitution can be made on many, but not all, occasions.

5. [t] FOR [d]. The simplest way to state this vocal effect is to say that when a voiced [d] is terminal in a word, it may be replaced by its voiceless counterpart [t]. Actually the sound of this substitution is neither [d] nor [t], but lies between the two—another case of the human tendency to slur, deemphasizing a voiced consonant so that it takes on a voiceless quality. The substitution is only occasional.

6. [z] FOR [s]. Several regional dialects in Italy cause a speaker to substitute the voiced [z] for a voiceless [s]

in medial and final positions. This inconsistent effect is heard most often in words like *baseball* ['besbɔl], which becomes ['bezbɔl], or *cross* [krɔs] changed to [krɔz].

7. . . . *tion*. The Italian equivalent of our syllable *tion* is *zione*, pronounced [tsjonɛ]. It occupies the same position and is close enough in sound for a substitution. The following English words and others like them would be easily understood if given the Italian ending: *demonstration, construction, ratification, destination, indignation.*

KEY-SOUND WORD DRILL

Space is left below both words and sentences for scoring phonetic or other symbols.

Essential Characteristics

(*Voice:* Mario Tartaglia.)

1. INTERJECTED [ə]. Cap, rib, put, brag, been, trees, garage, bobwhite, something, diphthong, midnight.

2. DROPPED AND ELIDED SYLLABLES. Tomato, paper, postcard, there, friend, best, vacation, politician, wonderful, pocketbook; want to, that is, what do.

3. ERRORS OF SYNTAX.

   a. NUMBERS. These girl, their cloth(es), two eye, all baby, each person, one times.

   b. TENSES. We eat eight o'clock, he go yesterday, tomorrow she talk.

   c. PRONOUNS. These dress, she . . . ; them dog; many people, he . . . ; is you ball, they shoes, her talk fast.

   d. CONTRACTIONS. (*Can't*) he no can; (*won't*) he will no pay; (*mustn't*) he mus' [ə] no' cough; (*isn't*) it is no come; (*don't*) you no do it.

   e. COMPARATIVES. (*Faster*) more fast; (*biggest*) most big.

   f. PREPOSITIONS. We go Rome, he go back Italy, they move Chicago.

4. [i] FOR [ɪ]. Italy, in, ill, river, invisible.

5. [u] FOR [ʊ]. Put, bush, could, pull, woman.

6. CONSONANTS.

   a. [r]. Radio, report, carbon, script.

   b. [d] FOR *th* [ð]. The, they, these, father, although.

   c. [t] FOR *th* [θ]. Think, thank, author, with, month.

   d. [ʜ]. Have, handball, hide-and-seek, perhaps, behave; *and in reverse:* the *h*episode, at *h*us, come *h*up.

   e. [w] FOR *wh* [hw]. What, why, wheel, which, white.

Occasional Characteristics

1. [a] FOR [æ]. Antonio, land, salad, dance, happy.

2. [ɛʳ] FOR [ɜ]. Her, girl, first, worm, worse.

3. [ɑʊ] FOR [ɔ]. Pause, bought, caught, thought.

4. [e] FOR *and*. Father and son, salt and pepper, old and young.

5. [t] FOR [d]. Did, head, banged, fished.

6. [z] FOR [s]. Baseball, vase, best, these.

7. . . . *tion*. Demonstration, destination, indignation.

KEY SOUNDS IN SENTENCE CONTEXT
Essential Characteristics

1. INTERJECTED [ə]. Mind you papa—you come home before midnight. / What do you mean, just look, that place has lots trees.

2. DROPPED AND ELIDED SYLLABLES. I'm going to see the politician. / This tomato is the most best. / You want to go there?

3. ERRORS IN SYNTAX.

   a. NUMBERS. These girl have much pretty ring. / All baby are cute.

   b. TENSES. Yesterday he go baseball game, tonight he go too. / Tomorrow I feel much better—you watch, I get up.

   c. PRONOUNS. These dress, she not fit. / Many people, he going to vote today.

   d. CONTRACTIONS. He no can do like he say. / You think he will no pay?

   e. COMPARATIVES. You like the dress more long? / That horse, he run the most fast of all.

   f. PREPOSITIONS. Pack you things; we go *Roma*. / You want eat, you sit table.

4. [i] FOR [ɪ]. The sister plans go visit *Italia*. / I think the river is too big.

5. [u] FOR [ʊ]. These womens push and pull in the subway.

6. CONSONANTS.

   a. [r]. Raphaelo read the radio script rapidly.

   b. [d] FOR *th* [ð]. They want those other things.

   c. [t] FOR *th* [θ]. She thought she say thanks for all things.

   d. [ʃ]. Perhaps Giuseppe still have the handball.

   e. [w] FOR *wh* [hw]. Which whip are she going to whirl?

Occasional Characteristics

1. [a] FOR [æ]. Antonio was not happy with the last dance.

2. [ɛʳ] FOR [ɜ]. The worm turned just a little.

3. [ɑʊ] FOR [ɔ]. Marcello thought he caught the most

big fish.

4. [e] FOR *and*. All you do is talk and talk and talk.

5. [t] FOR [d]. He pushed and pushed before it budged.

6. [z] FOR [s]. These baseball is most best.

7. . . . *tion*. This illustration makes a very nice demon-

stration.

Common Expressions

How are you?—*Come sta?*	Good-by.—*Addio.*
Well, thanks.—*Bene,*	Thank you.—*Grazie.*
grazie.	Please.—*Per favore.*
Good morning.—*Buon*	You're welcome.—*Prego.*
giorno.	Pardon me.—*Scusi.*
Good evening.—*Buona*	Mr.—*Signore.*
sera.	Mrs.—*Signora.*
Good night.—*Buona*	Miss—*Signorina.*
notte.	Teacher.—*Maestro.*
See you again.—*Arrive-*	Professor.—*Professore.*
derla or *Arrivederci.*	Doctor.—*Dottore.*
So long.—*Ciao.*	Countryman.—*Paesano.*

A Dear Lady

The following voice is that of an Italian-American lady, recorded under difficult circumstances. As you will hear, the tape is not free of obtrusive sounds, but since both the speaker and the subject content possess value as primary-source materials, unique of their kind, the selection is included for your study.

But I like Rome. When I was to Rome, I see the beautiful flower in the window, and the beautiful thing, trees with the flower and all, all those beautiful building.

— And we hear once Caruso sing the opera. Oh, that was beautiful. Very beautiful. We never hear those beautiful voice again, and I know Mario Lanza is next Caruso. I was a School della Bella Arte to Rome and they was beautiful white building. All the young girls and young boys was there. They was study over there. They learn from somebody color, make flower, somebody do the design, somebody, any kind, any kind of work, they were so beautiful.

At San Pietro Church, we went, we walk on the steps way high, and when we look down the people was so small, look like chicken. We visit Naples, we eat in a beautiful restaurant. We went down to Sorrento. We have the boat. That's really beautiful down there. You eat in a big restaurant on the side, way high. After you go down on the ocean, that's all flower round, and you take the boat, till you go on ocean play for hour or two, or one day—how much you like to stay, that was very, very beautiful, I can't forget that.

It's true when you see Naples and die, you see all those beautiful girl and boy play the accordion and sing —the voice, oh, they make you feel look like you in heaven, so beautiful, sing so nice voice, when they sing *Torn'a Sorrento*, oh, that's beautiful. Lots of Naples song that's real, real beautiful, all love song.

We take the boat to (from) Naples, August the twenty-four. Everybody was feel bad on the boat when I enjoy, really, I enjoy the, the trip on the ocean. On the boat we was nine days, and I enjoy—we went to dance every night, we see the show, and when I reach in this country, it was so beautiful. I went to New York. It was so nice, I see those big building and since I come this country, I love this country, I never went back in Italy.

You know, Louise, when I came to New York and I have a dime *e* (and) five cents. I have the dime and I went buy grapes. The fellow give me about a big bag grapes because dime was worth more. A friend of mine, she has a nickel, she went buy, she has half a bag. She ask the fellow, "You tease, you teach, you, you, you must steal me because they not give me much grapes." I say, "Don't you know, the, the dime, and it's small but it's ten cents, and the, the nickel, it's big but it's five cents, it's half-way worth." And she say, "Oh, Mama Mia, we gotta learn lots in this country." I say, "Mama Mia, *niente*—" and the fellow was a sturdy young fellow. After he give us the grapes he say, "Lady, we no steal nobody—we Italian too."

INDIVIDUAL-PRACTICE EXERCISES
Key-Sound Word Drill

The following key sounds are placed beside each other so that you may practice the change of lip, tongue and jaw positions necessary for the making of the proper sounds.

Want to go there—each; diphthong; brought; stop— fish; fast; foot; further—sister; has; red; pocketbook —what; radio; will; pause—think; them; thank; those —most; whisker; have; hallmark—the episode; held;

superstition—Italy; girl; could; dance—her; demonstration; not; worse—pretty; race track; with; thought—although; handball; ask; what—tomato; is; something; white—suggestion; all right; rehearse; first.

Key Sounds in Sentence Context

There are many sentences to read aloud.

Do not wait for me because I must go down town.

Wait a minute; you do not have your shopping bag or your pocketbook.

I do not think I like the American game of baseball.

In Italy we play a wonderful game called rugby football.

What do you think you are going to get by hanging around here?

The churches and buildings in Rome are very beautiful.

Genoa is one of Italy's biggest and busiest cities.

The *autostrada*, what you call the freeway, is straighter than the old road.

Bring the rope you bought to the big river.

Was it your father or his sister's mother that joined the group?

We will have rings and things and fine array.

There will be a big rush because many people will go to the racetrack tomorrow.

A bus will take all of you to St. Peter's in Vatican City.

Piazza Venezia and the Forum and the Coliseum are all very close together.

Please come and sit down at the table before your food gets cold.

It is longer to go to Chicago this way, but I can't help it.

All right, all right, there will be plenty of gifts for all the babies and the older children, too.

Mr. and Mrs. Furio and their daughter Silvana will see her professor before going to the doctor's office.

Avanzi mustn't travel the quickest way; it will spoil everything.

These girls are to wear white dresses, but those boys shouldn't put on white shirts.

Take your choice, either the paper or the postcard.

Where are you going to go?

What's the matter with them, they can't drive their cars in Venice?

It is harder to walk in these shoes; I can go faster if I am barefooted.

SIGHT READING AND FLUENCY PRACTICE

Transpose the following into the idiomatic expression of an Italian dialect such as would be used by a person with little formal education.

Buying and Selling Vegetables

What is it you want, lady? Anything I can help you with? You can see everything we have, it is all in the trays, nice and fresh. Do you see the spray coming from the little pipe there? It keeps all the vegetables cool. There is no hurry; take your time. The best shopper looks the longest and gets the freshest, the best of everything, that's what I always say.

You see the cucumbers; they are a very good buy today, special, just like advertised. Italian cucumbers just in, picked first thing this morning. No, they are not shriveled, that's the way they grow, very natural.

Have you ever tried them? No. My goodness, I'm surprised. Italian cucumbers have a remarkable flavor. Now you will pardon what I'm going to say, and it is not that I'm prejudiced, but Italian cucumbers absolutely have the best taste—old-fashioned, like these things used to taste—and with salt and oil, oh my, none like them. Go ahead, try them. If you are disappointed you come in tomorrow and tell me so and I will give you all the others in the box. So what can you lose?

And tomatoes, they are very good today, red and juicy, just feel. No, don't pinch, take in your whole hand—now, just feel a little. Is good, yes? Sure, I pick 'em out for you. How much you want—you say two pounds and I'm going to give you two and a little more. That celery you got there is very crisp, not all wilted— and clean, I bet you ain't going to find no worms there. Good for salad.

You know what my wife does when the weather is hot like this? She never mixes a salad. She just takes all the nice crisp vegetables, the cucumbers and celery and lettuce and radishes and carrots, and cuts them up, you know, slices them this way and that, what you call dices 'em, and sets them on the table separately and lets everybody make his own dish—with lots of good oil, we always have much oil, is good for many things.

What? No, I didn't come from Rome. We are from the south of Italy, where most Italians in America come from. It's not so good there as in the North; that's why everybody leaves. My father and mother and brothers and sisters lived in a very small place, a town so little I bet you nobody ever heard of it, below Naples, near Castellammare. That's where Sorrento and Amalfi and Positano are, and Capri and all those beautiful places. But I visited Rome once, only I was too young to remember what I saw. It was just before we came to the United States—papa and mama and those of us who were the youngest, we were the ones that came. My other brothers and sisters stayed there. They were all married before, you know how it is. Those others, they are still there, living in Italy, but better now than before.

They want me to come back for a visit. And you know something? I'm going to go—why not, what's to prevent? Everybody goes on a trip, even the boys and girls. All you need is a passport, and some money. So that's what I'm going to do, get the passport and the money and take my wife and the kids for the biggest trip of our lives—tourists, with cameras and credit cards and everything.

A Marriage Proposal, *Anton Chekhov*

Lomov's speech from this classic comedy lends itself to the pace and utterance of an Italian dialect.

LOMOV: I'm cold. My whole body is shaking, just like the time when I must take an examination. So, I will talk to myself: Now, see here, you must settle down. Do you know what you must do—be decisive, that's the thing—don't think, don't make the hesitation, whatever you do, do not permit the subject to be a distraction. What's the use waiting for an ideal love, it is never going to come. Right? Right! And that takes care of that. So, now I have got myself in hand,

I am in control, I am calm. (*He stands still, relaxes, smiles. But then his body begins to shake again, a leg first, then the torso.*) It's cold! I'm cold. Mother of Heaven, why can't I just think about this without so much jerking! Take care, take care, everything is all right—reason is on my side. Natalia, she is a fine housekeeper, first class—and she is very beaut— very beaut— well, she is not bad looking, and what is more, she can read and write. So, what more could anybody ask? (*He groans.*) I'm so nervous. What's that? I hear something—no, it's not anything, my ears making a roar. Now I'm hot. Where is the water —the wat——ah. That's better. I must get married, that's for sure. To live a regular life, that's the thing. Now I can't sleep. I just start to doze and the muscles on my left side jump. I itch, right where I can't scratch, in the middle of the back. My hand, it twitches. My heart goes thump, thump, thump, and my head pounds. I have to leave the bed to walk up and down, up and down, so I can make myself calm. Then, when I crawl back into bed and am just about ready to close my eyes for sleep, what happens? I get a cramp in my leg. That's the way it goes, every night, night after night after—

(NATALIA *enters.*)

—Oh!

XII

*

GERMAN

*

A German dialect is an emphatic speech, characterized more by the strength of its vowel and consonant substitutions than by idiomatic expressions. Definiteness of utterance negates slur in syllable formation. The result is that the key sounds of the dialect are relatively easy to detect. In most cases they are also easy to form. The same is true of an Austrian dialect.

The German tongue itself is one specific branch, perhaps the principal one, of the Teutonic language group. Present-day Dutch, Danish, Swedish, and Norwegian are also members of that group. So is English, although it is the least noticeable member, its words and sounds being the farthest removed of any from present German speech. Between those cousin languages which are located on the Continent—German, Dutch, Danish, Swedish, Norwegian—some understanding is possible in written and oral communication. Not so with English. A study of the German language is required before an equal understanding can come to an Englishman or an American.

Consequently, the number of German words of transferable use to the dialectician is limited, causing a speaker to rely heavily on the use of key sounds in the German dialect. On the other hand, the advantage to an English or American dialectician is that a German dialect introduces only a few new sounds—the rest are native to us.

One of the new sounds, the vowel [ɛʳ], has already been studied as one of the key sounds of Scots, and of the French dialect where it was heard as [œ:]. Another,

the [x], as in *loch* (*lake*), is very like its aspirated Scotch cousin. A third is [ç], *ich*, also strongly aspirated. These last two have limited use for the dialectician. For the rest, the majority of the dialect differences fall in the consonant category.

Within the territory of the modern German nation itself—disregarding the political East-West division—there are the usual dialectal inconsistencies. Some Germans speak High German, some Low German. The descriptions are geographical, not social. The term High, a reference to altitude, includes the South German areas of Bavaria and Baden, and some portions of Switzerland and Austria, those which are located in or on the edge of the Alps. There the dialectician listens almost in vain for the sound of a back-trilled [r], a sound which, in contrast, is heard often and strongly in the lower flat areas of North Germany, centering around the city of Hamburg.

On the other hand, some citizens of Berlin claim that only they speak a proper German, to which statement some non-Berliners have been heard to reply heatedly that there is a question whether the Berliners really speak German at all. To understand this we only have to compare the above situation to that of an American Southerner who evinces a special attitude toward the speech of a northern city, Boston or Brooklyn, for example.

In consequence of the above, the usual twin problems of the dialectician are also present in this study. First, when listening to primary sources, that is, to Germans speaking in English, certain key sounds may not be present, causing doubt of the legitimacy of the use of those key sounds, as in the instance of the lack of a back-trilled [r] in the speech of someone from Munich. Second, a comment by a German person, one from the province of Silesia, might be disturbingly critical of a failure to substitute a [z] for an [s].

For the above kind of problems, the actor-dialectician has this knowledge to sustain him: that the inclusion of a sectional dialect in a national dialect in any non-English speech is an unnecessary refinement of his work, one that would require a detailed study and practice beyond legitimate limits. Fortunately it is never a matter of pertinence that an actor be required, in his use of a German or French or Italian dialect, to prove to an audience that the character he portrays comes from Hamburg or Marseille or Naples; no audience has the knowledge necessary to detect localized differences, nor a desire to do so.

Consequently, in the section which follows, certain arbitrary but legitimate choices between key sounds will be made. The choices will be explained, after which, in turn, the student is given an opportunity to choose for himself which practice he will follow.

Many Standard English pronunciations can be heard in the speech of a German talking in English. If the speaker did not learn his English from another German, the chances are he learned it, because of geographical proximity, from an educated Englishman. Before World War II the above explanation was consistently true. And today, among most older German public figures the precise accents of Oxford or Cambridge are heard repeatedly. This aspect of a German dialect could be used to advantage in certain instances. On the other hand, the restriction need not be an extra requirement for a proper German dialect. Since the war, in those areas where American personnel have been stationed, American pronunciation and American idiom ("Can't lube your car today, Bud, all filled up.") have made their expected impress.

KEY SOUNDS OF A GERMAN DIALECT

As indicated above, the family relationship between English and German is responsible for the large body of similar sounds in the two. In most instances the differences lie in consonant substitutions. In the main, distinctiveness comes into a German dialect by interchanging fewer than a score of them, most of which are simple plosives and fricatives. Add the vowel [εʳ], as in *air*, and the two heavily aspirated sounds [ç] as in *ich* and [x] as in *ach*, further add a couple of vowel substitutions, and the basis for a German dialect is established.

One factor, not previously presented in these studies, must now be considered. It is the element of choice whereby the student dialectician determines for himself which of two alternate dialectal sounds will be used. This choice will be made between (1) using the front- or back-trilled [r], (2) using a [d] or [z] substitute for the voiced *th* [ð], (3) using the more American [æ], as in *at*, or the English [ɑ], as in *father*, and (4) substituting or not substituting the heavy-sounding [z] for [s].

Some French words are established in the present-day German vocabulary. Typical are *fiancé, lingerie, bonbon,* and *salon.* Generally such words are spoken with a French pronunciation, but the less educated the speaker, the more Germanized the sound.

Not all distinctive German sounds are heard in the dialect. The three below are cases in point. While all three are legitimate and can be used where applicable, their inclusion is not mandatory for the reason that they are seldom heard when a German speaks in English. The three are:

[y], a sound made by saying [i] through closely rounded lips.

[ʏ], which is [ɪ] spoken through closely rounded lips.

[ø], [e] also spoken through closely rounded lips, as in the name *Goethe.*

Vowel Substitutions

1. [εʳ] FOR [ɜ]. Except in final syllables, the [εʳ] combination replaces the English *er* [ɜ] as in *earth.* [εʳ] is produced by sounding [ε] as in *yet,* followed closely by a uvular [r], that is, an [r] slightly trilled by the back of the tongue and uvula. Thus *earth* [ɜθ] becomes [εʳθ]. This pronunciation contrasts with the Scots' formation of [εʳ], in which the tip of the tongue, not the back, provides the trill.

The American pronunciation of *her* is subject to this change. When *her* is found in a two-syllable word, as in the German name *Hermann,* the sound is uttered with full strength. Unlike the French-dialect speakers, Germans drop the terminal *r* in such words as *father* and therefore do not pronounce the [εʳ] in such cases. The words *word* and *German* themselves are useful references to bring this sound to mind.

2. [ɑ] FOR [ʌ] OR [æ]. The "broad *a*" [ɑ] of Standard English or Standard American speech is employed by the Germans to a greater extent than we Americans use it. This characteristic is embodied in the German tongue, and reinforced by an English influence. Thus *alp* [ælp] is [ɑlp], *alto* [ælto] becomes [ɑlto], *after* [æftɚ] changes to [ɑftə], and *love* [lʌv] might alter to [lɑv]. However, the above substitutions may or may not be made, at choice. Since some Germans do not strongly use the "broad *a*" [ɑ], its use or nonuse becomes a matter of individual preference.

3. THE TERMINALS *e* [ə], *ed* [ɛd], AND *mann* [mɑn].

a. THE TERMINAL *e* [ə]. Unlike an Englishman or American, a German pronounces the unstressed vowel *e* [ə] when it is in a terminal position. He does this in his own language and the habit is readily transferred to English, especially when he encounters in the new language a word similar to one of his own words, such as *name* or *machine*. Unaccented, the final vowel is heard as [ə].

b. THE TERMINAL *ed* [ɛd]. Many foreigners—Germans, Italians, Greeks, Japanese—often regard this English tense ending *ed* as a complete syllable in itself and pronounce it as such, unaware of the tradition throughout the English-speaking world of eliminating the vowel completely. Especially when a foreigner is reading from an English text is he likely to give the *ed* ending full treatment, saying ['wɔlkɛd] for *walk'd* or ['dʒʊmpɛd] for *jump'd*. If a German character were reading from a script, it would be good practice for him to use this dialectal idiosyncrasy.

c. THE TERMINAL *mann* [mɑn]. When *mann* appears terminal in a name, the vowel is pronounced [ɑ] as in *father*. Although terminal, the syllable is not sloughed off but is given some stress.

Diphthongal Changes

More as subtle rather than broad changes, the two diphthongs [eɪ], as in *eight*, and [oʊ], as in *oat*, can be shortened to the vowels [e] and [o].

Consonant Substitutions

The switching of consonants from English to German usage is of critical importance in the attainment of a proper German dialect. Nor are the substitutions to be made merely a matter of a simple exchange, as of a [t] for a [d], for example. In the majority of cases, good

dialect usage requires that the consonant which is substituted be softened or modified somewhat as it is uttered. Thus the [d] that supplants the voiced *th* [ð] in *those* will sound better if it is not given with its full plosive value, but is softened somewhat by lessening the usual hard contact between the tongue and upper gum ridge when the consonant is formed. The result will be a [d] that might sound a little like [t]. The same modified action holds true on the other two plosive substitutions of [p] and [k], as well as on the fricative [f].

1. [r]. Again the [r] leads the list of consonants which undergo alteration in a new dialect. Here again the sound is accorded distinctive treatment, and in more than one way. In a German dialect the uvular [r] is delivered with greater strength than it is in a French dialect. This is the result of adding a guttural sound to the back-trilling action of the tongue.

Harshness is the natural result of this addition. It must be noted, however, that it is a harshness which is softened both by the action of a very flexible tongue and by constant repetition. The sounds which are produced by the first trials on a German uvular [r] generally are too strong and noticeably harsh..This fact does not indicate that practice on the making of this consonant should be avoided; on the contrary, such practice should be increased. Nor should the first sounds be permitted to become, by habit, the accepted sound for this consonant. The idea of modified strength should be continuously kept in mind even as the first overstrong utterances come forth.

Some Germans front-trill the tongue when forming the [r]. This fact will be welcomed by those student dialecticians whose more sturdily-muscled tongues have difficulty shaping the uvular [r]. As with the back-tongue action, the front trill is relatively slight, sometimes it is made with no more than a single or a double tongue tap.

There are certain areas in the German nation in which the inhabitants do not employ any kind of a trilled [r] at all. Nevertheless, because the sound is thoroughly established as a distinctively German sound, its consistent use is recommended.

The possibility of either a front- or a back-trilled tongue action provides a legitimate choice to the dialectician. But since a front-trilled [r] is also distinctive of Scotch, Italian, and Russian dialects, a second recommendation is made that a uvular [r] be practiced and employed in a German dialect in every case where such employment is possible.

2. [v] FOR [w]. The substitution of a [v] for a [w] is probably the best-known characteristic of a German dialect. The change occurs in initial and medial positions, and is effective for both the voiced *w* [w] and the unvoiced *wh* [hw]. Thus *wear* and *where* receive identical treatment.

The opposite substitution of a [w] for a [v], *winegar* for *vinegar*, has sometimes been used by comedians to achieve comic responses. But this interchange is a sometime Slavic rather than a Teutonic trait and is not justified in an authentic German dialect.

3. [f] FOR [v]. This change is between two fricative consonants and consists of substituting a voiceless [f] for a voiced [v]. Thus *five* [faɪv] becomes *fife* [faɪf]. It is necessary to express a caution, however, like to one of those above, to the effect that the substitution is made in modified rather than full strength. By an act of breath control, by restraining slightly the amount of air usually exhaled on [f], the desired result can be achieved. When heard in sentence context, the [f] which is substituted for a [v] should be easily detected, but in delivery it should not be emphasized to the point that it calls attention to itself. In no case would it be as obvious as the [v] for [w] substitution.

4. [d] FOR [ð]. A [d] is the usual replacement for a voiced *th* [ð]. The principal act of substitution occurs when the *th* [ð] is in an initial position. More restricted is the substitution when a [ð] is medial. For example, *feather*, *neither*, and *rather* are words which, with the [ð] in a medial position, could sustain the change, but *smoother*, *whither*, *bathed*, and many others, could not. A test of whether or not [d] should be substituted for [ð] in a medial position can be made by sounding the questioned word. In the majority of cases, the substitution will be unworkable, or will be so awkward in formation that the substitution obviously should not be made. In the limited number of cases where the exchange is possible, a weaker rather than a stronger enunciation will benefit the speaker; let the [d] be there, but call no attention to it.

There is a second substitution which may be made for the voiced *th* [ð]. It is the one made by the French, in which [ð] is replaced by [z]. The same substitution is also one of the key sounds in a Japanese dialect. Because two other dialects replace [ð] with [z], it becomes reasonable for a German dialect to retain distinctiveness by mostly using the [d] replacement. But since both substitutions can be heard in primary-source speech throughout Germany, and since the same individual has even been heard to use both within a short space of

time, it must be recognized that either is proper. Both are heard on the accompanying tape.

5. [t] FOR [θ]. The voiceless *th* [θ] receives the simple substitution of [t] without competition from any other consonant. The exchange is best noted in an initial position. *Thought* [θɔt] becomes *tot* [tɔt], and *thank* [θæŋk] becomes *tank* [tæŋk]. But the [θ], when in an medial or terminal position, does not always take [t] in substitution. Care must be taken that clarity is not lost because of the exchange. *Author* could accept a [t] substitute, as could *aesthetic*, but *ether* or *youthful* could or should not. When a [θ] is in a final position, equal care must be taken. *North* would sustain a change, *myth* would not. The reasonableness of the sound itself indicates whether or not a substitution can be made.

6. UNVOICED TERMINAL CONSONANTS. Four voiceless consonants are exchanged for four corresponding voiced consonants when in a terminal position: [p] for [b], [t] for [d], [k] for [g] and [s] for [z]. There are no complications in this exchange. The only instruction is that the substitution be effected by a soft rather than a strong attack. If the articulatory action is light enough the resultant sound will often seem to be halfway between the consonant that is being replaced and the one that substitutes for it. In any case, *bread* becomes *breat*, *knob* changes to *knop*, *dog* to *dok*, and *was* [wɑz] to *vas*.

7. [z] FOR [s]. An abrupt reversal of the item immediately above indicates that it is also proper to substitute [z] for [s], primarily on the initial but sometimes on the medial syllable as well. The explanation is that both [z] and [s] are used in equal abundance in German speech, even as they are in English. However, since only a limited number of Germans employ this substitution, the exchange is not absolute; not every [s] becomes [z]. A sense of proportion tells the dialectician when too much use overbalances his work and calls attention to the substitution.

In some instances the choice of [z] for [s] can be based upon the comic potential in this particular exchange. To the English ear there are comic impulses coming from the sounds themselves, as in such a combination as "Zusy zipped her zoup with (mit) a zingle zip." Of course care must be taken to insure that a comic element does not intrude where it is not wanted. *So*, pronounced [zo] and *also*, pronounced ['ɑlzo], are good words to bring this substitution to mind.

8. [tʃ] FOR [dʒ]. This substitution provides a German dialect with one of its most distinctive key sounds. The exchange takes place in initial, medial, and final posi-

tions: *Jane* [dʒeɪn] becomes *chain* [tʃeɪn], *agent* ['eɪdʒnt] *achent* ['eɪtʃnt], and *badge* [bædʒ] *batch* [bætʃ].

9. [ʃt] FOR [st] AND [ʃp] FOR [sp]. Only in an initial position do these two exchanges occur. Somewhat limited in use, they still provide distinctive key sounds for the dialect. In the first substitution *street* [strit] is pronounced *shtreet* [ʃtrit], while in the second *spill* [spɪl] becomes *shpill* [ʃpɪl].

10. SPECIAL GERMAN SOUNDS: [ç] AND [x]. Two typically German consonants are the last key sounds to be considered. (Both are also heard in a Scots dialect.) Because there are no English equivalents for these closely related sounds, their use is restricted to a few instances, such as those in which the dialectician would substitute *ich* [ɪç] for the pronoun *I*, or be called upon to exclaim *ach!* [ax]. The first sound is best made when the tongue is placed as for the vowel [i] and then is subjected to a strong current of air. The [x] is produced when the position taken for any back vowel, [a], [o], [ɔ], [ʊ], [u], is also treated to a strong current of air.

Special Stress

One particular effect, peculiar to German speech, is the habit of stressing, by elongation, the second or third syllable of a multisyllable word. The result can be heard clearly on the tape which accompanies this text. It is achieved by holding on to the natural accent or stress in such a word as *vacation*, which would be heard as *faK-AAtion* [fe'ke:ʃn].

KEY-SOUND WORD DRILL

The material of this section is to be practiced in coordination with the German Dialect tape. The voice on the tape will pause after each word so that you may repeat it immediately, checking your pronunciation against that of the speaker. Space is left below each line for scoring phonetic or other symbols.

(*Voice:* Larry Moss.)

Vowel Substitutions

1. [ɛʳ] FOR [ɝ]. Earth, Hermann, word, German, first, hurt, scourge.

2. [ɑ] FOR [æ] OR [ʌ]. Alto, after, love, laugh, and, theater, propaganda.

3. THE TERMINALS [ə], [ɛd], AND [mɑn].

  a. [ə]. Name, machine, parade, episode, minute.

  b. [ɛd]. Walked, jumped, asked.

  c. [mɑn]. Thomas Mann, Hauptmann, Sudermann.

Diphthongal Changes

1. [eɪ] TO [e]. Aid, may, age, vase, weigh.

2. [oU] TO [o]. Old, open, boat, sold, row.

Consonant Substitutions

1. [r]. Rose, role, pray, married, every, script, beer.

2. [v] FOR [w] and *wh* [hw]. Was, wagon, witch, always, forward, swindle; what, which, whistle, horsewhip.

3. [f] FOR [v]. Vivid, very, average, oval, love, dissolve, arrival.

4. [d] FOR [ð]. The, them, those, father, rather, other.

5. [t] FOR [θ]. Thank, thought, theater, diphtheria, deaths, thousandth.

6. [p] FOR [b]. Bob, cab, verb, rubbed, carbon.

  [t] FOR [d]. Bad, head, made, canned, saved.

[k] FOR [g]. Bag, dig, fog, rug, zigzag.

[s] FOR [z]. Was, does, is, crazy, tongues, please.

7. [z] FOR [s]. So, soup, sit, also, gas, suitable, cycle.

8. [tʃ] FOR [dʒ]. Jar, Johnny, George, agent, changes, badge, major.

9. [ʃt] FOR [st]. Stable, still, stump.

[ʃp] FOR [sp]. Space, Spanish, speak, spick, spoil.

Special German Sounds

(*Voice:* Marianne Hofmann.)

1. [ç]. Milk, light, right, Brecht, dramatish, break.

2. [x]. Ach, book, cook.

Special Stress

Civilization, television, examination, celebrated, exaggerated.

KEY SOUNDS IN SENTENCE CONTEXT

(*Voice:* Larry Moss.)

Vowel Substitutions

1. [ɛʳ] FOR [ɜ]. She earned her first wages from the work. / Hermann was the first person to circle the world.

2. [a] FOR [æ] OR [ʌ]. The alto sang after the Austrian

band played. / It was bad propaganda to laugh at the aunt.

3. THE TERMINALS [ə], [ɛd], AND [mɑn].

The parade was stopped because the machine broke down. / Herr Hauptmann and Herr Sudermann both composed serious dramas.

Diphthongal Changes

1. [e] FOR [eɪ]. At her age the old woman required aid at the gate. / What does the child weigh today?

2. [o] FOR [oʊ]. Her old boat was sold. / *Meine* goat eats the oats.

Consonant Substitutions

1. [r]. Heinrich rushed around the rosebush. / Gertrude was married in a red robe.

2. [v] FOR [w] AND *wh* [hw]. We were in the wagon when it moved forward. / The witch's whistle will always keep you awake.

3. [f] FOR [v]. He arrived at one of the five curves. / The violin music was very vivid.

4. [d] FOR [ð]. They would rather gather feathers. / The other fathers and mothers were there.

5. [t] FOR [θ]. We should thank the author for his aesthetic thoughts. / The theater cannot be both north and south.

6. [p] FOR [b]. Bob was perturbed because he struck the cab.

   [t] FOR [d]. Bud was mad because she hid the deed in the sand.

   [k] FOR [g]. The stag and the pig got lost in the fog.

   [s] FOR [z]. Who cares which one is lazy and which one is crazy?

7. [z] FOR [s]. The gas also was unsuitable.

8. [tʃ] FOR [dʒ]. The agent brought charges against Jane and George.

9. [ʃt] FOR [st]. We should not steal the statue from the stage.

   [ʃp] FOR [sp]. The spinster made the room spick and span.

   (*Voice:* Marianne Hofmann.)

Special German Sounds

1. [ç]. Brecht ate some fish and drank some milk during the break.

2. [x]. Ach, the cook took the cookbook.

Special Stress

There was a special celebration after his examination was over.

She made a strong recommendation on television.

German-English Words

German words, similar in pronunciation to English equivalents, may be used to strengthen a dialect.

(*die*) *Mutter*	*Sommer*	*wunderbar*	*Butter*
(*der*) *Vater*	*Winter*	*Propaganda*	*wild*
(*die*) *Schwester*	*kalt*	*Automobile*	*blond*
(*der*) *Bruder*	*warm*	*Minute*	*still*
(*das*) *Haus*	*Glas*	*Machine*	*Finger*
Garten	*Sport*	*Radio*	*Buch*
Freund, Freunde	*gut*	*Theater*	*Milch*
Stu'dent	*Bier* (beer)	*dramatisch*	*nicht*
Universität	*Kaffee*	*Mann*	*Nacht*
Registrar	*Kindergarten*	*Name*	

Familiar German Words and Expressions

ja-ja	*über* (over)	*Strasse* (street)
ja wohl	*klein, kleine*	*Soldat* (soldier)
	(small)	

nein	*Schule* (school)	*Kuss* (kiss)
ich (I)	*Herr, mein Herr* (Mr.)	*Dummkopf* (block-head)
ach!	*Frau, meine Frau* (Mrs., my wife)	*danke* (thank you)
und (and)	*Fräulein* (Miss)	*Hundert*
mit (with)	*Onkel* (uncle)	*Tausend*
also	*bitte* (please)	*Million*
Guten Morgen! Good morning!	*Wie geht's?* How are you?	

Gute Nacht. Good night!	*Sehr gut.* Very good.
Danke schön. Thank you very much.	*Was ist los?* What's wrong?
Auf Wiedersehen. Good-bye.	*Ich weiss nicht.* I don't know.

READING FOR FLUENCY

Touring Germany

(*Voice:* Marianne Hofmann.)

The tourist who wishes to visit Germany may journey there by sea, air or land. When arriving by boat the traveler will probably come in from the North Sea to one of the two great port cities, *Bremen* or *Hamburg*.

Also it is quite possible to move up the Rhine river from Holland into the Rhineland by a small boat, not too quickly perhaps, just slow enough for good sightseeing. *Düsseldorf* and *Köln*—Cologne in English—*Koblenz* and *Mainz* are the largest cities on this historic route.

By air the Western tourist most likely would fly in from London or Paris, setting down at *Hannover* or *Frankfurt* or even *München* (Munich). Unless of course the polar route brought the traveler in from Sweden or Denmark. In which case the landing would be made at *Hamburg* or *Hannover*. And it is generally from either of those cities, or from *Frankfurt* or *München* that one flies into the divided city of *Berlin*.

By auto, access to Germany is principally from the west and south. The *Netherlands, Belgium,* and *Frankreich* (France) form the western boundary while Switzerland and Austria border the southern side. Always, when a car enters Germany, it is not far from one of the famous autobahns which crisscross the countryside.

As soon as the tourist arrives an involvement in past history takes place. While in the rebuilt cities modern buildings are everywhere, yet there is (are) also many sturdy reminders of past centuries. City halls, theaters, churches and guildhalls in the large and small cities, and farmhouses and castles in the country give testimonials to the continuity of community life from the time of the medieval period through the last century. Decorations in wood and stone and plaster are always evident. The architecture is beautiful or interesting or spectacular, or even all three of those things at once.

Birds of a Feather [1]

(*Voice:* Larry Moss.)

A number of us some years ago were taking supper in Halifax after a performance, when a gentleman who has now retired from the stage, but who is living in New York, suddenly entered the room and said, "Oh, yes, I see; birds of a feather, &c." The thought instantly struck me on the weak side, and, winking at my brother actors and assuming utter ignorance, I said, "What do you mean, birds of *a* feather?" He looked rather staggered and replied, "What, have you never heard of the old English proverb, 'Birds of a feather flock together'?" Everyone shook his head. That was my cue, and I began to turn the proverb inside out. I said to him, "There could never have been such a proverb—birds of *a* feather! the idea of a whole flock of birds having only one feather! The thing is utterly ridiculous. Besides, the poor bird that had that feather must have flown on one side; consequently as the other birds couldn't fly at all, they couldn't flock together. But even accepting that absurdity, if they flocked at all they must flock together, as no bird could possibly be such a damned fool as to go into a corner and try to flock by himself." Our visitor began to see the point of the logic, and was greeted with roars of laughter. I made a memorandum of the incident, and years afterward elaborated the idea in writing Dundreary.

---

[1] From *Talks with Sothern*, ed. F. G. De Fontaine (New York: G. W. Carleton & Co., Publishers, 1878), pp. 27–28.

INDIVIDUAL-PRACTICE EXERCISES

Key-Sound Word Drill

These key sounds are placed beside each other so that you may exercise the change of lip, tongue, and jaw positions necessary for making the proper sounds.

Hauptmann was never forward—old; wagon; hurt; propaganda—gate; here; world; was—asked; swindle; soap; thought—major; bag; stable; is—twelve; feather; spoil; head—cab; lodge; name; whistle—circle; shrimp; spoil; tug—vivid; good; rush; crazy—alto; television; staccato; braved—celebrated; which; gag; minute—bob; bad; bag; was—so; jar; stable; sphere—cab; glad; dig; does—advent; rather; illustrated; always—the world is round—the westward movement—what is his age—the student's imagination—the music of Beethoven—Fritz is working.

Key Sounds in Sentence Context

Never would we rush anyone with the name of Herr Hauptmann.

Johnny and George had no soup for supper.

Bob was glad he had a cab for the theater.

The machine carried the band in the big parade.

Please rush the shrimp to the white wagon.

Those altos were the first persons to dare to laugh at the major.

He is guessing who is kissing her now.

The world is very vast and quite round.

Jane was very perturbed by the Spanish steward.

Here the beer is both cold and warm.

The judge with the whiskers celebrated the examination.

Doug carved his name in a suitable style.

It was easy to wipe away the strange word.

The other wound was what hurt the worst.

The Examination

Rudolph will be coming from work in just a few minutes. He called and gave Frieda the message. When he gets here he should be able to inform all of us what the old judge said. After that, we will know better what to do. In all events, I have the expectation that each one of you will be instantly ready to go into action. Of course, it is entirely possible that Herr Grotesmann had already spoken to the old judge before Rudolph arrived.

In which case the results of the examination will not be broadcast, and Rudolph will be able to tell us nothing.

If that is so, then all we can do is to stop our work and sit here, just as we have been doing for so long, and wait and wait and wait.

(*Substitute German pronunciations in the following sentences.*)

Her brother left the large book in the kindergarten.

A glass of warm water is good in the winter.

The friend waved a single finger.

Suddenly the wild wind was very still.

The soldier said thank you before he called good-bye.

Please do not startle the students in the small school.

Herr and Frau and Fräulein Müller also spoke to Uncle Anton.

Gertrude spilled the milk in the street.

Strauss and Wagner are as well known as Bach and Beethoven.

Both Goethe and Schiller wrote serious dramas.

The play at the state theater was wonderful.

SIGHT READING AND FLUENCY PRACTICE

Birds of a Feather [2]

Here was produced for the first time the piece known as the "American Cousin," by Tom Taylor. I was cast for the part of Lord Dundreary, a fourth-rate old man, with only forty-seven lines to speak. I refused the part at first, but finally agreed with Mr. Burnett, the stage manager, to play on the condition that I should entirely rewrite it. Miss Keene was also full of objections, which however she finally yielded. In rewriting the part I threw into it everything that struck me as wildly absurd. There is not a single look, word or act in Lord Dundreary that has not been suggested to me by people whom I have known since I was five years of age. It has been said that I have cut the piece down for the purpose of Dundrearyizing the performance. This is not true.

Freddy

Once upon a time there was a little boy. His name was Freddy. Freddy was not very strong, so he could not run about and play like all the other little children.

---

[2] From *Talks with Sothern*, ed. De Fontaine.

So Freddy had to stay in his house and just sit by the window, looking out on the garden. Hour after hour he would sit there, thinking to himself. Many times he would make up little stories for himself. He liked to do that. After some time he got so he could make them up very easily. And then the stories got to be not so little, they became very *gross*—er—how do you say, big. And that is why today Freddy is one of the most accomplished liars that I know.

The Red Auto

We were just walking down the road, my friends and I, when I first saw the great big auto coming towards us very fast. It was painted a shiny red color, like the material the girls put on their fingernails. What made the episode so startling was that neither I nor my friends could see anyone at the wheel of the car. It just appeared to come around the corner, without any driver at all, and head straight for us. Of course it was on the wrong side of the road, at least I thought so, and there was no one guiding it at all. I think someone, per-haps Gertrude or maybe Elsa, or one of the other girls, gave a big scream. Whoever it was must have been standing very close to me, for the sound seemed to be right in my ear. Then someone else, and it might have been me, let out a large shout. If I were the one who shouted, I know I must have been trying to tell the big motor car to get back on the right side of the road. Like a flash it went past us, going on its way so rapidly that in no time whatsoever it was just a red dot in the dis-tance. There we stood, all of my very good friends and I, with our eyes and our mouths very wide open. "Did you see her?" someone asked. "Yes," another replied. "It was a very small woman, maybe just a small girl, and she was grinning at us as if she was having a very good time." "Such little girls," I said, "should not be driving big red automobiles on a narrow road. They should be staying home with their fathers and mothers and playing with dolls."

I submit this episode to you as an illustration of what is happening to all of us in this civilization.

XIII

*

RUSSIAN

*

The Slavonic language group includes many geographic areas: westward from the Urals to the borders of Germany, southward from the Arctic to the Aegean and Black Seas. Many regional and national groups are contained within that area, each with a language or dialect of its own, but all stemming from a Slavonic base.

One of the principal characteristics of this family of tongues is the large number of similar sounds found in the major and minor groupings, indicating that there are more oral characteristics held in common than is usual in so large and extensive a language body. In contrast, the national and regional differences within the Celtic language group are much more marked, as was indicated in the chapters on Irish and Scots speech.

In demonstration of existing similarities, two girls, one from Eastern-Central Europe and the other a Russian, when recorded in succession, sounded so like each other in major characteristics it was difficult to distinguish between them; the main difference was non-critical, caused by the fact that one had spent some time in France while the other had not. Also the accents of a Lithuanian forester matched those of an emigré Russian pastor and a Polish businessman to a remarkable extent.

In consequence, it is possible to work from the theory that the key sounds studied as part of the Russian dialect can also be applied to many of the other divisions of the Slavonic language group.

A major division itself, the Russian language is des-ignated as Eastern Slavonic, and includes the geographical area generally designated as Russia proper. Within that area, as is expected, are many regional subdivisions of the national speech. Concern with all of them is neither possible nor necessary. Our concentration centers upon those key sounds held and uttered in common. These are fewer in number than those in most dialects, but lack of quantity is made up by strength and distinctiveness. For example, the effect of regional speech, personal mannerisms, and the extent of education could cause ten Russians to speak in ten different ways. But when all ten spoke in English the similarities would be sufficient in quantity and strength to give solid foundation for a Russian dialect.

A few bold linguistic strokes can serve to characterize this study. None are so divergent from English formations as to require the practice of new and difficult muscular patterns. Distinction comes, rather, from an emphasis upon the fullness of dialect sounds. Oral Russian is a full-bodied language. Both muscular energy and vigor in attack are necessary to achieve the requisite strength. In contrast to our own utterance, in a Russian dialect no articulatory member (lips, jaw, tongue) nor any area (front, middle, or back of the mouth) may remain inactive during speech.

The alterations that occur are matters of degree rather than difference. The jaw must drop down in a larger than usual motion to permit an enlargement of the oral cavity; the plosive consonants must be delivered with more than usual energy and be cut off with greater sharpness; vocal slurs or glides must be given with more emphasis than is customary with us; and both the tongue and the walls of the pharyngeal cavity must accommodate themselves to the action necessary to achieve a full-bodied throatiness.

All dialects have occasional effects that creep into speech outside the rules. Russian has more than most. Single sounds and single words in variety in the work ahead will bear testimony to this phenomenon. Two particular sounds, both glides, are especially susceptible to a kind of elision that is most prominent in the Russian language itself. [j], as in *ya*, and [w] are the consonants in question. Both are the result of an enlarging action by the articulators, and both will be heard in expected and unexpected places.

KEY CHARACTERISTICS OF A RUSSIAN DIALECT
Grammar and Language Structure

Because of differences in grammatical construction, a Russian speaking in English is prone to omit both definite and indefinite articles. Although the lines of a part might be written with all necessary articles included, it would be a proper practice to omit many of them during delivery, especially in moments of excitement or tension. Example: "Give me book."

Plurals are not always observed. As a consequence, the singular may be substituted to the extent knowledge of English suggests—the less the grasp of the new speech the more times a plural may be reduced to a singular. For example, "I have many picture," or "These shoe hurt me."

Tenses also constitute a problem for those Russians not thoroughly grounded in English grammar, but this circumstance applies with equal stress to nearly all persons who study a new speech. Less uniform is the enunciation—mostly when reading, less when speaking —of an *ed* ending. On occasion such stress might be given as, "They look'ed at the building," or "She danc'ed very fast."

In like manner a final *e*, as in *parade, vacate*, is sounded rather than dropped; unstressed, the vowel is sounded as [ə]. Also an *ous* or *tion* ending might be given full enunciation, thus: [ous] or [rjɔn].

As in all instances when a dialect represents the speech of a non-English speaking person, misplaced stress in phrasing becomes a usable characteristic for the dialectician. Thus, "We were just 'going," could

properly be changed to either "We 'were just going," or "We were just go'ing." The tendency can be of equal use in speaking and in reading. In either case it should not be overused.

Vowel Substitutions

1. [i] FOR [ɪ]. Whether due to the prevalence of French as a spoken language in official and social circles a century and less ago, or because of some other reason indigenous to Russian speech, the front vowel [ɪ], as in *it*, is altered to the value of [i], as in *eat*. Used less by a Russian than the same idiosyncrasy would be by a Frenchman or Italian, this substitution is still a notable part of the dialect. Thus *it* becomes [it], and *live* is [liv].

2. [ɛʳ] FOR [ɝ]. In a manipulation similar to that found in Scots, the sound of [ɝ], as in *her*, is reshaped into a combination of [ɛ], as in *eh*, and front-trilled [r] which, for our purpose, we score as [ɛʳ]. In consequence, *first* [fɝst] becomes [fɛʳst], and *learnt* [lɝnt] changes to [lɛʳnt]. Not as extensively nor as forcefully employed as in Scots, the sound still has a steady use in a Russian dialect.

3. [ɑ] FOR [æ] OR [a]. The sound of the "broad *a*" [ɑ] is substituted freely for [æ] and [a]. *Had* [hæd] and *ask* [ask] are typical, changing to [hɑd] and [ɑsk]. Even such strong alterations as *bad* [bɑd], *and* [ɑnd], *add* [ɑd] and multisyllable words like *propaganda* [propɑ'gɑndə] and *vacate* ['vɑketə] are commonplace and give substance to the need for the full-throated sound so often heard in the dialect.

4. [ɔ:]. This symbol must do to represent a phoneme not heard in American speech. The closest sound to it is the Standard English vowel [ɔ:] as heard in the Standard English pronunciation of *law* [lɔ:] and *all* [ɔ:l]. Yet even the Standard English [ɔ:] falls short of the hollow throatiness of the Russian vowel.

To produce the proper sound, the jaw must be lowered more than usual, the lips partially rounded and slightly protruded, while the back of the tongue arches slightly toward the soft palate as the walls of the pharyngeal cavity enlarge and tense themselves. When these placements and actions are effected the resultant sound is both hollow and throaty, thus forming the most distinctive vowel sound in a Russian dialect.

This phoneme, which we have arbitrarily designated as [ɔ:] acts as a substitute for several middle and back vowels: [ɝ] as in *her*, [ʌ] as in *up*, [o] as in *go*, [ɔ] as in *ought*, and [ɑ] as in *father*. For example, each of the following would change its nominal vowel to the sound of [ɔ:]: *word* [vɔ:rd], *love* [lɔ:v], *gold* [gɔ:ld], *Slav* [slɔ:v], and *watch* [vɔ:tʃ].

Diphthongal Changes

1. [ɑʊ] FOR [ɔ]. When a Russian, not too familiar with English, sees the two letters *au* linked together in a word, he will be inclined to give them a diphthongal evaluation rather than allow them a single vowel sound. Having read *au*, which he pronounces as [ɑʊ], he will be inclined to repeat his pronunciation when talking. Thus to a limited extent the *au* combination, which we usually sound as the back vowel [ɔ], as in *caught*, will creep into his vocabulary in the shape of the above diphthong. Under these circumstances the recommendation is made that the [ɑʊ] substitution be employed judiciously. Where a sentence or passage is already strongly supported by other key sounds of the dialect, the [ɑʊ] diphthong need not be called into play. In all cases its use should be moderate.

Consonant Substitutions

Consonants, especially those that can sustain vigorous action, are strongly emphasized in a Russian dialect. The initiation and termination of the plosives (*p, b, t, d, k,* and *g*) is sharp. The aspiration of a dropped *h* is marked, and the tip-of-the-tongue action on an *r* is pronounced. But the number of consonantal changes or substitutions is not large, indicating that each alteration must receive full attention to sustain a dialect that always seems to be more radically altered than it actually is.

1. [r]. The Russian trills the [r] with the tip of the tongue, sometimes with the vigor of an operatic star. The medial [r] takes more action than does an [r] in an initial or terminal position; when initial it may receive no more than a tap, and when terminal may lose some strength because of the human tendency to slur final sounds. In over-all use, however, the [r] should be employed as one of the strongest key sounds of the dialect.

2. [d] FOR [ð]. [d] is consistently substituted for the voiced *th* [ð] in certain positions. This change occurs in a German dialect, and once in a while can be heard in the French and Italian, but in neither is it as heavily sounded as when used by a Russian in speaking English.

The change is employed mainly when the *th* [ð] is the initial syllable, but only occasionally when [ð] is in a medial position. No substitution at all is used for a final [ð] syllable, principally because the change generally renders the subject word unintelligible. Accordingly, *the, that, they* are consistently pronounced [dʌ], [dæt], and [de], while *father, gather,* and *weather* are only intermittently sounded as ['fadə], ['gædə], and ['vɛdə].

3. [t] FOR [d]. A minor substitution occurs when [t] replaces a terminal [d]. The substitution is not consistent, or it may be that it is just not complete. In a final position it is somewhat easier to form a voiceless [t] than to make a voiced [d], and in the process of neglecting terminal sounds, which happens everywhere and in all languages, an incomplete [d] can sound like its voiceless companion, [t]. Thus *mind* [maɪnd] may become [maɪnt].

4. [f] FOR [v]. In like manner to the above, and for much the same reason, a voiceless [f] may replace a voiced [v] when the latter is medial and terminal. When this substitution does occur, for it is not consistent, such words as *movie* and *Slav* would be pronounced ['mofi] and [slɔ:f].

5. [k]. Strong, consistent, and necessary is the addition of the sound of [k] to an *ng* [ŋ] syllable, especially when the latter is terminal. It is a simple addition, and easily formed. In contrast, the resultant sound is one of the most striking effects in the dialect. To form the required [k], the back of the tongue will momentarily block passage of the sound wave, so that the air, when released after the stop, makes an audibly sharp click.

In the majority of cases a [k] is added to a terminal [ŋ] when that syllable is part of the present participle ending *ing*. Thus *running* ['rʌnɪŋ] becomes ['rʌnɪŋk].

In contrast, a [k] sound should be used but rarely when *ng* or *ing* is terminal in a one-syllable word. Accordingly *tang* would not become *tank*, or *sling, slink*.

In a few instances, when *ng* or *ing* is medial in a present participle, the [k] may be added both there and again at the end, but such a double use in one word should be saved for those times, for example, when the intent is strictly comedic. It is possible for *singing* to become ['sɪŋkɪŋk] or *longing* to be ['lɔ:ŋkɪŋk]. But the double use of [k] in one word is awkward at best, as is demonstrated in *thronging* ['ɵrɔ:ŋkɪŋk], and so should be very sparingly employed. A [k] added to the *ing* ending of a present participle is sufficiently strong in its own right to preclude additional use in any instance short of farce.

6. [j]. The *ya* sound of [j] is a Russian insertion that subtly or strongly is made to fit between a consonant and a following vowel. It is a glide connecting the two and may be heard plainly in some instances but only hinted at in others. There are known places to insert this slurring sound, and there are others where its presence comes as a surprise. Two of the usual places follow the consonants [l] and [n] when either letter is followed by a front vowel. Russian pronunciation of *nyet*, their word for *no*, is key to this sound. So also is the [j] sound in *onion* ['ʌnjən].

As a rule this glide, connecting consonant to following vowel, should be slightly rather than fully heard. Since an [lj] combination is more difficult than [nj], the former will be a more subtle sound than the latter. *Next*, pronounced [njɛkst], is a key word to bring this sound to mind.

In contrast to the above, three words, common to both English and Russian, lose the [j] glide in the latter tongue: *music* [mu'sik], *communiqué* [komuni'ke], and *communist* [komu'nist].

In still another variation the [j] glide is heard in a number of words beginning *uni-* which we pronounce ['junɪ]. The Russian will drop [j] as the first sound of the word and then insert it as a glide between the *n* and *i*, so that *uniform* ['junəfɔrm] becomes ['unjəfɔːrm].

Beyond the coverage of rules are those instances in which traces of [j] can be heard in such disparate words as *men* [mjen], *mascot*, heard as [m'jæskɑt], or *Russian*, heard as ['rusɪjən].

7. [x̸]. Since there is no [h] in his language, the Russian does not pronounce it in English. However, he does not merely drop it as a French person does but, on sight, attempts the sound by a rush of air against the hump of the back of the tongue. The result is similar to the Scotch sound represented by the symbol [x] and in the word *loch* [lɔx]; there should be no vibration, however. Occasionally, as the [h] is aspirated a slight sound of the [j] is inserted—*help* [hɛlp] then becomes [x̸jɛlp].

8. [v] FOR [w] AND *wh* [hw]. The substitution of [v] for [w] and [hw] is consistent in a Russian dialect. Many times the substitution, while employing the [v], will retain a slight sound of [w], so that *work* would be either [vɔːrk] or [vwɔːrk].

9. [w]. The [w] is not entirely eliminated by [v]—it comes back as a conditioning sound, mostly in connection with [ɔː], and is caused because phonation is begun when lips, jaw, and tongue are moving into place for the full and somewhat throaty sound of [ɔː]. The result is subtle rather than strong, indicating that [w] is never fully formed or emphasized. The practice of this insertion varies from individual to individual; it is most noticeable in those who round and fill out the lower back vowels. *Gold*, pronounced *gwold* [gwɔːld] is a good illustration of the sound.

KEY-SOUND WORD DRILL

Space is left below both words and sentences for phonetic or other symbols. A pause after each word permits repetition.

(*Voice:* Jerry Blunt.)

Vowel Substitutions

1. [i] FOR [ɪ]. If, Italy, his, dentist, suspicious, capitalist, socialist.

2. [ɛʳ] FOR [ɜ]. First, learnt, erstwhile, curve, prefer.

3. [ɑ] FOR [æ] OR [a]. Had, baggage, bank, passport, propaganda.

4. [ɔː]. War, world, workers, gold, come, host, vogue.

Diphthongal Changes

1. [ɑʊ] for [ɔ]. Caught, brought, pause.

Consonant Substitutions

1. [r]. Wrong, Russkie, arrow, heard, girls, Boris.

2. [d] FOR *th* [ð]. The, this, though, others, neither.

3. [t] FOR [d]. Told, loud, land, world, glad.

4. [f] FOR [v]. Advent, movie, Slav, Kiev, love.

5. [k]. Working, loving, banking, young, pausing; *and*

occasionally for comic purposes: bringing, singing,

wronging.

6. [j]. Next, near, neck, niece, nucleus, lack, leap, limp,

men, guest, Ranevsky, uniform, unilateral, uni-

versal; *in contrast:* music, communiqué, communist.

7. [h̸]. His, home, host, humored, inhabit, rehearse.

8. [v] FOR [w] AND *wh* [hw]. Where, watch, work, choir,

one, language, quake.

9. [w]. Gold, hold, coffee, most, Volga, boat.

KEY SOUNDS IN SENTENCE CONTEXT
Vowel Substitutions

1. [i] FOR [ɪ]. He visited his dentist in Italy. / The capi-

talist and the socialist limped into the office.

2. [ɛʳ] for [ɝ]. Vassily learnt it first and early. / The

erstwhile communist preferred to be heard.

3. [ɑ] FOR [æ] OR [a]. That was bad propaganda for the

bank. / Anna had her passport in the baggage.

4. [ɔ:]. The host gave gold to all the workers. / No war

must come to the Volga. / The vogue for love took

the world by storm.

Diphthongal Changes

1. [ɑʊ] FOR [ɔ]. He thought the Czar ought to have

caught the old communist.

Consonant Substitutions

1. [r]. The Russkie ran on the ramp. / Boris was four-

teen before he performed.

2. [d] FOR *th* [ð]. The others got these and those. / They

wanted this, but the others wanted that.

3. [t] FOR [d]. The words were loud. / Leonid told the

world the bad news.

4. [f] FOR [v]. They love Kiev. / The avenue runs over

the cave.

5. [k]. The young girls were laughing and working. /

Wearing shoe was hurting feet.

6. [j]. We need to look at the next uniform. / The nu-

cleus was near the neck. / *Nyet*, do not give it to the

men.

7. [h̸]. He is good-humored. / Perhaps the host will help

the huskers.

8. [v] FOR [w]. When will the world have one language?

/ Once or twice during the day we will work.

9. [w]. Tolstoy told a story about the Volga. / The gold and coffee were put on the boat.

Russian Place Names

(*Voice:* Irene Zmurkevych.)

Moscow, Leningrad, Murmansk, Arkhangelsk, Yaroslav, Vitebsk, Kiev, Kharkov, Odessa, Mariupol, Taganrog, Magnitogorsk, Minsk.

Names from The Cherry Orchard, *Chekhov*

Lyubov Andreyevna Ranevskaya, Leonid Andreyivich Gayev, Yermolay Alexeich Lopakhin, Peter Sergeyich Trofimov, Boris Borisovich Semyonov-Pishchik.

Famous Russian Names—Literature, Music, Drama

Tolstoy, Chekhov, Pushkin, Peter Ilyich Tchaikovsky, Nikolai Andreevich Rimskii-Korsakov, Konstantin Sergeevich Alekseev (who is known to Americans as Constantin Stanislavsky), Nemirovich-Danchenko.

READING FOR FLUENCY
Tom Sawyer, *Mark Twain;* Chapter II

(*Voice:* Jerry Blunt.)

Saturday morning was come, and all the summer world was bright and fresh, and brimming with life. There was a song in every heart; and if the heart was young the music issued at the lips. There was cheer in every face and a spring in every step. The locust trees were in bloom and the fragrance of the blossoms filled the air. Cardiff Hill, beyond the village and above it, was green with vegetation, and it lay just far enough away to seem a Delectable Land, dreamy, reposeful, and inviting.

Tom appeared on the sidewalk with a bucket of whitewash and a long-handled brush. He surveyed the fence, and all gladness left him and a deep melancholy settled down upon his spirit. Thirty yards of board fence nine feet high. Life seemed to him hollow, and existence but a burden. Sighing he dipped his brush and passed it along the topmost plank; repeated the operation, did it again; compared the insignificant whitewashed streak with the far-reaching continent of unwhitewashed fence, and sat down on a tree-box discouraged. Jim came skipping out at the gate with a tin pail, and singing "Buffalo Gals." Bringing water from the town pump had always seemed hateful work in Tom's eyes before, but now it did not strike him so. He remembered that there was company at the pump. White, mulatto, and negro boys and girls were always there waiting their turns, resting, trading playthings, quarreling, fighting, skylarking. And he remembered that although the pump was only a hundred and fifty yards off, Jim never got back with a bucket of water under an hour—and even then somebody generally had to go after him.

Utopia, *Sir Thomas More;* Book One

(*Voice:* Irene Zmurkevych.)

Here I should describe to them the law of the Macariens, who are not far distant from Utopia, and whose king on the day of his coronation is bound by a solemn oath that he shall never at any time have in his treasure over a thousand pounds of gold or silver. They say that a very good king, who took more care for the wealth of his country than for the enriching of himself, made this law to be a check and bar to kings against heaping and hoarding up of so much money as might impoverish their people. For he foresaw that this sum of treasure would suffice to support the king in battle against his own people, if they should chance to rebel, and also to maintain his wars against the invasions of foreign enemies. Further, he perceived that the same sum of money would be too little and insufficient to encourage and enable him wrongfully to take away other men's goods, which was the chief cause of why the law was made. Another cause was this: he thought that by this provision his people should not lack money wherewith to maintain their daily business and traffic. And seeing the king could not choose but spend and bestow all that came in above the sum prescribed for him, he thought that he would seek no occasions to do his subjects injury. Such a king shall be feared by evil men, and loved by good men. This and such other information, if I should offer to men wholly inclined and set in the contrary direction, how deaf hearers think you I should have?

INDIVIDUAL-PRACTICE EXERCISES

Key-Sound Word Drill

The following key sounds are placed beside each other so that you may practice the change of lip, tongue, and jaw positions necessary for the making of the proper sounds.

This; are; word; drill—first; gold; over; land—ascot; young; bird; bank—next; loud; working; script—host; love; uniform; propaganda—choir; heard; singing; music—suspicious; workers; rehearse; guest—laughing; girls; parade; Kiev—unilateral; food; vogue; men—twice; these; socialist; danced—war; bringing; dentist; coffee—other; movie; were; wrong—Moscow; had; baggage; coming—those; boys; perform; leap—Vassily; rose; near; roaring; river—watch; bird; leap; boat—in; most; early; work—neck; old; was; bad—ago; net; humored; them—this; communiqué; quite; wrong; was.

Key Sounds in Sentence Context

Fourteen bad boys were coming over the river.

The next baggage will have gold.

Young men is too loud.

Many apple are too old to eat.

Da, that is right. *Nyet*, that is wrong.

Both boys and girls play many game.

The bank in Kiev had lots uniform.

These capitalists had plenty passport.

They read the script in Italy.

We was working and sweating in the hot old office.

Boris gave thirteen girls money for the sad movie.

The scientist caught birds and butterflies in his net.

Marya was laughing and dancing with her boy friend Nikolai.

Neither of the others wanted a long parade.

Where is first passenger to go aboard vessel sailing to Odessa?

The quake woke all people living in big city.

Always beware singing workers in office.

The world did not want another war.

Peter rehearsed the difficult language of his new role.

The singing of that aria is banned in this area.

Natasha held the magnifying glass in her left hand.

Chekhov told many humorous story about country people.

Everyone wrote cook that food was good.

Konstantin Sergeevich Alekseev is proper Russian name of great actor, teacher, regisseur whom we call Constantin Stanislavsky.

SIGHT READING AND FLUENCY PRACTICE
Tom Sawyer, *Mark Twain;* Chapter II

Tom gave up the brush with reluctance in his face, but alacrity in his heart. And while the late steamer *Big Missouri* worked and sweated in the sun, the retired artist sat on a barrel in the shade close by, dangling his legs, munching his apple, and planning the slaughter of more innocents. There was no lack of material; boys happened along every little while; they came to jeer, but remained to whitewash. By the time Ben was fagged out, Tom had traded the next chance to Billy Fisher for a kite, in good repair; and when *he* played out, Johnny Miller bought in for a dead rat and a string to swing it with—and so on, and so on, hour after hour. And when the middle of the afternoon came, from being a poor poverty-stricken boy in the morning, Tom was literally rolling in wealth. He had beside the things before mentioned, twelve marbles, part of a jews'-harp, a piece of blue bottle-glass to look through, a spool cannon, a key that wouldn't unlock anything, a fragment of chalk, a glass stopper of a decanter, a tin soldier, a couple of tadpoles, six firecrackers, a kitten with only one eye, a brass door-knob, a dog-collar—but no dog—the handle of a knife, four pieces of orange-peel, and a dilapidated old window-sash.

He had had a nice, good, idle time all the while—plenty of company—and the fence had three coats of whitewash on it! If he hadn't run out of whitewash, he would have bankrupted every boy in the village.

Tom said to himself that it was not such a hollow world, after all. He had discovered a great law of human action, without knowing it—namely, that in order to make a man or a boy covet a thing, it is only necessary to make the thing difficult to attain. If he had been a great and wise philosopher, like the writer of this book, he would now have comprehended that Work consists of whatever a body is *obliged* to do, and that Play consists of whatever a body is not obliged to do. And this would help him to understand why constructing artificial flowers or performing on a treadmill is work, while rolling tenpins or climbing Mont Blanc is only amusement. There are wealthy gentlemen in England who drive four-horse passenger-coaches twenty or thirty miles on a daily line, in the summer, because the privilege costs them considerable money; but if they were offered wages for the service, that would turn it into work and then they would resign.

The boy mused awhile over the substantial change which had taken place in his worldly circumstances, and then wended toward headquarters to report.

Henry the Fifth, *Shakespeare;* Act IV, Scene 3

WESTMORELAND. O, that we now had here

But one ten thousand of those men in England

That do no work today!

KING.   What's he that wishes so?

My cousin Westmoreland? No, my fair cousin.

If we are mark'd to die, we are enow

To do our country loss, and if to live,

The fewer men, the greater share of honor.

God's will! I pray thee wish not one man more.

By Jove, I am not covetous for gold,

Nor care I who doth feed upon my cost.

It yearns me not if men my garments wear;

Such outward things dwell not in my desires.

But if it be a sin to covet honor,

I am the most offending soul alive.

No, faith, my coz, wish not a man from England.

God's peace! I would not lose so great an honor

As one man more, methinks, would share from me

For the best hope I have. O, do not wish one more!

Rather proclaim it, Westmoreland, through my host

That he which hath no stomach to this fight,

Let him depart. His passport shall be made

And crowns for convoy put into his purse.

We would not die in that man's company

That fears his fellowship to die with us.

This day is call'd the feast of Crispian.

He that outlives this day and comes safe home

Will stand a-tiptoe when this day is nam'd

And rouse him at the name of Crispian.

He that shall live this day and see old age

Will yearly on the vigil feast his neighbors

And say "Tomorrow is Saint Crispian."

Then will he strip his sleeve and show his scars,

(And say "These wounds I had on Crispin's day.")

Old men forget; yet all shall be forgot,

But he'll remember with advantages

What feats he did that day. Then shall our names,

Familiar in his mouth as household words—

Harry the King, Bedford and Exeter,

Warwick and Talbot, Salisbury and Gloucester—

Be in their flowing cups freshly rememb'red.

This story shall the good man teach his son.

And Crispin Crispian shall ne'er go by

From this day to the ending of the world,

But we in it shall be remembered—

We few, we happy few, we band of brothers.

For he today that sheds his blood with me

Shall be my brother. Be he ne'er so vile,

This day shall gentle his condition.

And gentlemen in England now abed

Shall think themselves accurst they were not here,

And hold their manhoods cheap whiles any speaks

That fought with us upon Saint Crispin's day.

Utopia, *Sir Thomas More;* Book One

Moreover, a man can have no opportunity to do good, falling into the company of those who will sooner ruin a good man than be made good themselves— through whose evil company he will be marred; or else, if he remain good and innocent, yet the wickedness and foolishness of others shall be imputed to him, and laid on his shoulders. So that it is impossible even with that crafty wile and subtle trickery to turn anything to better. Wherefore Plato in a goodly simile declares why wise men refrain from meddling in the commonwealth.

For when they see the people swarming into the streets and daily wet to the skin with rain, and yet cannot persuade them to come in out of the rain and take to their houses, knowing well that if they should go out to them they would nothing prevail, nor win anything by it, but be wet also in the rain, they keep themselves within their houses, content to be safe themselves, seeing they cannot remedy the folly of the people.

INDEX

78 79 80 81   8 7 6 5 4 3 2